Y0-BOA-604

smart women ™

Barbara L. Thrasher & Madelon A. Smid

MACMILLAN CANADA TORONTO

Copyright © Barbara Thrasher and Madelon Smid 1998

All rights reserved. The use of any part of this publication reproduced, transmitted in any form or by any means, electronic, mechanical, recording or otherwise, or stored in a retrieval system, without the prior consent of the publisher is an infringement of the copyright law. In the case of photocopying or other reprographic copying of the material, a licence must be obtained from the Canadian Copyright Licensing Agency (CANCOPY) before proceeding.

Canadian Cataloguing in Publication Data

Thrasher Barb, 1947.
    Smart women

ISBN 0-7715-7573-4

1. Women-owned business enterprises — Canada — Management.
2. Businesswomen — Canada. I. Smid, Madelon. II Title.

HD6072.6.C2T47 1998   658.02′2′0820971   C98-930950-9

1 2 3 4 5 TPI 01 02 00 99 98

Cover and text design by Kevin Connelly
Smart Women logo designed by Oliver Nemeskeri

This book is available at special discounts for bulk purchases by your group or organization for sales promotions, premiums, fundraising and seminars. For details, contact:
Macmillan Canada, Special Sales Department, 29 Birch Avenue, Toronto, ON M4V 1E2.
Tel: 416-963-8830.

Macmillan Canada
A Division of Canada Publishing Corporation
Toronto, Ontario, Canada

Printed in Canada

This book is dedicated to God's Greatest Network:

WOMEN

To all women, the Smart Women who ask the questions
and
the Smart Women who have the answers.

With special thanks to our mother,
Kathleen,
who both asks and answers.

Smart Women

Smart women grow up
make choices
Choose
beauty, grace, endings, beginnings
buy their own flowers
make love, have babies or not
face loss and death
and laugh anyway
look in the mirror
face their face in all its phases
smile frequently and weep seldom.

Smart women play,
dress up, dress well and dance
especially alone.
Smart women take advice
forgive, forget or remember and move on

Smart women find themselves and commit
help others to help themselves
work hard with passion or work hard anyway
love to love
love to learn
plan and save
and spontaneously take risks in new directions.

Smart women stay focused
then change
and change
and change
constantly re-balancing, in the connection
of mind/body/spirit…

Smart women are transformed by the power of gratitude
healed, they live WHOLE lives
filled with family, friends, self and the community
in relationship with, and co-creators of, life.

Valerie Pusey

Acknowledgements

We would like to thank the following people for their help:

Judy Adams	Rick Harcus
Kathy Aitken	Noreen Jackman
Sonya Anderson	Ashley Jones
Nicole Beaudoin	Pat Leece
Kay Blais	Linda Leier
Maria Boublile	Andrina Lever
Lianne Chacra	Bev McMurray
Monica Corry	Pat Moore
Dr. Don Daly	Kathy Mutch
Madeleine Daly	Guy Paproski
Caroline Dillard	Judith Richards
Anne Ellenberger	Shelley Stewart
Maureen Forsyth	Karen Titanich
Mary Gunn	Dorothy Waller
Karen Hahn	Rob Waller
Lorraine Harcus	Margo White

Thanks also to the Manitoba Arts Council. Thanks to Susan Gajewski, CIBC; Debra Wilton, Royal Bank; Leslie Dancause; Hazel Muise; Muriel Baribeau and Helen Webster.

Special thanks to Shawn Jorgensen for his formatting skills and infinite patience. And thanks to Cathy Ferguson, Claire Paradis, Ila Stevens and all the Human Resources Development Canada team for the thousands of small businesses they have created.

And thanks finally to our editor, Susan Girvan, who uses her talents to help women move forward.

Contents

Preface 1

Introduction – Murdering The Money Myth 5

Section 1 – Leadership

Introduction 11

Chapter 1 Planning 15

What frustrations do you experience when you try to plan? 15

Planning Quiz 17

1. How do I define my vision? 19
2. Why do I need a mission statement? 22
3. Can I bring my personal values to the business? 23
4. How do I create a Strategic Customer Advantage (SCA)? 25
5. How big should my business be? 29
6. What should be in my plan? 31
7. Who can help me plan? 32

The Whole Person Action Plan for Planning 35

Chapter 2 Finding and Keeping the Right People 37

What frustrations are you experiencing in finding and keeping the right people? 37

Finding and Keeping the Right People Quiz 39

1. What people issues do I need to deal with? 41
2. How do I find the best people? 43
3. How do I grow good people into great people? 48
4. How do I prevent burnout in my staff? 53
5. How do I evaluate the people in my business? 53
6. How do I get an evaluation? 54

The Whole Person Action Plan for Finding and Keeping the Right People 56

Chapter 3 Delegating 57

What frustrations are you experiencing in delegating? 57

Delegating Quiz 59

1. Why do I need to delegate? 61
2. How do I learn to let go? 61
3. What do I stand to gain if I let go? 62
4. How do I go about delegating? 63

The Whole Person Action Plan for Delegating 73

Chapter 4 Communication. 75
What frustrations are you experiencing in trying to communicate? 75
Communication Quiz 77
1.   What are some barriers to communication? 79
2.   How can I be better understood? 79
3.   How can I encourage my employees to communicate better? 85
4.   How can I communicate when I'm not there all the time? 86
5.   How much communication is enough? 88
The Whole Person Action Plan for Communication 91

Chapter 5 Conflict Resolution 93
What frustrations are you experiencing in trying to resolve conflict? 93
The Conflict Resolution Quiz 95
1.   What is conflict resolution? 97
2.   How do I handle conflict in a professional way? 98
3.   When should I stand up for what I believe? 101
4.   How should I behave when conflict occurs? 103
5.   When is the best time to deal with conflict? 105
6.   How much of this is my responsibility? 107
7.   How can I stop staff conflict from happening in the first place? 108
8.   How do I handle a difficult customer? 110
The Whole Person Action Plan for Conflict Resolution 112

Section 2 - Management
     Introduction 113

Chapter 6 Marketing Systems. 117
What frustrations do women experience in trying to
     market their product or service? 117
Marketing Quiz 119
1.   What is marketing? 121
2.   What is promotion? 121
3.   How do I define my market? 122
4.   How do I know what my customers really want? 123
5.   How do I ensure good merchandising? 124
6.   What is the key to good customer service? 125
7.   How do I ensure good public relations? 126
8.   What type of advertising can I do? 128
9.   How do I get publicity? 130
10. Will I benefit from participating in trade shows? 131
11. How can I maximize my sales? 132
12. How can I be proactive in planning my promotions? 135

13. How do I evaluate my promotions? 140
The Whole Person Action Plan for Marketing Systems 142

Chapter 7 Operating Systems 143
What frustrations do women experience in setting up and using systems?. 143
Operating Systems Quiz 145
1. Why are operating systems important?. 147
2. When do I need a procedures manual?. 147
3. How do I evaluate my systems?. 148
4. What is the most important system to develop first?. 148
5. How do I manage a paper-trail system? 149
6. What do I need in my purchasing system? 152
7. How can a phone service help me? 153
8. What can computers do for my business?. 154
9. How can I find the right software for my business? 156
10. How important is a system to monitor my inventory?. 157
11. What other systems are important to my operation?. 158
12. How can I handle growth? 161
The Whole Person Action Plan for Operating Systems 164

Chapter 8 Financial Systems. 165
What frustrations are you experiencing around your finances?. 165
Financial Systems Quiz 167
1. What is a financial system? 169
2. How do I structure my business?. 170
3. How do I know how much money I need? 171
4. How do I understand my financial statements?. 172
5. How do I price my product/service properly? 174
6. What financial systems do I need to have in place?. 175
7. How can I control my costs?. 176
8. How do I find the right financial expert to help me? 178
9. How do I find the money I need? 179
The Whole Person Action Plan for Financial Systems 185

Section 3 – Self-Development
Introduction. 187

Chapter 9 Body. 193
What frustrations are you experiencing in the area of physical wellness? 193
Physical Wellness Quiz 195
1. How will owning my own business affect my health? 197
2. How do I find time to exercise?. 198

3. What kind of exercise should I do? 199
4. What else do I have to do to keep my body healthy? 202
5. What does how I look have to do with it? 205
6. What does how I behave have to do with it? 208
7. What are those little things that count? 210
The Whole Person Action Plan for Physical Wellness 212

Chapter 10 Mind 213
What frustrations are you experiencing in keeping up-to-date? 213
Education Quiz 215
1. What are the three Cs of learning? 217
2. How can I learn faster? 218
3. What is the difference between a coach and a consultant? 218
4. How can I learn from my competition? 221
5. Why are conferences one of the best methods of growing my mind? 223
6. How can I find the money for learning? 224
7. What should I be learning? 226
The Whole Person Action Plan for Your Education 227

Chapter 11 Spirit 229
What frustrations are you experiencing in nurturing your spirit? 229
Spiritual Wellness Quiz 231
1. How can I simplify my life? 233
2. How do I find a little peace and quiet? 234
3. What else will enrich my life? 238
4. Where will I find the money to look after me? 239
5. How can I get the emotional support I need? 240
6. Can I run away from home if it gets to be too much? 244
The Whole Person Action Plan for Nurturing Your Spirit 247

Conclusion 249
What trends are developing in women-owned businesses? 249

List of Smart Women Business Owners 253

Resource Directory for Women Entrepreneurs 257

Preface

Smart Women is the most important business book you will read this year. It is:

- a coach-in-a-book
- a practical daily tool
- a guide with advice from more than 100 women entrepreneurs

The women in this book are real women. We found them in the oil patch, in the fashion, trucking and meat processing industries, in the arts and in wellness businesses. They are running successful businesses and have a wealth of information to pass on. By combining their wisdom with business expertise and personal philosophy we have written a book to show you how to:

- work *smart* not hard
- increase the profitability of your business
- become a whole person
- deal with specific business frustrations

These women are not just real women, they are also *Smart Women*, a term we use throughout the book to describe women with great strengths in certain areas who are still working on weaknesses in other areas. A *Smart Woman* is striving to be a **whole person**. A **whole person** is a person who has developed within her/himself a balance of body, mind and spirit. This person is self-reliant and grounded because all of his/her choices are based on a set of values, which are based on the message from their inner voice. Because their values guide their choices, they come from a position of confidence that creates a sense of peace. A **whole person** draws from the full range of characteristics inherent in all humans (but which our culture has divided over time, designating some as more common to males, some more prevalent in females). By blending the best of all human traits within us we develop a **whole person** attitude to life. Few *Smart Women* are **whole people** yet. Some may never be. Only you can decide if you fit the category.

Smart Women is also about women and money. The problem we need to address is *why aren't women making money?* We tackled the issue and went a step further. We concluded that we could not tell women how to start making money without examining why the majority of them haven't been, so far. It's a complex question, and our answer will be controversial to say the least. One of our test readers wrote "This makes me mad" in bold letters across one of the pages. Whether you agree with what is said here and have outgrown old paradigms and moved on towards new thinking or you refuse to see the new, we hope you will read on. A *Smart Woman* will.

Money with all its power and promise dances elusively just beyond the reach of most women. Why? "Why indeed?" asked Barbara Thrasher, Executive Director of Communicating Power Inc. *The Business Builders.* "My marketing company's mission is to secure entrepreneurs worthwhile work that they love, by enhancing their communicating power—with bankers, suppliers, staff and customers. CPI's Enterprise & Innovation™ is one of the top small business programs in the country. My company has worked with more than 1000 small business owners in the past five years."

During a conversation the spring of 1996 I (Barbara) shared with Madelon my dismay at the results of an informal survey I had taken while working with owners of businesses. When I suspected the majority of these women were laboring for minimal return I decided to try to find out, by asking more than 100 of them, if the problems they experienced running profitable businesses were any different from those encountered by male entrepreneurs. Out of the hundreds of frustrations they shared 11 were consistently mentioned by the women. They make up the areas we discuss in this book, under the headings of leadership, management and self-development. Indeed some of them were clearly small business problems period. But even these problems, because of the way the women tackled them, took on a gender-specific spin that led to money problems.

A book to assist and encourage women entrepreneurs who are having difficulty making their businesses successful, appealed to me (Madelon), a published writer. Examining my own frustrations as an owner of MAS Production, a small business specializing in writing and editing, I identified with the problem.

Our journey to find answers to the question "Why are women entrepreneurs not making the profits they should?" took us back and forth across the country—by phone, fax, e-mail, airplane and car. We tackled interviews on a national basis to ensure the answers weren't dependent on regional governments or geographical conditions. We asked each woman how she overcame specific hurdles, how she became profitable and how she moved from working hard to working *smart*. We conducted 100 formal interviews.

We interviewed women business owners who have operated profitable companies for more than five years and we interviewed women struggling in the first years of a new business. Our interview subjects ranged from the owners of businesses that were barely scraping by to multimillion-dollar companies. Many of the *Smart Women* represented have won business awards and recognition, including entrepreneur-of-the-year citations. Many have proven women entrepreneurs *can* make money.

We interviewed women in partnerships who owned 50% of their respective businesses. We interviewed a woman whose company has gone public. We interviewed women who combined business and nonprofit organizations and women who run local, national and international companies. We interviewed women in their 20s who had barely begun their businesses and women in their 70s with 50 years of business experience.

Trying to identify who these women should be taught us a new phenomenon. It is a new twist *Smart Women* are bringing to networking—the mystique of synchronicity. Synchronicity is an intuitive sense that what is happening is not just coincidence but meant to be. It is a universal energy receiving and sending out messages. Suddenly the right person walks into your life, or a check arrives in the mail. Using synchronicity as a tool requires you to be "tuned in," aware of its power and able to recognize when you are receiving a message.

When the project began, we put the word out and within days our antenna started picking up information, ideas, contacts and support. As the interviews progressed, *Smart Women* taught us to move our skills from old thinking networking to new happening synchronicity. The concept evolved and the book took over. It began driving us, instead of us forming it. Even today we get gooseflesh as we write about it. It is awesome to understand the power of women working together. It is an honor to be part of the energy radiating from this sphere of influence and experience.

If you continue to read, you will be given the opportunity to test your strengths in every aspect of business and being. A truthful assessment will tell you if you're s*mart* enough to have made, or are in the process of making, the necessary changes to become a **whole person**. We have included action plans to assist you in this process and dozens of quick, practical tips that you can use tomorrow morning. The book has been formatted so that you can turn to your burning question of the day. Whether it's How can I afford a vacation? or How can I obtain financing? we provide immediate answers. Read them, adapt them, implement them. Even though you may be feeling short of being a **whole person**, the fact you are working on yourself makes you a ... *Smart Woman.*

Murdering the Money Myth

Call it the Cinderella Complex. Call it anything you like but the ugly truth is there are far too many women entrepreneurs toiling away in the wee hours of the morning for starvation wages. We know women are opening more businesses, hiring more people and their businesses are lasting longer than those of their male counterparts. The appalling reality, though, is that 75% of women in business are not running operations capable of providing them with secure, above-the-poverty-line incomes. This is a depressing statement, particularly if you consider the fact that one of the major forces driving women to choose self-employment is the need to get out from under dead-end jobs in the hope of doing better than cost-of-living raises allow. They are attempting to move beyond the reality of being paid 62 cents on the dollar earned by their brothers and husbands.

Statistically, women-owned businesses are surviving longer than those owned by men. How is it possible that they are not profitable, if they are lasting longer and employing more people? We're not sure, but our guess is that men simply refuse to work so hard for so little, while women sacrifice their own wages to pay others. The proof is in the Stats Canada figures from 1993—women business owners that year took home an average $18,400, while men business owners took home an average of $33,400. These numbers are even worse when examined more deeply. If you work for someone else for minimum wages, you get to go home at 5 p.m.; if you work for yourself, you slug on for another four hours. Add up your income over a seven-day week. Guess what ... you're working for $3 an hour!

What surprised us even more was that no one was talking about the lack of profitability in women-owned businesses. We wonder if entrepreneurship is yet another societal ghetto for women?

"Women constitute more than half the world's population, are the main producers of wealth, carry out two-thirds of all work performed but only receive one tenth of the world's income and own 1% of property."[1] This is not just depressing, it's unacceptable.

We are not psychologists and do not pretend to be experts on human behavior. The ideas we feel compelled to present come from searching discussions with the women we interviewed and from an examination of our own *paradigms* (a business and psychological term for a personal perception based on a deep-rooted belief). We recognized that 92% of the women we interviewed refused to be associated with or defined by money. We asked each woman, What is your impression of a rich woman? Most were upset by their answers. It is puzzling that this late in the 20th century women still have the little voices inside their heads that say:

A Rich Man is sexy, exciting, powerful, dynamic and obviously intelligent (or he couldn't have made that much money).

A Rich Woman is a manipulative, unattractive, tough, hard-nosed bitch who is forced to hire a gigolo if she wants any attention. Only when she surrenders control of her money to some big, strong man does she once again become a gentle, loving and lovable person to those around her.

Where do these insane ideas originate and how have they become so deeply ingrained in many of us? We need look no further than the fairy tales read as bedtime stories to us as little girls, Disney movies—romantic tales such as *The Little Mermaid*, where the heroine sacrificed her greatest gift, her voice, in order to win the prince.

We acknowledge, with relief, that some women have grown beyond these mental prison bars. However, the majority of new women entrepreneurs appear to be trapped by the old beliefs. They struggle daily against both the ambition that led them to become their own boss and the subconscious fear of how they will be perceived if they become too good at it.

---

[1] Andrina G. Lever report on "Globalization and International Trade" as taken from Franscisca Nennasar Tores, in the European Commission's Annual Report from the Committee On Women's Rights, 1995.

In addition, the greater part of women's work is unpaid work. Their enormous contribution in both the home and the community is given no financial remuneration. This makes it difficult for women to equate money as a measurement of success. Instead, their impulse is to give of themselves as generously in their businesses as they do elsewhere in their life and for as little return.

Having money interferes with what has been a woman's prime directive for centuries—to attract a man to provide for her and their young. Women who have pushed past this to acquire independent means have often paid dearly. Consider only a few of the statements made by women we interviewed—statements that reveal deep, throbbing wounds. We heard the pain in the voices of the women who said: "When my paycheck first topped his, he couldn't handle it"; "When my business became profitable, he told me I obviously didn't need him anymore and found a 20-year-old bubblehead who did"; "He couldn't stand the competition so he undermined my business decisions until I handed the books over to him"; "He siphoned off funds until my company was bankrupt and then walked out, leaving me to pick up the pieces." Faced with these kinds of statements, we concluded that rather than risk this kind of outcome, most women **sabotage themselves and their business profits.**

Smart Women—those who became aware of what they had done—assured us that this sabotaging is not done on a conscious level. This, however, is a rather terrifying demonstration of the power of our subconscious. Many of the women we interviewed told us that though their businesses had almost gone under because of self-sabotage, a crisis enabled them to overcome personal paradigms, move to a more integrated point of view and get their businesses back in the black.

"We ask ourselves, Who am I to be brilliant, gorgeous, talented and fabulous? Actually, though, who are you not to be? Your playing small does not serve the world. There's nothing enlightened about shrinking so that others won't feel insecure around you. And, as we let our own light shine, we unconsciously give other people permission to do the same."[2]

Many women entrepreneurs are confused by the "money message." They were raised hearing the words, **Nice girls don't ask for money.** They appear to believe money is evil and wanting it makes them a "bad

[2] Harriet Ruben, *The Princessa: Machiavelli For Women*

person." They do not seem to realize all their so-called "good goals"—saving the rain forest, educating their children—depend on how successful they are at creating the money to make that work possible.

Deciding to tackle this testy subject takes a lot of courage. Although the almighty dollar serves as a god in much of the world, women don't like to talk about it. They especially seem uncomfortable about admitting a desire for it. Only 3 of the 100 women interviewed said part of the reason they were in business was to make money. With an overwhelming statistic like 97% telling us it's not important to them, we have to think twice before we say, it better be.

Your fear of money manifests itself in your daily life. Do you chronically overspend and are you, therefore, regularly in a debt crisis from which you need to be rescued? Do you constantly worry that there isn't enough—hoarding and measuring each dollar? Women's personal money issues are transferred to their businesses. The overspender has a constant, perilous cash-flow problem and the woman with the poverty mentality refuses to invest her cash in the growth of her company.

You may want to take a minute to probe yourself. Find out your attitude to money by answering these questions:

- How do you feel when you ask someone (husband, father, banker) to give you money?
- How do you feel when you hand someone (customer) a bill for your services?
- How do you feel when you have to collect money owed to you (from a client, supplier, friend)?
- How do you feel about handling money (budgeting, balancing your checkbook, tipping, splitting a bill)?
- How do you feel about spending money?
- How do you feel when the subject of money comes up?

If the questions and your honest answers to them produced immediate, negative reactions in you, then continue your inner exploration to grasp the extent to which you might be tempted to sabotage yourself.

New studies show women have great management styles, and men in top corporations are adopting our female team-building, empowering characteristics. But the only way we're going to ensure we have money to retire on is if our strengths are balanced and we dig deep enough to reach the traits inside that society presently labels "masculine."

We can tell you that the *Smart Women* we talked to who owned successful, profitable businesses reached beyond the male and female stereotypes, to find and nurture within themselves the best and strongest of all characteristics—the appropriate behavior for the occasion regardless of gender bias. Somehow we must peel away the layers of societal restraint to find the wondrous part of us that got lost when we turned 12 and the hormones kicked in. Where is the little girl who delighted in math, was inquisitive about bugs and climbed trees to survey the world? A female, in short, who could handle the numbers, manage the business and go global.

What is this woman like? Believe us, she's **all** woman. In fact our *Smart Woman* knows that success breeds the confidence to explore who she is. She doesn't avoid ruffles or lace, flashing good pieces of jewellery or a nice pair of legs or tearing up when she talks about her new grandchild. She has rediscovered in herself the lifetime explorer who climbs high trees. She is, in fact, becoming a **whole person**, learning to draw on the traits buried within her that she's been denying in order to "win a prince." Each of us is born a **whole person**. The yin and the yang, as taught in Eastern philosophy, create harmony through balance in every one of us, male and female. The *Smart Women* we interviewed are no longer content to be "half people." They want to live in a world where a woman is assertive when she is right, and a man may "tear up" without making everyone in the room uncomfortable.

The greatest challenge of the 21st century will be the re-creation of ourselves and the acceptance of others as **whole people.** We will celebrate what is strongest in each of us. Hundreds of *Smart Women* have created crazy, exciting, vitally unique companies and made them profitable. They represent a new kind of woman entrepreneur—one who makes money, and who is a **whole person.**

SECTION I

LEADERSHIP

"**M**anage things, lead people,"[1] is a much-quoted line in business today. Leading people is a Herculean task if you haven't acquired leadership skills, either through experience or by observing other women leaders. Until recently, very few women achieved the supervisory and management ranks that provided opportunities for them to learn to lead. To further incapacitate Western women, role models have been Hollywood beauties such as Marilyn Monroe or political icons like Margaret Thatcher. Both groups offer little in the way of leadership skills that we could relate to our daily lives. So forgive yourself if you are encountering difficulties in leading the people connected to your business.

What does a leader do? A leader inspires. A leader offers people the opportunity to contribute to a worthwhile endeavor. A leader challenges people constantly to achieve their best performance. Influencing employees to surpass yesterday's efforts ensures the growth of the person and the growth of the company. Leadership begins with your vision—a picture you passionately want to bring to life. In the role of leader you must **formulate a plan**, or determine the steps necessary to ensure your vision comes true. Seldom can you accomplish the plan alone. Therefore, as leader, it becomes critical for you to **identify the right people** to carry out special pieces of your plan, to let go and **delegate to them**, in order to move your business forward. And you must be able to **communicate your vision** with enough clarity to inspire these people to want to join you in making it a reality. You must also **deal with conflict** and not allow the process to be slowed by negativity, infighting or apathy.

[1] Stephen Covey, *The 7 Habits of Highly Effective People:* Simon & Schuster (1989)

As you become a great leader, your business will begin to grow significantly. You stop working hard and start working *Smart*. Define your goals and lead your people forward to help you achieve them. Your goals might be as simple as creating a savings account that will put your kids through university or send the whole family to Hawaii, or as complex as endowing a library or a children's wing in a hospital.

Why do women sabotage their efforts to be good leaders?

Women want to be liked. It's as simple as that. The ***need to be liked by everybody all the time*** is deeply ingrained in most women. Along with this belief is the feeling that if someone doesn't like us, it is our fault. This subconscious impulse to "make nice" leads many women to sabotage their leadership effort. How do we do this?

> Kim Campbell, Canada's first woman prime minister, addressed an international gathering of women entrepreneurs at the 1997 Canadian Women International Conference in Toronto. She shared with them her willingness to be described as a "team leader," "negotiator" or "consensus builder," but said, "I mentally cringe when someone calls me boss." Two hundred women in the audience risked dislocated vertebrae as they nodded heartfelt agreement. "I was brought up to believe a bossy woman was not a nice person. It will be a long time before we overcome our own prejudices," Ms. Campbell lamented.

Leadership requires confidence. We must separate ourselves from the group, cross the line and turn to face them. We must persuade this gathering of people to believe in us and our ideas, follow us and do our bidding. Assuming a leadership position often goes against the mind-set instilled in women. Think about some of the lessons we learned and the behavior we observed in other women, while we were growing up. All along, women have been taught that if we are "good little girls," we will be valued by others. Another underlying message we hear in "be a good little girl" is that we must be different from boys in order to be accepted.

A lack of confidence is what keeps us from making bold, long-term plans. We paralyze ourselves with a lose/lose proposition. What if we fail? We will look foolish, we will harm those we drew into our plan, we will lose our dream and end up with nothing. What if we win? We will have to take responsibility and make sacrifices. We will have to work hard, and success may cause new problems of conflict with our spouse, or a loss of privacy or of friends.

Great leaders are charismatic communicators, able to sway their audience with the passion of the words. Women are often credited as the more emotional communicator—seen as a leadership strength. Yet, many women keep things to themselves, afraid to speak out in case they are wrong. The subconscious signal to "flee rather than fight" causes us to sabotage ourselves in the area of conflict resolution.

Traditionally, the fastest way to prevent a woman from going after what she wants is to tell her she's too aggressive. It very effectively stops her in her tracks. In fact, she is only asserting her right to be what she wants to be. Time and again we psych ourselves up to confront an issue, then slink away at the first sign of criticism, anger or intimidation.

If we want to be perceived as nice, we're not likely to order people around, fire them for sloppy work, demand that they stop spreading discord in the workplace or tell them they have certain targets to meet. We shy away, thereby destroying the process of delegation and limiting our ability to communicate. There goes leadership.

Instead of resigning ourselves to our weaknesses we must adopt the **whole person** philosophy and grow our leadership skills. These traits are in all of us, but they are like muscles that have rarely been used. Now it is time to flex and begin to build them up. For example, most women bring the strengths of creativity, attention to detail and personal ethics to the planning process. A **whole person** would augment these by developing his or her ability to see the big picture, be realistic and create support for their vision. In order to find and keep the right people we must combine the strengths, commonly thought of as feminine, of team-building and intuition with the objectivity and sense of fair play that come more naturally to men. A **whole person** delegates by combining a willingness to cooperate and empower others with good judgement of character and a hands-off approach. A **whole person** also communicates by painting evocative word pictures and using a direct approach, logic and a confident delivery style. Finally, the **whole person** deals with conflict by using a proactive approach to limit the occurrence of conflict. When it cannot be avoided, he or she balances feeling empathetic and desiring peace with objectivity, assertiveness and authority.

A **whole person** comes from a set of values that make choices simple. A **whole person** radiates positive energy because she or he is comfortable with where they stand. This immediately inspires trust and confidence, which attract others. If you are to make it down the prosperity path, you must lead with magnificence, courage and style.

CHAPTER 1

Planning

What frustrations do you experience when you try to plan?

The Chinese think nothing of formulating a business plan to cover the next two hundred years, while most North Americans have not yet accepted the need for a three-year plan. In a country where long-term strategic planning is almost nonexistent, many women entrepreneurs join the ranks of those who find reasons not to do it. "I get too caught up in the day-to-day details," said one. "The resources are exclusively aimed at males," complained another. "It wastes too much of my time," sighed a third.

Women entrepreneurs avoid planning for a myriad of reasons. The one we hear most often is, "I don't have time." Women are not managing their time well enough to make planning a priority. They are locked in a chicken-and-egg cycle—**not enough time to plan, no plan to provide more time.** Are you caught up in the little details? Do you procrastinate? Do you follow your gut feeling, cross your fingers and hope all will come out right in the end? Do you build great schemes in your head but never put them down on paper? Do you talk about it until all your enthusiasm, along with everyone else's, is depleted, but never take action to make it happen?

The second excuse we heard most often was **lack of money.** You may be reluctant to take the time to plan because it cuts into other work that puts immediate money in your pocket. You believe you must first take an extensive planning course you can't afford, or you feel you will have to hire extra staff (which you also can't afford) to cover for you while you are at the planning workshop. You are no longer chasing the almighty dollar, you're being run over by it!

Factors beyond your control may inhibit your ability to plan. Identify the activities wasting your energy. Some of them may be necessary because you are not able to anticipate events. You may be a good planner—with your days scheduled, your weekly planner filled out, your itinerary set for the month—then your personal life strikes. Your son must be taken to the dentist because he broke his tooth, your daughter is scheduled for three extra practices the week before the concert, and your husband's job is taking him out of town unexpectedly. As a mother, wife, partner, friend you have probably been programmed to sacrifice your plans for those of the people in your life. Frustration results.

You will also experience frustration if you don't know where your business is headed. Recognize that nothing stands still and you must be prepared to move with the times. Possibly you are in an industry where trends fluctuate and force you to be flexible. Perhaps you have a partner who refuses to plan. Do you never get beyond the daily crisis, to be able to plan?

The one thing that isn't beyond your control is your attitude to planning. Have some fun with it. It's not a "do or die" endeavor! To find the time and money to plan and overcome the obstacles, you must first adopt a proactive attitude.

You don't need a special education to do basic planning. And planning will allow you to take control of your business. As you define your vision, your mission, your advantage in the marketplace and your goals, difficult decisions will become easy. And leadership is much less difficult when you know where you're going.

Do you know what you're planning for?
Check out your planning quotient
on the next page.

 Are you sabotaging yourself?

Planning: Danger Signals

(Circle the appropriate answer for each question. Add up your numbers and check the next page to see how your planning skills are affecting your leadership ability.)

5 - always	4 - regularly	3 - occasionally	2 - rarely	1 - never

1. Do you take time to plan for the short term?

5	4	3	2	1

2. Do you have a written three-year plan in place?

5	4	3	2	1

3. Do you set interim goals to help you achieve your plan?

5	4	3	2	1

4. Do you review your goals and see what progress has been made?

5	4	3	2	1

5. Do you avoid getting caught up in day-to-day details?

5	4	3	2	1

6. Do you have a well-defined strategic customer advantage? (page 25)

5	4	3	2	1

7. Do you update your plans and change them when necessary?

5	4	3	2	1

8. Do you have a clear understanding of the values on which you want your business built?

5	4	3	2	1

9. Do you share with your employees/suppliers/clients values on which you want your business built?

5	4	3	2	1

10. Do you know what your competition is doing?

5	4	3	2	1

Your planning score _____

41–50   Excellent. Your planning ability will move your business ahead in its profitability and ensure it grows in the direction you desire. This allows you to do what you love to do.

31–40   Redefine your mission statement. What are you doing to achieve it?

21–30   You need a plan. Schedule a day just to sit down and write out your vision, mission, and ethic statements. Share them with those closely involved in your organization. Get their insights on how you can better live them. Order the Communicating Power Inc. business plan workbook.[2]

11–20   We suggest planning an activity workshop. Put serious effort into the **Whole Person** Action Plan on page 35. Take a day in the country and rethink your vision.

10   Your business is probably stagnating, with growth minimal and profits far too low. Your employees lack direction and you are spending too much time fighting fires instead of being proactive. You are probably experiencing depression and exhaustion. Read and reread this chapter. Go on a two-week holiday, don't even think business; then take three days to plan before starting up again. Get help from your accountant and other experts.

If your planning quotient is low, you are losing money in the following ways:

- By not knowing where your business is headed, you are unable to set goals and end up aiming low.
- By not properly identifying your target market, you miss opportunities to diversify and build your business.
- By not defining your strategic customer advantage, you give your competition the opportunity to cut into your market share.
- Because you do not have a strategic customer advantage, customers "shop you" based on price, not value.

[2] Call toll-free 1-877-444-1940 to order.

I. How do I define my vision?

Creating a three- to five-year plan is an overwhelming task. You can begin, though, by deciding on the basics of your business simply by answering the questions Where am I now? and Where do I want to end up? Then, one step at a time, plan the route in between. You will start out crawling, but end up sprinting.

a) Begin with a Dream

"My vision," says Danielle Medina, owner of Medina Foods Inc., "is to promote the Medina Seal of Quality as the world's guarantee of nutritious, delicious, safely prepared food." In 1980 she was a dietitian who didn't understand business; but she did understand food. She couldn't believe how overcooked and tasteless institutionally prepared food was, and the unsanitary conditions it came from. She felt that if standards could be imposed, it would be possible to measure the safety and nutritional value of meals by analyzing and measuring their components. She decided that if she could put a food assessment program on computer, she could provide nutritional status reports to the managers of food service companies. Danielle made the proactive choice to approach an executive at Air Canada. She knew an airline needed to use dozens of catering companies around the world. She felt they would be very interested in affordable quality food auditing for their passengers. She was granted a 10-minute interview. Shaking with nerves, she told the busy executive how she could make a difference for his customers. She painted a vivid picture of how even sodium depletion could hurt a regular flyer. "You want that customer to stay healthy, so he can fly," she pointed out. She flashed her arms out to demonstrate wing span; her passion sold the idea, and they agreed to a trial. She has set worldwide standards for all airlines. Danielle reminds her clients, who now include such companies as Canadian, KLM, Northwest and United, "An airplane has hundreds of people on board to mother and care for. They deserve good taste and good nutrition. But most of all, they deserve safely prepared food."

> "I believe we should leave this place a better world for our being here."
> **Joan Macdonald**
> **J.V.I. Commercial Driving School Ltd.**

This is Danielle's "vision" of her business. A vision is an understanding of what you want to accomplish. Your business is the means of accomplishing it. Most Industrial Age businesses are driven by their product/service offering. For example, the owner of the dry-cleaning store might think the business is *cleaning clothes*. An owner with a broader view—a vision—knows the business is *selling personal image*. We lay our money on their counter for a chance at the next job promotion, the attention of a new boyfriend or the respect of a boss. If this wasn't the case we would all buy wash and wear polyester. Once the owner comprehends the potential impact the business can have on our lives, she or he will make better choices that will change the way she or he does business. By identifying your business's potential contribution to your life and to your customers' lives, you determine if it is the right business for you. When your business concept meets and passes the following three criteria, you have the basis for your vision:

- Does it allow me to fulfill my childhood dream, the answer to the question, What do I want to be when I grow up?
- Does it allow me to live by the values and beliefs that are the foundation of my life?
- Does it provide me with a way of making a meaningful contribution to the community it will serve?

b) Find Your Genius

Sometimes it's hard to know what you want to be when you grow up. In order to write your vision statement you need to back up a step and ask yourself: What do I want to accomplish in my life? What is the reason I was put on Earth? What is my major purpose? David McNally's *Even Eagles Need a Push*[3] is an excellent guide that will help you through this process. To ensure balance, inner peace and prosperity in your life, your business vision must be aligned with your personal vision.

> "Anything I dream of is possible to do."
> *Valerie Pusey*
> *Northern Passage Gallery*

Your purpose is often discovered in those things you do best—your area of genius. If you have not developed an understanding of your area

[3] David McNally, *Even Eagles Need a Push*; Transform Press (1990)

of genius, spend extra time on Section 3, "Self-Development." Exploring yourself is an exciting treasure hunt that forces you outside your comfort zone. Looking deep inside yourself is hard work. Many people give up the search and settle for just "cleaning clothes."

c) The Power of Vision

Vision is about giving your life purpose. When you make your vision part of your business, you give meaning to the lives of the people who work for you and buy from you. Going to work every day to clean people's clothes soon becomes repetitive and boring. Who cares anyway? You soon feel anyone can do the job and that your work is not worthwhile and has little importance or value. If, on the other hand, you go to work every morning determined to enhance people's images so they'll achieve more success in their lives, you (and your team) have a reason to get out of bed. Your product and service line will change. You will improve your customer services and alter the role you play in your customers' lives. Soon your business will begin to look different from that of the average dry cleaner. Your customers will do a double take if you start helping them achieve their life's dreams. They will deluge you with loyalty, commitment and appreciation—qualities hard to come by in today's arid business world.

d) Wouldn't It Be Nice If...

When the purpose of your business is in place, you may want to include other issues of personal importance in your vision statement. For example, you might wish to address the size you want your business to be (home-based versus international). Do you wish to provide jobs? (Barb Housser creates work for university students as part of her vision.) Do you wish to grow other businesses? (Communicating Power Inc. subcontracts to more than 300 small business owners in a year.) Do you wish to have an impact on the environment or other worthwhile causes? (Bianco Nero raises hundreds of thousands of dollars for breast cancer research.) Do you want your family involved? (Gladys Saren is thrilled every day to work with her adult sons in two complementary businesses.) Do you

> "Build a good foundation. Don't try to build the roof first."
> **Nicole Beaudoin**
> **Quebec Business Women's Network Inc.**

want to win some special award or leave a legacy? (Seagull Pewter has built Seagull University, a wildlife sanctuary and education facility of world renown.)

Visions change, but this doesn't give you permission to act like a flake by constantly changing your focus. As your business develops over the years, both your and your customers' needs will change. Visions are not carved in stone, they must be allowed to grow and develop right along with you. This is a great relief, because it means you don't have to get it perfect the first time. Take a stab at it and fine-tune it at least once a year. After each change, ensure that everyone (financers, suppliers, staff and customers) is brought up to speed.

2. Why do I need a mission statement?

Your vision statement is very personal and because it can be quite lengthy, it may not be practical to share it with others. But it's important to communicate the core of your vision to your staff, customers and all others your business will touch.

> "Clarify your vision to all your employees. They need a reason to be there."
> *Bev McMaster*
> *WeCare Health Services Inc.*

The mission statement defines the business that will accomplish your vision. The mission is a flag you can fly to the world, one the whole team can raise together, even if your business is a do-it-yourself family carwash. In 25 words or less, it should tell the world your mission, including

- what business you are in (drawn from your vision statement—such as "to help families spend quality time together")
- what key product/service you are offering (e.g., a carwash)
- who your customers are (e.g., families with vehicles)
- what your growth direction is (e.g., families in St. Albert who want to spend more quality time together by turning washing the car into a fun, family outing)
- what makes you special (e.g., entertainment, the form of decor, children's games, family water fights)

Sample Mission Statement:

The Big Toy Wash Co. offers a safe, environmentally friendly and fun carwash service that helps the families of the St. Albert area clean together, play together and stay together.

3. Can I bring my personal values to the business?

Once you've established your vision and your mission, make sure they reflect your values. When your business's objectives are at odds with your personal values you cannot help but sabotage your efforts. And yet, the majority of business plans do not have an **ethics statement.** Business has acquired a nasty reputation: "capitalist pigs," "Businesspeople are only out for a fast buck." These labels scare women entrepreneurs. Often in trying to avoid being perceived as "rip-off artists," they give away business and end up working for free. An ethics statement provides standards for your business, while ensuring you still charge a fair price. You may not always achieve these standards, but they serve as a measuring stick that allows you to acknowledge when you fall short and encourages you to continually try harder.

> "You must live by your values," Danielle Medina cautions. A few years ago she sold the majority of her company to a large food chain. Eight months later she learned they intended to put the Medina Seal on artificial cream puffs. "I learned that the new owner would be at a special dinner I was also attending. I arranged to be seated next to him. During the meal, I asked him in front of a table full of journalists why he had decided to endorse the artificial product. He had no idea it was happening. He ended up helping me and sold the company back to me. He understood the importance of ethics."

Ponder the fact that *we are what we know*, before you decide whether or not it's worth taking the time to write an ethics statement. Each of us has all the worst characteristics of the worst bosses we ever worked for in our memory banks. You are constantly in danger of emulating their practices in your own business. It's like telling yourself, "When I'm a parent, I'll never do that to my kids," and one day, in horror, you catch yourself duplicating exactly the same pattern of behavior.

"We can change the business world by changing the way we do business."
Valerie Pusey
Northern Passage Gallery

Unethical behavior rubs off. If enough people within an environment are regularly practicing unethical behavior, it becomes the norm. For example, in many organizations employees help themselves to pens, paper, photocopies and the like. The practice is so common, the employees no longer consider it stealing. Unless you make a conscious effort to communicate your values, you will find yourself in similar circumstances. How will you feel when members of your staff take things from your business?

In trying to think of everything you want in your ethics statement you should move beyond the **Golden Rule**—*do unto others as you would have them do unto you,* and embrace the **Platinum Rule**—*do unto others as they would be done unto.*

Lori Donovan's shoe manufacturing company silk screens the leather of one of their children's boot lines to match the fabric in a designer's children's clothing line. By treating each customer so individually she lands premium licencing deals.

The Platinum Rule helps you deal differently with each person. You must recognize that what makes you happy and is part of your value system is not the same for everyone.

Other issues you may want to address in your ethics statements are:

- loyalty: Will you dump suppliers when someone cheaper comes along?
- natural environment: Have you already addressed it in your vision statement? If not, is it important to you?
- profits and pricing: Will you undercut competition or inflate prices?
- contribution to community: How will you handle the hundreds of requests you'll get every year to donate to worthwhile causes?
- crisis management: How will you react if something goes wrong?
- work environment: Will you leave staff standing on a concrete floor for an eight-hour shift? working without proper lighting? in strong fumes without proper equipment?
- discrimination: Is everyone on your team treated equally?

- harassment: What process do you have in place to report it and deal with it?

Your ethics statement can be written in point form. You should provide a copy to everyone who works for and with you. When you have an ethics statement many tough decisions become easy.

> Danielle Medina was offered $10,000 to do a margarine contract at a time when she couldn't afford to pay rent. She doesn't believe in margarine. "I look back and say 'Thank God, I turned them down.' A different decision would have negated all I have done since to build a worldwide reputation as the quality expert," she points out.

The development of the vision, mission and ethics statements will provide the key to the door of your customer's heart—and they will provide a solid foundation for all your plans.

4. How do I create a Strategic Customer Advantage (SCA)?

The saying is *Own their heart—and you own the market.* To own your customers' hearts (and gain their loyalty) you must have something special to offer. This is called your **strategic customer advantage** (SCA). Your SCA defines: (1) *what you have that the customer really wants* and (2) *where you fit in the marketplace.* Your SCA differentiates you from all the boring, look-alike businesses left over from the Industrial Age that still fill the marketplace today.

> It is not what you expect. The window is filled with exquisite glass shapes. Inside gently tinkling Eastern music and exotic scents waft over you. Immediately you are part of a sensory adventure. You find you have stepped onto a new spiritual plane, where, for the short time you are in this spa, your body, mind and spirit achieve a harmony that will move you further on your journey to inner peace.

Not the usual glitz here. No smooth plastic edges or the gold-leaf cherubs we are accustomed to. Instead we discover something "uncommon." This unique appeal that so captures your attention is LaRaffinage's

"Keep an ideas journal in the back of your time-keeping system. Review it every week and decide what you can implement in the coming week."
Barb Housser
Sam's Deli

SCA, its single most important tool to increasing sales in today's competitive marketplace. Renate Geier, the classic blonde who owns the business is herself a unique combination of flowing, feminine spirituality and solid business sense, a **whole person.**

Your SCA must position your business to meet the specific needs of a market segment large enough to financially ensure your profitability. Often these needs are so nebulous that if you ask the customer beforehand, they can't identify what it is they really want. They only recognize it when it materializes "in front of their eyes." A great SCA is reinforced over and over by a hundred little enhancements, that, when delivered all together, appeal powerfully to your sense of smell, sight, taste, touch, sound and the emotional sixth sense that signals when something is right for you.

> Barbara Balfour, owner of the The Gallery, located in a building that had last served as a library, says, "The building has charisma, a pull of its own. It is a piece of art in its own right. It feeds my imagination and helps to promote my work." The building has been declared a historic landmark and now Barb's business is on a tour route. A great SCA delivers a busload of clients to your door!

If your customers don't know what they want, how do you build an SCA that works? *Smart Women* positioned their companies from the beginning, though most of them will tell you they didn't know what an SCA was. So how did they get it so right? Unquestionably, it comes from their own *vision* of what they want the company to be. It takes shape, is reinforced and manifests itself throughout the first five years of operation. The farm in the west with its wild boar hunts, the dairy on the prairies with its special breeding program, the weaver in the south who makes wool clothing for large-sized women; all shared the same story of growing a place in their customers' minds and hearts.

Smart Women start with phrases like: **"I knew the industry needed something," "I couldn't find what I wanted," "I didn't feel it was being done right."** Their explanations end most often with the theme "We get constant feedback from our customers and implement their recommendations whenever possible."

Having an exclusive product line is one way to build a strategic customer advantage.

Wholesaler Doris Tan introduced two exclusive and innovative hair care lines to the marketplace. Even so, she cautions, you can't afford to forget that while the competition may not have the same line as you, they do have a competitive product. "If you're not backing up what you do with a hundred other special details that capture your customers' imaginations, you're still vulnerable to losing them."

Sometimes having it all works.

Debi DeBelser is a far cry from the flannel dressed "hard hat" you would expect to find running a multimillion-dollar company that supplies pipeline to the oil patch. She says survival for her company is a direct result of being involved in all of the three major areas of her industry: sales, production and trucking. In the 1980s, when the bottom fell out of the oil market, competitors who focused on a single service went under. Debi felt she was able to hold on simply because she could achieve some economies of scale when clients came to her to get the whole job done. "In boom times," Debi reminds us, "it's harder to manage a diversified company." But, knowing the roller-coaster nature of her industry, she has no intention of giving up her SCA. New clients constantly express their amazement that one company can do it all well. Her challenge is to build systems in which all three divisions can communicate with each other effectively and with the best interests of the client in mind.

Sometimes creating mystery and wonder around your business creates an SCA that draws increasing numbers of people who like sanitized adventures.

Phillipa Hudson located on the coastline, with the ocean as a backdrop to her merchandise. She imports minerals and semiprecious stones. Her unique offerings—such as chunks of meteorite—have combined both the exotic and the extraordinary. Tubs, canoes and

"We have incredible mental powers that we can harness and make magic happen."
Zandra Bell
at wit's end

other ingenious containers are filled to the brim with every kind of polished stone from all over the world. For $5 customers can buy a bag and spend a fascinating hour or more on a treasure hunt, filling the bag with the size, shape and color of stones that speak to them. By focusing on school children and booking classroom tours and birthday parties, she attracts a secondary market of parents. "We started the business with the idea of selling minerals from around the world in a unique way, and increased our sales 200% the second year." Profitability gives Phillipa a glow and allows her to travel the world bringing home new treasures to share.

In determining your SCA you must first know what your competition is doing. How can you offer something special if you don't know what's available already? The answer is a *competition analysis*. Competition analyses, which must be undertaken on a regular basis, examine only those businesses that compete in the marketplace where you sell, for example, a suburb of Vancouver, or Vancouver, or British Columbia, or Canada. The bigger your marketplace the more widespread your competition analysis must be. Phone, write, drop in and observe your competitors. Document everything you can discover—from their location (and how good it is), to their prices, service levels (e.g., How many rings before they answer the phone? Does a real person or a machine answer?), the number and quality of their staff, how diverse their product/service line is, how they promote and how they budget their promotions (check everything from their brochures to their Yellow Pages ad). Gather competition information on an ongoing basis. Often competitors will refer clients they don't have the resources to handle to you, and you may want to do the same for them.

The second area you will want to continually research is your industry. In strategic planning, this is called an *industry analysis*. Traditionally, Europe has led North America by one to two years in most industries. The southwestern United States has led Canada in trends by up to a year. Eastern Canada tends to be ahead of Western Canada by a good six months. By doing continuous industry analysis you can identify opportunities or an SCA and avoid pitfalls. Some of the best sources for this information are the Internet, international industry magazines, industry associations, library resources and international Yellow Pages. You can also make phone calls to selected businesses or ask out-of-province friends to track down what's happening in their city.

5. How big should my business be?

Struggling to clarify your vision and define your product may cause you to stretch your comfort zone. Do you want a business that could be successful beyond a local level? One that could employ a large number of people? If you do want to grow your business, identify, in your plan, what you need to do over the next three years in order to achieve profitability.

> **"Your business plan must be a living document."**
> *Joy Hanley*
> *Fine Food Investments Ltd.*

Businesses come in every size. They should be custom-made. You need to decide whether you want to operate a smaller business, with strict controls over the time and resources you are willing to invest, or whether you want to grow a huge corporate structure. Big or small, the goal of the business has to be to generate enough profit to continue to evolve.

> Donna Bell has strong motivation to operate a small home-based business. Two of her three sons have special needs. "My life is integrated. What happens in the home affects the business and vice versa. We operate like a wheel, not a juggling act," she explains. With skills in commercial sewing, Donna runs a company that manufactures safety vests. She has targeted the oil-driven seismic industry in Alberta. Donna has computed the number and size of orders she will take and the number of employees she will hire to keep her work hours under control, while still slowly growing her business. Her plan is "to increase revenue, pay down debt and be prepared to move my business into larger off-site premises by the time my sons are educated and self-sufficient."

Profitability is a big focus in Donna's business: she moved away from manufacturing products with poor margins and now specializes in an important area that gives a fair return on her investment and the profits needed for controlled growth.

In contrast, Bev McMaster, who is in the home health-care business, says, "My plans are very ambitious. They extend to 2010 and involve dealing with other big players in the health services field. I have people already working to pinpoint companies we will buy out in the global market. We are expanding into the U.S., Great Britain, Australia, Southeast Asia and France." In a strong, proactive move, Bev has established legal teams in designated countries who are working to protect her trademark. She is collaborating with government bodies and their respective health-care industries. She explains, "Because we are community-based and deal with ethnically diverse populations day in and day out, international expansion is a logical and natural next step." She is projecting a multibillion-dollar company by 2010, while still maintaining the highest quality of health service. She has designed and written strategic business plans but she says, "They are not written in stone and many times they still have to be reworked. When your plans come alive, they give you tremendous confidence in your ability to succeed because you have a clear picture of what needs to be done next."

This company was seeded by Bev's sudden awareness that the mother of a close friend could not get proper home care. Providing appropriate home care to many became her vision.

"The difference between those who do and those who don't is the do's continue to think in the washroom."
Bev Durvin
Benkris & Co.

She grew a desire to help one woman into a business that provides quality health services and home support across the country. Her corporation now employs 4000 people and has annual sales of $30 million. As long as Bev's core values of quality, caring and integrity continue to fuel growth and she continues to plan proactively, there is every reason to believe she will meet her goal for 2010.

Size decisions are very personal things. They need to address your lifestyle, concerns and ambition. But big or micro, they need to be profitable. Don't say you can't travel just because you don't know what the trip looks like at this moment. Once you have a destination in mind, you can draw a map, consult a few experts on travel hazards and be on your way.

6. What should be in my plan?

The planning process becomes straightforward once the foundation of your plan is in place—the vision, mission and ethics statements—and you have determined your SCA. The remainder of your plan addresses:

- how you will offer your SCA (your product/service plan)
- how you will communicate your SCA to your customer (your marketing plan)
- what systems you need in place to provide the SCA to the customer (operations plan)
- how much will it cost to do and how much will you make from it (financial plan)

Dozens of outlines of business plans are available to help you. Banks give them away free, public libraries stock them and some companies develop their own. Communicating Power Inc. has developed **Enterprise and Innovation**™, one of Canada's leading strategic business plans, along with a simple-to-follow workbook.[4] It provides you with a step-by-step, fill-in-the-blanks process to move you through the planning process to the completed document. Business plans, completed with the help of this workbook will wow any banker.

Surprisingly, with help so readily available, less than 20% of small business owners have ever written a business plan. A direct correlation can be seen between this figure and the small business failure rate of 80% within five years of setting up. Having a business plan is not a guarantee for success. However, statistics collected by small business programs such as SEA (Self-Employment Assistance—a government program that assists small business startups) show that the 20% of businesses that have plans and that implement them, are more profitable and move forward faster.

In 1987 Linda Naiman read *Prospering Women* by Ruth Ross. When she finished, she wrote down a five-year plan. She then opened a new business, training people for the graphics design sector. "I never looked at my plan for an entire year," she shared in amazement, "then I opened it and discovered I could tick off, as completed, everything I had projected for the next five years,

[4]Call toll-free 1-877-444-1940 to order.

and a few things I hadn't planned like addressing a sitting of a United Nations committee."

Now that is a quantum leap! Planning is the tool that moves you forward faster. A written business plan is not always necessary. However, banks these days will not consider first-time financing without a business plan. Aside from its necessity, writing it down is beneficial: it helps you lodge it in your subconscious and makes it much easier to share with others.

Next, develop contingency plans to deal with threats should they occur.

Jacqui MacNeill explains, "You make huge improvements in your company by making contingency plans around the vulnerable places in your business and safeguarding yourself before you're attacked there." Jacqui recognized that 95% of her aromatherapy supplies were purchased in bulk from one American company. "If they went under or raised their prices dramatically, it would have a terrible impact on my business," she pointed out. Jacqui made a proactive decision to eliminate the threat. She chose to import the pure essence from several sources and manufacture the product herself. And, she created her own label, which she now sells through her retail stores. This, in turn, provided a new opportunity: selling the new product to others on a wholesale, bulk basis.

> **"Be open to change as a constant in your life and see the opportunity in the change."**
> *Gaye Trombley*
> *The Avalon Group Ltd.*

7. Who can help me plan?

Possibly the most effective planning tool ever devised for growing your business is an advisory board. If the only thing you implement from this book is an advisory board, and you follow the bulk of their advice for the next year, you'll double or triple your profits. A large corporation has a board of directors responsible for helping the company grow. If you are a lonely entrepreneur, putting in 18-hour days, then you are certainly working hard, not *smart*. As an entrepreneur, you don't need to gallop bravely off into the sunset alone after a long day. Copy what's best from the big firms and get yourself an advisory board—a group of four to six people willing to donate two hours a month to growing your business. Choose people from diverse fields (e.g., finance, industry, marketing), who are willing to share their networks with you. Reach as high as you can to find these people. You'll end up with experience and skills it would take years to learn on your own.

Your advisory board's job is to:

- hold you accountable for producing your projected monthly sales figures
- provide you with their expert advice on your day-to-day operations
- help you gain a broader perspective on your strategies
- save you from having to learn everything in the school of hard knocks
- provide you with access to their networks and give you referrals
- boost you up when you're down
- kick your butt when you're not performing, and applaud you when you succeed

"There are a lot of resources out there. Use them."
Lori Donovan
First Step International Ltd.

What's in it for them? Most successful people are more than willing to invest a couple of hours a month, for a year, to help someone who appears very determined to achieve success (someone has probably done the same for your advisers). People like to give advice. It's also flattering to be asked and to have someone acknowledge their expertise. Since it's a new strategy, most businesspeople have no experience with advisory boards. This gives them the opportunity to test-drive yours and see how it works.

"When I began my wellness magazine I set a primary goal of making an impact and being credible," stated Elaine Kupser, publisher of *Impact* magazine. "I was new to the industry, so this was tough. I approached top people from the wellness field and asked them to sit on my advisory board. I put key people in every aspect of the wellness industry in place. As well as advising me, I asked them to contribute articles to the magazine, which provided immediate credibility for my product. They each enjoyed the payoff of increased

"Business is a creative act, a mystery to be revealed. Business is no longer a problem to be solved."
Linda Naiman
Linda Naiman and Associates Inc.

prestige, free promotion for their business, greater profits for their own business and the good feeling of knowing they were helping grow my business. Together we are making a genuine contribution to the industry."

Tips for Working with Your Advisory Board:

- Don't serve food. It stretches the time. Keep to the promised 1½ hours per meeting, per month. Save ½ hour potential follow-up phone time per month for crisis or celebration. You can throw a nice thank-you dinner at a time outside of that scheduled for meetings when you want to recognize your board members' contributions to your business.
- Do have a preset agenda and keep on track.
- Do lay all your cards on the table and be totally honest. Hiding your true financial picture will make it hard for them to provide appropriate advice to you.
- Don't pay them, but do show your appreciation in other small ways. Their main reward will be in seeing you grow and knowing they had a hand in it.
- Don't take it personally if someone says no. A jammed schedule is a legitimate reason for declining. Ask them if you can call them from time to time for advice or if you can approach them again next year if their schedule changes, and you are seeking a replacement or addition to your present board. Ask them also if they know of any other talented businessperson who might be interested in helping you. The more determined they see you are to succeed, the more keen they'll be to give you a hand.

We have watched new businesses with advisory boards quickly outdistance businesses that were equally viable but that did not have advisers.

Once you have a great plan in place, you need the people to help you implement it. Finding and keeping the right people is both a *Smart Woman* challenge and the next leadership skill we will discuss.

The WHOLE PERSON
Action Plan for Planning

1. Write your mission statement. What business are you really in? Has your thinking changed since you first began the business?

    _____

    _____

2. Identify your vision. Take a day (Monday is best) away from business. Pack up paper and pen, head for the park, your cabin, the country—anywhere that is away from people. Spread your blanket and dream. See the vision of your business five years from now. Write it down.

    _____

    _____

3. Make a list of every unethical thing you've done and every bad practice you've recognized in other bosses/owners. Use this "ugly" list to create a guideline for your ethics statement.

    _____

    _____

4. Determine your SCA. Write a list of all the ways you could appeal to your customers' "senses" in order to increase their perception of your SCA.

    _____

    _____

5. Form an advisory board. Make a list of potential candidates. Ask others for recommendations. Phone people on your list until you have six members.

    _____

    _____

... now you're working SMART

Call Communicating Power Inc. at 1-877-444-1940 for Enterprise and Innovation,™ *our business plan workbook. Make it an ongoing process to work your way through it.*

CHAPTER 2

Finding and Keeping the Right People

What frustrations are you experiencing in finding and keeping the right people?

When discussing their frustration around people issues, the women we interviewed most often smiled wryly and shook their heads. Perhaps the most exciting part of their dissatisfaction with finding the right people was the emphasis they put on values, ethics and integrity. More than 60% of the women mentioned their insistence in finding like-minded individuals to work with them. Unfortunately, 15% of the women have a bias against hiring young people. They identified "unwillingness to accept responsibility," an "entitlement attitude," "poor work ethic" and "lack of commitment" when they talked about the young people they refused to consider when looking for help.

There is also a general disappointment among women entrepreneurs over employees' lack of loyalty and the feeling their business is used far too often as a "training centre for higher jobs."

While more than 30% of the women talked about nurturing their employees, a large number of them are now *Smart Women* who see the negative results of doing so. They recognize that their mothering instincts increase the load they carry, exacerbate problems between employees and cost them their objectivity. Nurturing an employee is not the same as training and developing that person so that she or he is an asset in the business. Today's labor laws have placed a huge burden on small business-owners. They resent the time that must go into documenting each employee infraction. They feel betrayed by a system that penalizes them financially when they have a nonperformer on staff. In spite of the in-depth interviewing, such people get hired into a business and know exactly how far to push the limit of the law. In being prevented from dealing with the situation, an owner feels helpless.

Family is another area of frustration. Many small business owners are caught between feeling guilty if they don't provide a job for a needy relative and feeling anxious about hiring the relative though he or she may well be a poor worker who will hurt their business.

Some women say bad experiences have reduced their trust level. Some don't trust themselves to pick the right person for the job because of past mistakes that cost them dearly. Some say they go into the interview handicapped, closed against certain physical or character traits similar to the person who hurt them before.

Of course we can't talk about women entrepreneurs finding and keeping the right people without talking authority problems. Frustration is still rampant in this area. "My age works against me," said one budding entrepreneur, who was not yet 30 years old, "no one takes me seriously." "My looks work against me," said a slender, blue-eyed blonde. "People assume I'm too frail," she said, "they think I won't stay the course." Too fat, too thin, too shy, too female—these are some of the reasons women give to explain why they are not perceived as authority figures in their business. However, some women have seen these reasons not as drawbacks but challenges, and refuse to be treated differently than men. They are adopting some of the male-designated traits in dealing with people and finding they receive all the respect and attention necessary to lead.

**To test your ability to find and keep good people,
do the danger signals quiz on the next page.**

 Are you sabotaging yourself?

People: Danger Signals

(Circle the appropriate answer for each question. Add up your numbers and check your people skills quotient on the next page.)

5 - always   4 - regularly   3 - occasionally   2 - rarely   1 - never

1. Do you have a clear idea of the skills and attributes that will be an asset to your business?

| 5 | 4 | 3 | 2 | 1 |

2. Do you have staff training programs in place?

| 5 | 4 | 3 | 2 | 1 |

3. Are you willing to let people make mistakes they can learn from?

| 5 | 4 | 3 | 2 | 1 |

4. Do you have staff and friends help you find new employees?

| 5 | 4 | 3 | 2 | 1 |

5. Do you refrain from complaining about employees to other staff members?

| 5 | 4 | 3 | 2 | 1 |

6   When you discuss with an employee their unacceptable attitude, behavior or work do you have them sign something to verify that they have been told?

| 5 | 4 | 3 | 2 | 1 |

7. Do you have a pay structure in place that rewards productivity and meets your team's need to be appreciated?

| 5 | 4 | 3 | 2 | 1 |

8. Do you make objective people decisions based on business needs first?

| 5 | 4 | 3 | 2 | 1 |

9. Do you have written job descriptions for each position?

| 5 | 4 | 3 | 2 | 1 |

10. Do you regularly evaluate your employees' performances with them?

| 5 | 4 | 3 | 2 | 1 |

Your people skills score _____

41–50 You are great leadership material and have excellent people skills.

31–40 Although you exhibit talent in this area we suggest you take a hard look at your paradigms (beliefs) and assess why you are making mistakes with your staff.

21–30 You need to analyze this area carefully if you want to be an effective leader. We suggest you evaluate your staff members for energy and attitude. You may want to take a human resources workshop to gain a better understanding of people.

11–20 You definitely need a behavioral/personality profile workshop for the whole staff. Probably you need to retrain or fire several employees and replace them with qualified, high-energy people. We recommend you review all of your relationships and consider eliminating high-maintenance people from your company.

10 Your leadership ability is at risk if you are not enhancing the performance of your team members. We recommend that you read this chapter and work through the **Whole Person** Action Plan on page 56. Implement wherever possible.

If your skills in finding and keeping the right people are poor, your business is losing money because:

- You have not picked the right person for the job; it is being done poorly.
- Your customers do not get the service they want because of staff incompetence.
- Your energy is spent on staff issues instead of customer issues.
- Your poor people skills alienate your employees and lower morale, reducing productivity.
- The business is incurring huge costs in recruiting and training as a result of high staff turnover.

1. What people issues do I need to deal with?

a) You Get What You Pay For

Having a great plan with no one but yourself to carry it out is risky. What happens if you get sick, have a family crisis, or you just need to goof off? Fulfilling an ambitious plan with no staff is impossible. Growing a profitable business means, at the very least, having emergency backup staff. It also means honing your leadership skills to find and keep good staff and contract people.

As a woman, your major struggle with people issues may be your feeling that you can't afford to hire the best. You tend to hire someone who will work for less because they value themselves less. This often means you end up with a team lacking the skills you need. Many of your staff have personal esteem problems that affect your business. These lame ducks may bring out your "mothering" instincts; you might be spending your time caring for them, instead of caring for your business.

> "It takes a long time before you learn that employees, consultants and contractors are an investment not an expense," says Meredith DeGroat, echoing what many others in our survey shared.

Before you hire anyone, you must do your math to assess how much more business you can bring in with a new employee in a particular position. For example, if you hire an office administrator, you might determine they will free up the three hours per day you are now spending on those tasks. Your calculations might look like this—with those three hours you can take on one more major client each month at an average of $3000 per client. In addition you'll reduce your accounting fees at year-end, and have more control on your spending because your administrator will keep accurate, up-to-the-minute records. This will add up to another couple of thousand dollars. Your efficiency and your company image will improve, as less falls between the cracks, saving a few more thousand. Add all that together and it becomes evident you can afford to hire the best. If they are the best, they will double what you project they can do. With an excellent training program in place, you will know within 30 days if you have the

> "Don't just hire a warm body. Get the help you need. Then let people do their work."
> *Donna Bell*
> *Blue Dawn Originals*

right person. If they are good let them grow. If not, terminate immediately before the "expense" has a negative impact on your cash flow.

> "We consult at $100 an hour and pay a bookkeeper $28 an hour," says Liz Wyman of Office Compliments Ltd. "It's not hard to figure out whether I should be spending my time consulting or bookkeeping."

Are you making excuses—hiding in your administrative work rather than selling a new major client? Studies have shown a competent executive assistant can triple the sales of a top salesperson, simply by freeing up the salesperson's time to focus on what she or he is best at.

b) Energy Sources – The #1 Commodity

When it comes to finding the right people, energy—manifested physically, spiritually and mentally—is highest on the list of what *Smart Women* look for. If you lack energy you will be limited in your ability to move your business forward while juggling the necessities of family and outside interests. Are you going to be leading a charge with your staff, dragging them along, or worse still pushing them from behind? To get through a long workweek, you must be the proverbial "Energizer Bunny." You cannot do this if your energy is being siphoned off by the people around you. You must cut your losses by making objective decisions about who stays and who goes, from Aunt Jane, who never has a good thing to say about anyone, to the receptionist who tells her hard luck stories to all your clients.

"When you finish an interview, measure your energy level. If it's low, you're interviewing the wrong person."
Joan Teskey
Wajo Studios Ltd.

c) Letting People Go

It's difficult for women to say the three little words "You are fired" and usually by the time you get around to doing it you've lowered morale, and lost customers and sleep. You don't want to hurt the feelings of this laggard who has been hurting your business and taking your money without giving you a fair return. Get yourself a contact at the labor board— someone you can phone on a regular basis to ask employment questions. Then write down everything and be sure you know what you need in the way of proof that an employee deserves to be fired. Documentation is the rule.

2. How do I find the best people?

a) Use Synchronicity

Smart Women are cautious about social networking. Many feel network-ing produces few results, while taking up precious time. They have moved beyond networking to synchronicity to find the right solutions to their needs.

Synchronicity is not the same as intuition. Intuition comes from within and is a recognition of your deepest feelings, a sixth sense to help you make choices. Synchronicity is recognizing a source from without. Plugging into that source through the conscious and subconscious mind spreads your thoughts out into the universe, and the power, in turn, sup-plies what is needed. If you open yourself to this new way of receiving answers, they begin appearing from the most surprising places—words seem to jump off the page at you, phrases stand out in conversation, new contacts are introduced out of the blue. You catch yourself saying "**Aha!**" because you have your antennae up to snag information you would normally have let pass by. But remember, synchronicity only works if you are clear about what you need.

> "I hire people whose values are consistent with mine. Skills can be learned."
> *Mary Ann S. Turnbull*
> *Turnbull Learning Centre Ltd.*

> Meredith DeGroat, owner of a national success story—totally tropical interi-ors Ltd.—has one of the sharpest business minds in the country. She told us that when she wants answers, she walks into a business meeting focused on her particular problem. Within minutes someone else in the meeting will bring up the problem. A group discussion will ensue, producing several possible solutions. She can leave with an answer and not even have opened her mouth. Instead she opened her awareness.

Synchronicity is the new way many women find their best employees. First you must create a clear, precise picture in your mind of the skills and attitudes, the values and style of the person you want.

> Joan Teskey gave us an excellent example of this when she discussed her search for a new sales manager. She explained, "When I need somebody, I go to an event I know will be well attended by businesspeople and I put my need in the forefront of my mind. Before the event is over, the perfect person will

have introduced her- or himself, or someone will have provided the name and phone number of the right person for the job."

You might say synchronicity or energy has nothing to do with it. Simply having a clear picture allows you to see someone or something you might otherwise overlook. We're comfortable with whatever you want to call it. Just acknowledge that it saves advertising dollars, time and staff turnover, putting more coins into your coffers.

b) Test Drive

If you want to know if you have the right person before you spend a lot of time and energy on training them, take them out for a test drive. *Smart Women* have developed some uncommon hiring practices to help weed out what can prove to be costly mistakes.

• Interactive Interviews:

Terry Chang, who owns several businesses in Yellowknife, pays extra special attention when she is hiring trainers for her spa. "The job is so 'up close and personal,'" she says, "the wrong staff person can cost you customers for a lifetime." The sparse population in the North means only so many customers are available. She doesn't want to lose a single one. Terry interviews candidates for positions up to four times. With each interview she assigns harder tasks. This enables her to check the level of commitment and ability. The process looks something like this:

First interview: Explore people skills.

Second interview: Establish competency by having the applicant do a workout. Give the applicant a questionnaire she or he must take away, answer and return.

Third interview: Discuss results of questionnaire with applicant and assess how well she or he takes criticism and direction.

Fourth interview: Assign another trainer (staff member) to the applicant as a pretend client and have the applicant set up a complete program for the staff member. As a qualified trainer, the pretend client is capable of assessing the correctness, safety and fun of the program.

An applicant who responds positively and enthusiastically to all your requests, appears well groomed and on time at each stage will be a top performer on a regular basis. One who by the third interview is a "no show" or has excuses for why something can't be done, has effectively weeded out him- or herself and saved you time and money.

Exactly the same process could be used in other industry sectors. For example, in the retail sector have the applicant play the role of a customer while you demonstrate how you do things. Next, have them play the role of a salesperson while a staff member plays that of a customer. Finally, have a trial period. Many retailers have an in-store observation day before hiring, during which the applicant works in the shop for pay. You can quickly pick up on their willingness to help, whether they have initiative, what their energy level is like at the end of the day and whether their enthusiasm is genuine.

c) Interview Suggestions

"Expand your awareness to take in their ideas."
Karinna James
Catalyst Insights Ltd.

Before you can interview for a position you must have a clear picture of the job. Ask yourself, is it manageable, or have you created a Herculean task that only Wonder Woman could do? For instance, have you combined duties that require concentration (bookkeeping) with others that entail constant interruptions (reception)?

Three Key Interview Questions are:

- Why do you want to work for this company?
- What was the worst problem you had at your last place of employment and how did you solve it?
- If you had your dream job, what would your daily activities be?

A more extensive interview, which would allow you to measure different aspects of the person's character, personal philosophy, work skills and experience, might include the following:

- attitudes—What have you enjoyed most in your last employment? What have you enjoyed least?
- interpersonal skills—What kind of people (co-workers) do you work

with best? What kind of people are you most interested in as clients and why? Are there types of people you feel you'd be unable to work with?

- motivation—Why are you interested in working here? What are your long-range objectives? What kind of supervision do you prefer?
- values—What do you like to do in your leisure time? What would you consider to be the ideal volunteer job for you? Why?
- work habits—What is your energy level, and how would you describe your work habits?
- decision making—Thinking back, what are the most significant decisions you have made in your life and how do you feel about them?
- emotional stability—What makes you really angry (on the job or at home) and how do you deal with this anger? Describe your temperament. What do you like best about yourself? If you could, what would you improve?

d) Hiring Family

If you are hiring your own family, remember staff members need to accept them on equal terms. Some rules of etiquette for hiring relatives are:

- Be aware of how you address each other in front of staff: you shouldn't call them "Honey," or "Muffin," and they shouldn't call you "Mom."
- Make certain you are not "touchy feely" with them, and that you speak to them with the same level of respectful consideration and authority you use with other staff members.
- Don't bring personal issues into the business conversation.
- See that everyone on staff has a written copy of the family member's job description and a clear understanding of his or her level of authority.
- Assure all staff members they have the freedom to discuss with you instances in which they feel the family member is overstepping his or her bounds.
- Address the issues of boundaries with the family member privately when you feel they have overstepped.

Nepotism reigns supreme in small business. More than one-third of the women interviewed had family members on staff. Whether the relatives were part-time or full-time employees, the entrepreneurs generally appreciated the opportunity to strengthen the relationship. Just remember, as boss, you may be required to fire your son in the morning and go home that evening to hug him and tell him sympathetically you heard he had a bad day at work.

e) Try Contract Staff

For many the new way to grow is by contracting other small businesses to do the job. This creates new "virtual" corporations in which a small, almost invisible home-based business can be doing several million dollars of international project work by pulling in experts in specific areas. To grow with contract staff you must build a database (a resource list of top people with expertise you may need).

> Susan Nicol, owner of Lilyfield Communications, know it's imperative to have a current list of the best people in the fields that impact on her own. She emphasizes "You must be constantly adding to it, updating it and sectorizing it." Susan, who may be working on a 40-page agriculture report one day, and a 3-minute advertising video the next, subcontracts out much of her production work. She must be able to connect with experts she trusts. She has set up a sophisticated computer system that allows her to reach the right technical contractor and exchange accurate information quickly and effectively.

If you're doing a lot of contracting out, you need written documents outlining who is responsible for what, who is providing which services and resources, who gets paid what amount, and when and how you are going to communicate effectively. *No matter how much you trust your new temporary partner, a written agreement containing deadlines and escape clauses is essential.* Such agreements ensure accountability and make it possible for everyone to work well together. Also essential is meeting regularly (at least once a month) to deal with issues and communicate concerns.

3. How do I grow good people into great people?

a) Job Descriptions

Written job descriptions are essential, even in the early days when a staff member may be wearing three or four different hats. As the company grows, those jobs will start to break out separately. Job descriptions will not be used by good staff members to avoid other work. They are your best performance insurance tool for compensation and as such are very important. They allow you to ask, did they do the work? to what degree? how cheerfully? Each job should outline goals to ensure the staff member knows what they are striving to reach. This provides them the opportunity to reach outside their comfort zone, and a chance to achieve something. Both are important for job satisfaction. When an employee has been with the company for a year, you should try to build a career path for them. This can be difficult in a small business that isn't planning a lot of growth. At the very least, though, they need to be gaining new skills to remain interested in their work.

> "Peer pressure is the secret to getting people to perform without 'bossing.'"
> *Loretta Mahling*
> *Enchanted Forest Retail Group Inc.*

b) Limit Your Nurturing

Women are known for creating a caring environment. It is assumed to be one of their greatest strengths. According to *Smart Women*, it's also their Achilles' heel. Learn to care for your staff, yet not carry them on your back. Many women like to fix people. They think, "If I'm a little more patient," "If I train a little harder," "If I give them another chance … I can get this employee to work out." The result: hanging onto people months—sometimes years—longer than they should.

> Eveline Charles, the country girl who expanded a two-chair hair salon into a million-dollar spa, laughed when she explained, "My business taught me more about weeding than living in the country ever did. I learned the hard way to cut my losses early. Now I give people initial training and stand back and see what they do with it. When they come to me the first time with problems I re-examine my training method and work with them. If they keep coming back for help on the same issues following the re-training, I know I have pesky weeds. I pull them out. I need to focus my time on fertilizing, watering and creating room to grow my flowers. If you try to turn weeds into flowers by

caring for them, they grow so big they choke the real flowers out. A good hardy flower, on the other hand, if not strangled by weeds, blooms beautifully, with only a little care and attention from you."

c) Lots of Rewards

• **Cash on the Line:** Small businesses offer many advantages to entice talented people—advantages big business can't match. Human resources statistics tell us over 80% of people feel the size of their salary is not their number one motivator. *Smart Women* recognize this and build a stack of meaningful rewards to augment it and outweigh the attraction of the larger monthly paycheck offered by corporate competitors.

> **"Hire the best. If you can't afford cash, discuss other benefits they may be interested in."**
> *Linda Maul*
> *Corporate Source Inc.*

One way is to reward productivity. There are dozens of versions of profit-sharing programs in place across the country.

Debra DeBelser designed a gain-sharing plan to replace a profit-sharing plan that was not working for her employees. Her new plan enables the people in her pipeline company to keep track of their own department outputs and savings—things they can see and measure on the job. They are rewarded accordingly.

Bea Harks, owner of Visions of Beauty, redeveloped her commission sales structure by encouraging each staff member to build a VIP list of two hundred customers. They follow up with their customers on a monthly basis. This moved her high performers from salaries of $16,000 to $39,000 per year. She cautions, "Most women don't respond as positively as the average man to a commission pay structure. If you want to reward in this way you have to choose the right people, people who respond positively to reaching out to the customer instead of waiting for them to come to you. It will result in greater profits."

• **A Piece of the Pie:** The problem with commission is that it tends to break down the team, pitting staff members against each other. Statistics show the majority of women are not motivated by commission and feel their boss does not care about them when they work on a straight commission basis. This results in a lack of loyalty on the part of the employee. If this is your situation, try looking at bonus systems that reward all aspects of the tasks, not just sales. It should encourage a new type of team player within your business.

Several *Smart Women* have begun to offer their staff nonvoting shares in the women's companies. This entices staff to help the business grow better profit margins.

Your lawyer would have to help you set this up. Financially, you have to be in a position to buy the shares back if the employee chooses to sell. In addition, there are tax implications for you and the staff that you will have to review with your accountant. Ownership in the company is a huge enticement for some people.

> Barbara Hodges of Spadina Industries Inc., a mattress and futon manufacturer, believes that the traditional hourly wage and piecework formulas are inconsistent with her focus on quality and results. Therefore, all employees from the factory floor to the office are paid a monthly salary. Profit-sharing plans are being investigated. The idea is to compensate people for results, not just time worked. Employees will take the extra time to finish a job and load an important shipment; Barbara will send people home early when orders are current and the factory is shipshape. It's in everyone's best interests to focus on creating quality results rather than exchanging wages for time.

• **Creative Freedom:** A big reward for staff is giving them a say in how things are done. They can bring their own creative skills to their jobs; they can be encouraged to try new ways. While they have a job description, they can have more autonomy than they would in a big company. The entrepreneur who leads the small business is in touch with risk every day. People in big business tend to get in the "cover your butt" mode because they are not allowed to make mistakes. *Smart Women* say, "Go for it," "Figure out how to fix it," "If it doesn't work, just don't repeat it."

> **"I prefer to risk offering too much of a chance to someone than to accidentally offer too little."**
> *Nicole Beaudoin*
> *Quebec Business Women's Network Inc.*

No one is better at giving her staff room to learn than Val Petrich, who has owned several businesses and now is the serenely grounded owner of The Yoga Studio. Val reminds us, "If you risk and fail, you learn more. When you need to control your staff you are in trouble. You must understand that control is based on fear. If you are trusting, you are not fearful. Learn when someone is willing to try and eager to learn, it's a good sign you have someone you can trust to do the job."

- **Training:**

"We hear every day that knowledge is the key to prosperity in the 21st century and organizations need to create learning environments," says Linda Maul of Corporate Source. "What seems to get lost in the translation is that training initiatives need to be tied to business objectives, addressing specific performance gaps with measurable results. Training dollars not tied to performance issues are wasted dollars. Hiring the right individual is the other side of this equation. Today's successful employee is a positive, progressive individual, hungry to learn on a daily basis and accountable for their contribution to the business goals. When interviewing, it is imperative to ask for examples to illustrate the use of these skills in previous situations. Previous performance becomes the foundation for future performance," says Linda.

Helping staff to learn and grow is a guaranteed way to attract and keep good people. *Smart Women* have varying views on investing in staff training. Although all the women we interviewed agreed it should be done, several said they feel when staff pay for themselves, they try harder to succeed. A variation of this method is having them first pay for themselves, then reimbursing them when they train your other staff.

Some of the *Smart Women* pay some or all of the cost of both business and personal training for their employees. They believe that courses far removed from those covering business skills offer benefits, such as reduced stress and, therefore, that they make employees more productive. If the course expands the person's network and makes them a more interesting person to be around, you will see payoffs in your business.

> **"Pay according to the value of a service: if you pay peanuts you are apt to have monkeys working for you."**
> **Lisè Cantin**
> **Fishbowl Restaurant**

Valerie Hussey, publisher at Kids Can Press, uses a successful program where her company pays for much of the staff's professional development and gives time off without penalty for personal development.

Shelley Stewart organizes workshops for her employees, and makes certain the speaker and topic are of interest to the other businesses she invites to both attend the workshops and share costs. "It is extra work to put it all together," she says. "But it is worth the sweat equity to have the topic customized to my needs and timetable instead of having to fit into a prescheduled public course. Because those attending cover the cash cost, nothing is taken from my own pocket." A spin-off benefit for Shelley is a higher profile in the community. If you invite the media to attend, you may be written up in the local newspaper and gain some extra publicity.

• **The Watering Hole:** Socializing is another intrinsic reward that comes from being in a small business. You enjoy a sense of belonging on a small team that simply isn't possible in a company that has hundreds of employees.

Leslie Campbell, sophisticated publisher of *Focus on Women* magazine, has some great ideas. She rewards her staff with a late lunch once a month, on the day her magazine goes to press. "Everyone enjoys the great sense of accomplishment. We recognize the contribution of everyone on the team, as we celebrate making the deadline one more time."

Leslie also hosts countless parties at her house, which unite staff and contributors. Sometimes she has the event catered. She arranges plenty of potlucks, too, and never forgets a birthday.

> **"Kill them with kindness. It over rules any problem."**
> *Renate Wowchuk*
> *Renate's Hair Designers*

Leslie's biggest undertaking and success story is an annual community party she throws in September for approximately 300 people. This event helps her reward her advertisers, suppliers, financiers, staff and other people in the community. It also ensures that everyone feels they are part of the team.

• **Custom-Design the Rewards:** One key tip from *Smart Women*—when you reward behavior you like and want to see more often, be certain the reward is tailored to each individual's desires. We're back to the Platinum

Rule (see Chapter 1, "Planning"). You must know your people and understand what they would consider rewarding. For example, some might like their name on a plaque for a "Top Gun" award, but another might find such an award tacky. Or, if they don't like the cold and they're not into athletics, rewarding them with a ski trip will surely backfire.

4. How do I prevent burnout in my staff?

A fast-growing small business can drop increasing pressures onto the people working for it. We ask our staff to handle one more client, one more crisis, one more task until everyone is so overloaded the entire structure crumbles under its own weight. Lunch is the first to go. As a good leader, you should make certain all your employees take a proper lunch break, showing them the way by doing so yourself. This short respite increases energy levels for the remainder of the day. Also important is limiting the use of evenings and weekends for work. When you are paying out too much overtime it is a warning sign to take action—add someone to your staff, reassign jobs or say no to a client. Overtime is all right if it is needed to meet an important deadline and if the staff is rewarded accordingly; but it should not become a way of life in your business. Chronic overtime results in tired, cranky staff who have lost their creative edge and start costing you money with mistakes. That goes for you too!

> "Create a set of measurements of how each employee contributes to the bottom line. Ensure they understand it."
> *Bonnie Bond*
> *Seagull Pewter Ltd.*

5. How do I evaluate the people in my business?

Bev Durvin, of Benkris & Co., has a crystal-clear evaluation process. "You must start at the hiring stage by giving a clear picture of your expectations. Each staff member is evaluated by the supervisor, on the criteria agreed upon during hiring. This evaluation should occur semi-annually. It is a brief questionnaire on four key areas—the Big Cs:

> "Be consistent in your treatment of people and in the service you are providing."
> *Brenda Boernsen*
> *B's Fine Coffee & Teas*

- commitment—How well do they use their initiative and make decisions? How committed are they to the company and to developing themselves?
- communication—How well and how quickly do they move good information to the right people? How well do they refrain from poor communication like gossip, negativity and complaining?
- cooperation—How well do they work on a team?
- contribution—What did they contribute to the company in the past six months?

Bev advises, "Have their supervisor (maybe it is you) fill in one of these evaluation forms for each employee. Have the employees fill in one for themselves. The differing perspectives provide insight, as do conclusions around the legitimacy of the comments." Bev continues, "If there are weak areas, we give a coaching session. In the end we ask them if they are willing to change. If they agree, and do change, we follow up with a written thank you. This process gives them a sense of pride in their growth—its own reward."

Evaluations shouldn't flow in just one direction. Many *Smart Women* have their staff evaluate both their supervisors and the *Smart Women* themselves on how well they fulfill their roles as leaders.

6. How do I get an evaluation?

"If you want time for leisure you have to find the right people and train them to handle any situation that arises. That is your main job."
Simmone Power
Sunny's Family Restaurant

Debi DeBelser chuckles when she remembers the first time she asked for an assessment from her employees. "It was dreadful. It is a *walk of fear* for an employee to list negative things about their boss. It took a few times, but by placing the onus on myself and my supervisors to display more appreciation for the negative input than the positive, we made the process work. As individuals, on the management team, we then demonstrated a behavior change, with ongoing feedback from the employees over the next year. This encouraged trust and improved everyone's performance and fun. Now the staff are a lot less inhibited about their criticism."

Gulp!

Providing employment is no longer the way. It has been replaced by creating jobs people like to go to, and it is one of the most rewarding aspects of being an entrepreneur. When you have good people and you see them grow, you know you are a good leader. Remember each productive person adds to the growth of your business, your community and your country.

**People really can be
worth their weight in gold!**

Once you have found the best people for your business, let them do the work you hired them for. Concentrate on honing your delegating skills so you get the best investment from your business dollars. In the next chapter we will show you how to choose your area of interest, build it into expertise and hand the remainder of the work over to your team.

The WHOLE PERSON
Action Plan for Finding and Keeping the Right People

1. a) Write a complete description of a staff member you would like to have (a new position or someone to replace someone who is not performing). List their values and attitudes first, then fill in what skills and interests are required.

   _____

   _____

   b) When you have a clear picture of this person, put out an ongoing request to the universe until the person appears.

   _____

   _____

2. a) List the rewards your business can offer staff and contractors to entice the best. Get creative.

   _____

   _____

   b) Talk to other small business owners about what they offer their employees.

   _____

   _____

3. a) List the important things to include on an evaluation form if your family, staff, advisers, banker were evaluating you. How well are you doing?

   _____

   _____

   b) Using a calendar, make a list of each staff member's evaluation date and name(s) of her or his evaluator(s). Let everyone know. Implement the procedure.

   _____

   _____

4. Find out which training programs sponsored by your community match your staffing needs, and have a job-shadowing component for their students. Sign up to take on a student.

   _____

   _____

CHAPTER 3

Delegating

What frustrations are you experiencing in delegating?

Lack of confidence in themselves and in the people available to do a task prevents many women business owners from delegating. Of the women interviewed, 58% say they were poor delegators when they began their business. Owners who allow employees to take on some of their work sometimes end up in a frenzy of frustration caused by employees not meeting the owner's performance standards. The employees follow the owner's system but do the job incorrectly, don't do the job immediately, or don't produce the required results. The entrepreneur agonizes as she watches the process with alarm. She is all too aware that if she cannot empower one person to do a job well, she cannot build a team that will effectively complete all the work. In the process she wastes valuable time and energy.

Of the women interviewed, 30% take the job back after the employee hasn't done it correctly. Eventually they realize their refusal to allow their team to learn has left them doing all the work, which prevents their business from moving forward. Frustration indeed! The feeling that it will take longer to tell someone else how to do it than to just do it themselves often stops the transfer process.

The greatest frustration women expressed is the puzzle around why they can't delegate. On the surface it makes perfect sense—even sounds wonderful. Who doesn't want to have someone help them carry the load? But when they come to the actual decision around what part of the load they will hand over, they balk. Closer examination provided partial answers, such as: "I don't want to lose control over the job," "I feel anxious/fearful when I let it go, but can't identify why," "If I hand it on, I don't have the satisfaction of completing it myself." Perhaps a combination of these answers is at the bottom of why such overwhelming numbers of women are still struggling with the issue of delegating.

Some of the solutions women tried in order to improve their delegating skills caused a whole new set of frustrations. Partnerships seemed the way to go to 30% of the women. One targeted a partner to balance her own strengths, but chose the wrong partner and added to her workload. Another has a partner who refuses to delegate and therefore undermines any progress in this area. This is not to say partnerships can't be a successful solution to getting the help you need, but often they prove to be very, very tricky.

Some of the women we spoke to are competent delegators, but are frustrated by their inability to empower people and inspire them to take ownership of the task. Some explained they had no problem with the concept of handing on a task, but were weak in the area of communicating how it should be done. Some of them, in order to avoid asking an employee to do a job the employee disliked, ended up doing it themselves rather than confronting the employee.

An entrepreneur who is unable to delegate loses the opportunity to lead effectively. Eventually, her employees lose interest in learning. It encouraged us to hear one *Smart Woman* say, "I went from no delegating, to almost all delegating." You need to develop your ability to pick the right person objectively and hand on the job with confidence. This will make you a *Smart Woman* in the area of delegating and a step closer to being a **whole person.**

Are you an effective delegator?
Test yourself.

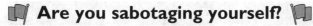 Are you sabotaging yourself?

Delegating: Danger Signals

(Circle the appropriate answer for each question. Add up your numbers and check your delegating quotient on the next page.)

5 - always   4 - regularly   3 - occasionally   2 - rarely   1 - never

1. Are you able to hand over a task you think you can do faster yourself?

5	4	3	2	1

2. Do you clearly define the task before delegating it?

5	4	3	2	1

3. Do you explain the resources, support and standards available when you assign a job?

5	4	3	2	1

4. Do you hand clients who have become your friends on to other experts?

5	4	3	2	1

5. Do you set reporting stages for employees doing a job?

5	4	3	2	1

6. Do you bring your team members together for support and sharing of ideas?

5	4	3	2	1

7. Do you assign tasks based on a person's strengths?

5	4	3	2	1

8. Do you spend 80% of your time on tasks related to your area of expertise and delegate your other work?

5	4	3	2	1

9. Do you schedule time to objectively review your workload and evaluate who can help lighten it?

5	4	3	2	1

10. Do you pass on a task without interfering in the details of how it is completed?

5	4	3	2	1

Your delegation score _____

41–50 You're doing very well. Check with your team to see if they're ready for even more responsibility.

31–40 Keep working on those delegating skills—it's time to pass a few more jobs on.

21–30 We recommend you find a good role model. Order the *Smart Women* audiocassette and workbook: *You Don't Have to Do Everything ...* **Delegate.**[1] Review the patterns influencing your decisions (e.g., are you refusing to express your needs?).

11–20 Your team is not working effectively. You are wasting a great deal of your time. Your business is suffering. List the jobs you want to let go of and immediately get someone to do them. Make a separate list for your personal life. If you have a bad delegating habit at work, it is likely you have a similar problem at home.

10 Your business is in trouble. Staff stands idly while you do the work, or you need to hire more staff to help carry your load. Work through your "delegating hang-ups" with a mentor/role-model to gain insight into what is holding you back and how you can get better at delegating. Take time to work through the Action Plan on page 73 and make the decision to adopt a **whole person** approach.

If your delegating quotient is low, you will lose profits for the following reasons:

- You are squandering a great resource—your employees.
- You are squandering a great resource—yourself.
- You are paying for services you are not receiving.
- Your company is not working efficiently.
- Staff will have low morale and they will not use their initiative to make your vision a reality.

---

[1] Call toll-free 1-877-444-1940 to order *You Don't Have to Do Everything ...* **Delegate.**

1. Why do I need to delegate?

Allowing someone to look after any aspect of your new creation—your business—may bring beads of sweat to your brow. All your protective, mothering instincts rise to the surface. As is the case with a first-time mom, you're convinced no one can possibly mix the formula as well, change the diapers as carefully or rock the baby as lovingly.

> "It took me ten years to discover that if I want to grow, I have to quit phoning for more toner for the machine."
> *Hermante Ayotte*
> *Clinique De Médecine Industrielle & Preventive Du Quebec Inc.*

In spite of the anxiety and worry, the only way a new mom can get some rest is if she's willing to let go—to trust someone else. As the child grows his or her needs expand. A good mother will trust others to help guide her child through life. Likewise, if you are going to make the kind of money you need to make your dreams happen, your business must grow and you must be prepared to turn over certain aspects of its development to staff and contractors.

As long as the business is just you and perhaps a few unempowered, front-end workers, you are limiting your profit potential and putting your business at risk of going under. What will happen if you are incapacitated for a period of time?

> "It's important to learn to let go of your child (business) and trust it to others."
> *Shelly Stewart*
> *A La Mode Fashions Inc.*

If you want to ensure a strong, healthy business you must build a strong, healthy support team to share in looking after it. You must ensure others believe in your vision of what this business can be. Then let go and allow them, in their own way, to help your business meet its potential.

2. How do I learn to let go?

It's as simple as deciding that it's more painful in the long run to hang on. Ask yourself two simple questions: (1) What will hanging on, doing what I'm doing now feel like in two years? and (2) What do I stand to lose, if I let go?

> "Know what you expect and what you are not prepared to give up."
> *Dr. Susan Vertefeuille*
> *Optometrist*

Linda Maul, an extremely feminine, yet hardheaded, businesswoman and a partner in Corporate Source, laughed gently as she told us, "Two years from now I want to be running a successful office in Calgary, close to the mountains, from where I get my greatest strength. That means I have to let go of the Edmonton office, and trust others to not only maintain it, but also to grow it. If I keep on doing what I'm doing now, going down the highway two or three times a week, I'll end up in a ditch, dead from exhaustion."

Bev Durvin didn't want to upset the lifestyles of her husband and children when she started her business. Her first efforts were to track down good home help and teach them how to run the house to her standards. She perfected her delegating skills with the home staff and created a smooth transition for her family. Several years later, her children, backed by her husband, came to her and said they would like to take care of the house themselves and use the money saved on more family holidays. Bev agreed because she felt it was important for her children to learn these life skills at this stage of their development. Each member of the family determined their areas of strength and interest. They laid claim to their share of the workload. Bev laid out her expectations of the final results and firm timelines for the tasks—but how the task would be done was left up to the family member. Bev explains, "Weeks later I opened my once impeccable color- and size-coordinated linen closet. The contents appeared to be moving, so poorly were things stacked. The temptation was there to put it back the way I liked it, but I knew if I did, I would own the task. Instead I spent three careful weeks on laundry day, working with the family to redefine the standards around sorting and folding the laundry. Now when I open my linen closet I know I will be able to find a washcloth. It will never be color-coordinated again," she sighs, "but I guess I can live with that, especially when I'm sitting with them on the beach in Mexico."

> "If you make a decision to delegate, make a decision to accept the consequences."
> **Lynne Sutton**
> *Totally Pets*

> "There are only so many hours in a day and you have only two hands. Someone else can help with the task."
> **Peggyann Boudreau**
> *JDP Computer Systems Inc.*

3. What do I stand to gain if I let go?

Manon Pilon, a miniature fireball, has been working for herself since her early teens. Her ability to let go allowed her first to hand over her day spa, her Montreal salons, and her international markets to top managers. An expert in skin care, she focuses on teaching top practitioners in the field. Her ability to find good people and let them grow has helped her to do what she loves to do, on an ever-expanding scale, for increasing amounts of money.

4. How do I go about delegating?

a) Examine Your Strengths

Delegation begins with having the right people to delegate to (see Chapter 2, "Finding and Keeping the Right People"). Begin by deciding what type of person with what type of skills you need. *To do this you must first identify your personal areas of strength.* All too often new women entrepreneurs feel guilty if they are not good at every aspect of running their business. Consequently, they make the huge mistake of hiring people for the wrong tasks in their business.

> Laurie Peck, who owns a speakers' bureau, can pull you in with her warmth and charisma. These traits were growing her new small business with sales increases of 50% per year. Her energy and quick, well-thought-out, needs-based solutions make her an extraordinary salesperson. While she was out bringing in dozens of potential orders for speakers, her small staff was unable to keep up with the paperwork in the office. She would return from sales calls and run flat out until midnight trying to catch up, but two days later find herself far behind again. As the various areas of her business went increasingly out of control, she hired a salesperson and disciplined herself to spend time in the office pushing paper. The results were her sales plummeted and her income fell. The office still wasn't well run, simply because it wasn't what she liked to do. A few months later, the salesperson left, and Laurie hired someone with strong computer and bookkeeping skills and stepped back into the sales role. Her business tripled its sales over the next two months because she was focusing on her strengths and follow-up was being performed in a timely manner by someone else.

"Never do anything you don't like to do if you can delegate it to someone else."
Zandra Bell
at wit's end

Once you know your area of strength you must develop the skills connected with that area in order to become an expert. What does expertise have to do with delegating? Only when you are clearly focused on your best area will you be ready—and not just ready but eager—to let go of other tasks. When you understand your *major purpose* (the reason you are here on Earth) you can marry your purpose to the skill areas in which you excel (see the section on vision in Chapter 1, "Planning"). Test the validity of your purpose by checking if your energy level zooms when you do a task. If it does, you probably have identified your *area of expertise*. Each of the *Smart Women* has become a recognized expert at something her customer base wants. An expert is someone who has extensive knowledge that can enhance others' lives.

> Marlene Pearce started her business in a new province by decorating show homes. She joined the Canadian Decorating Association, and became president. Working with the association, she wrote and published a training manual. Today, she is asked to lecture on drapery decorating all over North America. Her reputation as an expert brings her two to three large commercial jobs with decent margins each year.

Being an expert is also a marketing tool for positioning your company. Usually your area of expertise is closely linked to your business's strategic customer advantage (SCA). When you focus on your area of expertise, you will stay energized. Believe it or not, you will be able to find people who are energized by the tasks that sap you. Do not let yourself be bogged down in tasks that can be done more effectively by someone else.

"Just because you can do a lot of things doesn't mean you have to."
Valerie Pusey
Northern Passage Gallery

> Lara Lauzon has a Bachelor of Arts in human performance (kinesiology) and a Master of Fitness. She has been featured in her own television show, *Body Moves*, out of Victoria, gently easing us in and out of exercise on a daily basis. Brought on board *Body Moves* as a consultant, she soon went from backroom adviser to center stage. Lara is an expert on the human body. Her mission is to motivate people to take care of their bodies, and teach them how to avoid stress through exercise. Her business, Lauzon Consulting Inc., is set up to meet this goal. She is a sessional university lecturer and is constantly on the speaking circuit. With the birth of her son, Lara turned her focus to helping women meet the physical demands of motherhood. She has become an expert in the field, often quoted by reporters and health-care providers.

By building your reputation as an expert, more opportunities come your way. But you can take advantage of them only if you are willing to let go and delegate other work.

Research has shown that it takes ten years of focusing to gain a reputation as an expert in one area. By year five things should really be starting to cook. If you are rushing around answering phones and photo-copying, it will never happen. Becoming an expert moves you from get-ting paid $30 per hour, to $1000 per day, to $100,000 per project.

Becoming an expert is important if you want to quit working hard and begin working *smart*. It moves you from worker role to leader role. If you continue to find yourself back doing old tasks, think about why this happens. It may be that the tasks fulfill some need in you. Once you know what it is, you may be able to channel it in more effective ways.

b) Find Out What Is Stopping You

Renate Geier kept finding herself at the cash and wrap waiting on customers. It made her staff feel like she didn't trust them to do the job properly, and their confidence level fell. They hung back more and more, waiting for her to do the work. She found herself paying them to stand around, while the paper on her desk piled up. Finally, she recognized that she contin-ued to interact with the customer to fill her need for information. She needed feedback from them in order to keep her business on track. This was important to her, but she knew there were more effective ways to achieve the same results. She stopped waiting on the front counter and started holding focus group sessions. These provided her with more useful information for her visionary, leadership role. Her staff eagerly picked up the slack and sales went up.

> "If you don't delegate, your employees won't grow in the job and they'll leave you."
> **Anne Miner**
> **The Dunvegan Group Ltd.**

Time is the other destructive force in the delegating game. How often do you find yourself saying "It's faster to do it myself"? When you add up tomorrow and tomorrow and tomorrow of continuing to do that task, then obviously it isn't so. At some point you're going to have to show others how to do it, and sooner is better. Without a doubt, it means you have to take the time to think through and perhaps even better, write down the specifics of the task. Keep a copy of what you've written down in a safe place. Eventually it will end up in your training binder.

c) Hire the Best

In order to successfully develop your own expert status, you are going to need to bring more players onto your team. Hiring or contracting becomes a question of looking for top people in the fields needed to balance your own skills. It means making the proactive decision to pay for the best. In making this choice, you know you have not only bought yourself an excellent resource, you have also purchased freedom. As Bev McMaster says, "You don't just hire someone who is good at the job, you find a person who is better than you." Set your sights high because the better you hire, the more freedom you buy yourself.

"Always hire someone smarter than yourself. Set parameters and just let it happen."
Beverley Keating MacIntyre
BKM Research & Development Inc.

> Anne Miner, who owns The Dunvegan Group, a market research firm, uses the Russian doll analogy to demonstrate hiring the best. If you create a business where everyone hires below their own skills level, little Russian dolls come out of each other, each one successively smaller than the other until finally you're hiring someone with midget skills.

d) Create a Process for Letting Go

> Phillipa Hudson knows the value of using her leadership role to move her vision forward. She quickly saw that if she spent all her time on the premises of her busy retail operation, she would get caught up in the day-to-day details and never find time for the creative process that would improve the profits of her business. She made the decision to hire a manager and an assistant manager. She carefully selected and trained women she knew had the right skills and attitudes to take over her management role. Then she removed herself from the premises. Creating an office in her home was a positive step towards maintaining growth. From her home office, Phillipa has opened a wholesale business, introduced a new clothing line and increased the sales on her mineral retail operation by 20% every year. She has done all this in just 5½ years because she knows how to let go.

"An assistant can double and triple production."
Judy Harcourt
Harcourt & Associates

Once you have the right person in place you begin the process of prying your fingers, one by one, off a particular task—first with reluctance, then with relief. Comfortable delegation starts with good communication skills that keep you plugged into progress and problems. With the proper training and your leadership, your team can grow new skills to help your business. Learn and practice the delegation process at home, at work and in your community. Practice **IDEAL**—the basic steps of the **delegating formula:**

"Be open enough to teach your staff everything you know. Don't hold back. You will benefit in the end."
Renate Wowchuk
Renate's Hair Designers

- **Identify:** You must either find the person with the appropriate skills set to do the task you wish to hand on, or help someone you've selected obtain the skills they are missing before handing it on.
- **Describe:** You must describe/outline the position to yourself first; then clearly communicate the task in question to the person. This includes exactly what the task entails, what the chain of command is, what resources are available, and what guidelines already exist or which methods have been used previously.
- **Explain:** You must share your vision with the delegatee, and explain why the task is an important part of it.
- **Agree:** The delegatee must buy into the task and formally accept responsibility. You must both agree on the final outcome, the timelines and the consequences or rewards. At this point a contract is signed, if one is necessary, and physical changes, like new work space and changed hours, are implemented.
- **Let go:** You must hand over the task and walk away, checking on progress only at agreed-upon times.

To reinforce your learning of the IDEAL formula, here is another way to think of it:

IDENTIFY: WHO will do the task.

DESCRIBE: WHAT the task is.

EXPLAIN: WHY the task is important.

AGREE: WHERE and HOW the job will be done.

LET GO: WHEN you have a timeline in place for checking on the progress of the task.

If you don't get agreement, you find yourself in the position, for example, of having delegated doing the dishes to your teenager without his or her full cooperation and you return home to find them undone. With family and volunteers who can't be fired it's especially important to follow the delegation formula. We said one of the reasons women have trouble delegating is they've had so little practice. Role playing is a great way to practice. As previously mentioned, Communicating Power Inc. has an audiotape and workbook called *You Don't Have to Do Everything ... Delegate*[2] that walks you through dozens of delegating situations, demonstrating where delegation breaks down and providing practical dialogue for working towards more successful outcomes.

"Have faith ... with checkpoints."
Charlotte Semple
Victorian Women In Need Society

One *Smart Women* method for doing this is called "A Skeleton of Expectations": Terry Chang delegates effectively. She starts by providing her staff with a clear outline of what is expected. It works like this:

- Define what you think the project would look like in an ideal situation. (If you don't know what it looks like, you are not going to be able to pass on the task of doing it.)
- Work backward from the end to the beginning.
- Get input from staff on what they think an ideal picture will look like when this task is completed.
- Compare their picture with your own and address the differences. Ask yourself, "What would be the impact of different results?"

"Step back and watch them blossom."
Phillipa Hudson
Mineral World & Scratch Patch

- Ask your staff what resources and help they might need to get the task done.
- Provide clear timelines and checkup points for the task
- Assign the task and let the delegates put some "meat" on the skeleton.

[2] Call toll-free 1-877-444-1940 to order *You Don't Have to Do Everything ... **Delegate**.*

Explain to your staff member the whole picture so that she or he can understand the importance of the seemingly unimportant aspects. Their performance will improve dramatically. Delegating will become a snap.

Stephen Covey's *First Things First* explains delegating in a useful, easy-to-apply manner. He uses a "Green and Clean" story to talk about delegating within the family. This is excellent reading when you are learning to delegate.

There is a difference between hiring someone to do the books and having someone who will talk cash flow with you—or help with long-term planning. Delegation becomes more than freeing up time.

> "When someone is willing to try and eager to learn, it's a good sign you have someone you can trust to do the job."
> *Val Petrich*
> *The Yoga Studio*

e) Team Approaches

Many *Smart Women* use team-building skills to enhance their delegating abilities.

• **Create a Culture:** Creating a culture that encourages staff members to use their initiative and to be resourceful and responsible moves you beyond the simple supervisory steps of delegating to the role of leader. You create this environment by allowing people to make mistakes. If you have an unwritten "cover your butt" policy in place, everyone will be too afraid to try something new and risk its not working. Give your team the latitude to do things their own way, provided everyone has the same vision of the end results.

If your team is very small, you may be able to find external alliances (people) that would benefit from the process and therefore be willing to help in order to gain experience, get a reference or feel good.

> Charlotte Semple uses what she calls "End Point Visioning" to get the job done. She uses this technique to grow new skills in her people in order for her business to prosper. She brings together a team of people who have a common interest in a project. (Quite often it includes community volunteers.) The members brainstorm, identifying goals. This encourages creativity among the staff members and demonstrates to them, early in the process, that there is more than one way to do things. Then the group prioritizes goals and picks the top three. Action teams are made up of people who are willing to pursue the goal, along with their regular work. One of the results of this technique

was a team that decided the company needed a training video. They wrote a script and collaborated with the local college to get equipment and producers, then proceeded to complete the video. It is now part of the company's program and many people are reaping the rewards. A second team identified the need for a country retreat for battered women. They made finding the perfect piece of property a priority and went out and found it. Then they worked out the cost and how to pay for it, inspired by the reality of a beautiful oceanfront lot.

• **A Commitment Contract:** A commitment contract, in which your team signs off on something, makes goals real and immediate.

Renate Geier brings her team together for weekly staff meetings and once a month to share in defining the major goal for the coming month. Together they identify what they can do to achieve the goal (for example, creating a more peaceful atmosphere in the upstairs spa) in the next 30 days. Each staff member makes a written commitment to a specific action in that direction. Then everyone makes a commitment not to put blocks in the way of change.

Staff members delegating to themselves in this way makes for fast and easy delegation. Now it is up to you to stay out of it and let them achieve it.

"The best lesson I learned is that I am expendable."
Julie Tubman
Tubman Funeral Homes

• **Personal Projects:** Personal projects create an enthusiastic atmosphere. If you encourage each of your employees to create a personal project, of course, they are going to work harder on it. Once they own the project, they have a huge personal stake in having it succeed.

Wendy Brownlie and her partner bring all the staff of their physiotherapy clinic together for monthly meetings. Each staff member puts forward a personal project they feel will improve some area of the business in the next six months. The project is outlined and displayed on a huge chart in which the end goal is identified. The staff members set target dates and plot the progress. This information is available to everyone. Wendy says, "The chart encourages forward movement and enlists affirmation and support from other members of the team. This concept allows for commitment and ownership by our staff. They have the reward of working on a project that makes a difference and allows them to share leadership. It also looks good on their résumés."

- **Team Building:** By creating an environment where people can live the task, they take so much ownership that they move easily forward without a lot of babysitting.

> Bonnie Bond manufactures pewter and silver products. Deciding on the newest line is a team task. She builds her team from management, artisans, designers and retail buyers. She looks to them for input on which direction the company should go. The final results of these discussions are made into "documents." Once they focus on an area, like designing jewellery and other items to promote the only sanctuary for wolves in eastern Canada, Bonnie educates the team. In this instance, she loaded team members on a bus and took them to the sanctuary to study the behavior of the wolves. A plan was developed by the participants for the right way to bring the wolves' plight to the attention of the public. They wanted a product that would interest buyers and educate the public, while bringing profits to the business. Bonnie says, "There is a hierarchy of decision making with regard to vision. But after that, everyone must be involved in a team process to see that the vision happens. We check and recheck when starting the process of delegation. It is important to share with your employees when making decisions."

If you are not prepared either to clearly define the task or enforce the consequences you have set out for nonachievement, don't put the task out there in the first place. For example, don't just put up a sign (something women are prone to do when they want to avoid the issue) that reads "Please wash your own coffee cup." The sign is ignored and then you're angry because not only is the job not getting done but also your requests are being ignored. Either be certain you communicate why the task is important (sanitary, clean environment) and what the consequences for nonachievement are (a fine donated to a charity) or stop griping and pay a secretary extra to do this task as part of his or her job description. Alternatives are hiring an outside service to come in and do it or installing a dishwasher.

> **"Assign tasks according to strengths."**
> *Linda Naiman*
> *Linda Naiman & Associates Inc.*

Good delegation means imparting a clear understanding of job performance and the consequence that will result for nonachievement. Naturally, there are rewards for achieving company standards, like a paycheck, the respect of your peers, continued employment and bonuses for surpassing standards.

Many women have huge problems with delegation. If you don't learn to delegate, your business will never grow. You won't make it to the **whole person** style of life because you'll be too busy changing the toilet paper rolls.

Once you stop expecting those around you to read your mind and start clearly defining what you want done, you will need to be able to figure out which is the small stuff (color-coordinated linen) and which isn't (hiring the right personnel, staff and customer satisfaction). When you do that, you'll finally be able to accept that the job may get done in a different way; it will get done—but not by you.

"Treat your staff with respect. Fear is a great inhibitor to initiative. Give them room to make mistakes, as long as it isn't the same one."
Anne Miner
The Dunvegan Group Ltd.

Knowing you must become an effective delegator means polishing up your communication skills. It's time to take a hard look at how good you are at having people understand what you want.

The WHOLE PERSON
Action Plan for Delegating

1. a) Identify what you are really good at. What are the tasks that energize you and leave you looking for more?

   _____

   _____

   b) Identify what you are merely competent at. What are the tasks that leave you drained and exhausted?

   _____

   _____

2. a) Identify the people on your team who could take on more responsibility in those areas where you want to let go.

   _____

   _____

   b) Identify the skills they need in order to do so.

   _____

   _____

   c) Determine whether they need to be financially compensated (a raise) for the new work.

   _____

   _____

   d) List and schedule the training that must occur before they can handle the task.

   _____

   _____

3. Using the delegating formula (IDEAL) on page 67, review the steps you will use to delegate one task (at home, at work or on your volunteer committee). Carry through tomorrow.

   _____

   _____

CHAPTER 4

Communication

What frustrations are you experiencing in trying to communicate?

The highest degree of frustration in this area revolves around the means you use to get your message across—your communicating style. If people often say to you "I don't understand," or "You didn't tell me that before," you are probably expending a lot of energy having to repeat yourself. You need to work on clarifying and simplifying your communication style. If you see a lot of eyeballs roll up and back, you may be caught up in rhetoric and the person you are addressing is tuning you out. Or you may use vocabulary or technical terms they don't understand. Some women fail to organize their thoughts prior to speaking and jump from topic to topic, confusing their listeners. Or you might be dealing with physical issues. Do you speak too quickly? slur your words? turn your head away or cover your mouth while giving instructions?

Maybe you belong to a smaller, though equally frustrated, percentage of women who feel they lack skills in receiving the message. They ruefully admit to multitasking while a staff member is talking to them, or impatience with people who speak slowly or who speak at length. Fast thinkers make assumptions about what the speaker is saying and move beyond without taking time to ensure they understand. Perhaps you don't ask the speaker to repeat her- or himself, or question something you don't understand, for fear you will appear ignorant. You may go without important information because you don't want to admit you weren't fast enough to take it all down, or that you tuned out and missed some. Is a lack of focus impeding your ability to give or receive a message?

As your business grows, the need to communicate with more people increases. You must be certain your channels of communication are clearly set out and working well. How many people are between you and the desired outcome? Is the message getting through or is it lost somewhere between employees C and D? Is the right message getting through because it was clearly written down and passed to its intended recipient, not altered as it was passed verbally from mouth to mouth.

Along with growth comes an increasing amount of technical equipment and paperwork. Simple things can cause a great deal of frustration. Do you receive unreadable faxes or send them because you don't bother to use a dark pen? Do you get messages from your staff members that are not properly completed, or that lack necessary dates or have incorrectly spelled names? Are important messages lost in unimportant piles of paperwork? Is important information buried in the middle of a wordy memo?

As the number of personalities you work with grows, you will be further frustrated by the number of ways in which you must communicate to reach each person effectively. Do you understand what motivates each employee, or how he or she best absorbs information?

Emotion is, as ever, the most energy costly frustration around communication. Do you react instead of being objective? Do you take criticism personally? Perhaps, in speaking your mind, you are labeled insensitive or intimidating. One woman said she has a hard time empathizing with another person's viewpoint. "I'm too caught up in my own," she admitted. If you are nodding your head, this is something you need to work on.

There's one other touchy area to address. Your communicating style. Do you use proper grammar, have good diction, enunciate clearly and keep colloquialisms and cursing to a minimum? Some women find they are not given respect because of the way they talk. People they address are distracted by the delivery and miss the message.

A question of image goes along with communication. *Smart Women* are conscious of the need to present the proper image, use the best body language and exude a confident style. You may find it hard to break through stereotypes to get the look that gives just the right message. It is an ongoing struggle.

Test your communication skills by checking the following danger signals.

Are you sabotaging yourself?

(Circle the appropriate answer for each question. Add up your numbers and check the next page for your communicating quotient.)

5 - always	4 - regularly	3 - occasionally	2 - rarely	1 - never

1. Do you keep your message simple and clear?

5	4	3	2	1

2. Do you listen when someone is talking to you?

5	4	3	2	1

3. Do you use proper grammar?

5	4	3	2	1

4. Do you take time to be certain your listener(s) understand you?

5	4	3	2	1

5. Do you hone your communication skills through workshops or coaching?

5	4	3	2	1

6. Do you encourage staff/clients/suppliers to share information with each other?

5	4	3	2	1

7. Do you have regular staff meetings?

5	4	3	2	1

8. When people have difficulty articulating their needs, do you dig further?

5	4	3	2	1

9. Do you use humor to get your message across?

5	4	3	2	1

10. Do you recognize personality types with whom you may clash and adjust your communication style to prevent it from happening?

5	4	3	2	1

Your communicating score_____

41–50   Excellent communicator.

31–40   Able communicator. You may want to work on a few skills. You may be sabotaging yourself in some areas, while showing strengths in others. You may have conquered a great many communicating issues, but still need to deal with a few weak spots.

21–30   We suggest you start asking questions, first of yourself about why you are weak in this area, next to employees and others in your life to get their point of view. Order the *Smart Women* workbook *A Shared Message: Your Communication Profile* for your staff and you in order to gain a better understanding of each other.[1]

11–20   We recommend attending a communication workshop or following some of the suggestions in this chapter. Take yourself seriously in this area.

10   Your business is in danger. Improving your communication skills should become your number one priority. You probably have trouble leading anyone, and you are not getting your message across to customers, suppliers or staff. *Smart Women* work to overcome communication deficiencies and learn from their mistakes. Examine communication problems you had last week—list them and write solutions beside them.

No one can follow your leadership when you can't communicate well. Poor communication means your business loses profits in the following ways:

- Your staff become frustrated and angry when they don't understand what is required of them—morale drops and productivity drops along with it.
- Your staff do not share your vision and therefore do not work towards it.
- You lose time repeating yourself, and time is money. Communication crises result in both unhappy customers and suppliers.
- You are boring; no one listens to you; and you don't win "the deal."
- People who need to know aren't told in a timely fashion, resulting in inefficiencies and dropped balls.

[1] Call toll-free 1-877-444-1940 to order *A Shared Message: Your Communication Profile*.

1. What are some barriers to communication?

We live in a world in which we are bombarded daily with thousands of messages. In order to retain our sanity, our brain puts up screens to filter information for us. Sometimes these screens work too well. They filter out important things we need to know. Effective communication is about how good you are at getting your message through other people's screens.

We experience further barriers to communication because of such simple facts as age (think about talking to your teen), culture, sex, language and different personality types.

> "If the same problems keep cropping up, you should recognize an area lacking in good communication."
> *Jacqui MacNeil*
> *escents Aromatherapy*

It is your job, as leader, to ensure your business is moving forward in the direction you want it to go. To do this you must inspire others, through good communication, to want to do what is necessary to make this happen. Yet, being the boss throws up all kinds of barriers. People rarely screen out the boss, but they interpret everything you say through a different set of filters. You must find ways to break through the communication barriers and create an ambiance that encourages open dialogue with all around you. You must develop your persuasive skills if people are going to follow you.

Smart Women, even though many already have superior writing and speaking skills, make a daily effort to find new and improved ways to get their messages across.

2. How can I be better understood?

a) Ask Questions

Stephen Covey tells us "Seek first to understand, then to be understood."[2] *Smart Women* who ask questions that begin "Do you?" and "Are you?" can only get yes and no answers. These are closed-ended questions. They do not encourage dialogue and understanding. Learn to ask more open-ended questions, ones that begin with the words *who, where, what, why, when* and *how,* and you will be probing more deeply and gaining more understanding. To prove this to yourself, ask yourself the following two questions then look at the difference in your answers:

[2] Stephen Covey, *The 7 Habits of Highly Effective People*: Simon & Schuster (1989)

- Do you like your job?
- What do you like about your job?

Debi DeBelser is a soft-spoken woman who runs Northwest Pipe Ltd., a multimillion-dollar oil patch company. She put a profit-sharing plan in place for all levels of employees in her company in the belief it would improve and reward productivity. Her managers quickly adopted the plan, but for the majority of employees nothing changed. Undaunted, she tried harder to communicate to the employees who worked on the floor and in the field that this could be a win/win situation. Months later, with no improvement, she finally withdrew the plan. After a respite she asked individuals why they didn't go for it. She was stunned when they told her they thought the numbers the accounting office gave them were made up, and not actual. To them this meant the harder they worked the more the numbers would be tampered with, ensuring they never took home more money. Debi had never given them cause to distrust her, but some of the men had had previous bad experiences in other companies. They shared their distrust with co-workers, thereby destroying the opportunity.

> "Good communication happens when you ask questions until you are certain you understand the answers."
> *Donna LaChappelle*
> *Coldwell Banker Accord Realty*

Debi changed her tactics. She asked, "What do you want? Why do you want it? How would you make it work?" The responsibility for the new plan's success was transferred to the staff. Out of this process a new GAIN SHARE program was successfully implemented. Developed, in part, by the staff themselves, it measures things they can see with their own eyes. Of the experience Debi says, "You never know what is in people's minds unless you probe to see how they feel. Not knowing can cost you the deal."

b) Keep It Simple

Ask yourself "What is my objective in this communication?" Distill your message, get to the point, reinforce it, don't get sidetracked and when you're delivering it, look them in the eye. Bear in mind that if you build in too many layers, the receiver is left wondering who or what it was about.

c) Improve Listening Skills

Go back to your listening skills. Think about how you can create openness. What about a weekly one-on-one session, where staff members can ask **any** question, and bring up any issue, they want.

There is a technique to listening that allows the person speaking to know you are trying to understand. Show them you are listening by nodding your head, making eye contact and being involved with what they are saying. If you're a poor listener, you may want to avoid having important conversations on the phone. You may be handicapped because you might have learned to absorb much of a message visually (through body language). A poor listener is usually allowing themselves to be distracted by other things—visual stimulation, the answer they are formulating, or they are still thinking about point three while the speaker is on point four. To be a good listener, it follows that you must work on developing your ability to concentrate. Reaffirm with the speaker what you think you heard.

> "Set an example for your staff by writing down what they say to you in front of them. It will encourage them to write down what you say."
> *Karen Farkas*
> *Heart Smart Foods*

At the same time be aware of the listening skills of the person you are talking to. This is especially important when giving instructions. Have them repeat back to you what they think you just said. Doing so will save time and prevent frustration even though asking people to repeat what you said can be embarrassing. You don't want to imply they weren't listening. However, it is becoming increasingly important, as communication overload continues, to say in a pleasant tone, "Would you repeat to me what I just said, please, to be sure we clearly understand each other."

d) Go to Clown College

Clown college (where you are taught lessons in clowning) isn't about learning how to squirt club soda. Clowns understand that only 7% of all our communication is verbal, the rest is aural and visual. You can be saying the right words, but communicating an entirely different message through the tone of your voice or your body language. This is because our brain operates on two levels. The primitive brain (i.e., our unconscious) responds emotionally, taking in

> "Laughter makes life easier."
> *Dr. Susan Vertefeuille*
> *Optometrist*

information through the senses—touch, taste, smell, sound and sight. If the message isn't delivered in a stimulating manner the senses don't pick it up. As a result, it is not passed on to the new (conscious) brain where the information is processed in a logical manner. The unconscious brain acts as a screening device, constantly filtering messages. This is one reason you can hear something and two hours later flatly deny ever having heard it; it simply didn't have enough emotional impact to be passed on to your conscious brain for processing.

"I tell staff they have to laugh 5 minutes a day or they are no use to me."
Hermante Ayotte
Clinique De Médecine
Industrielle & Preventive
Du Quebec Inc.

Carol Ann Fried, one of Canada's top communication trainers, demonstrates how to get your message across. She stimulates all the senses during a session, using music, vocal changes, balloons, aromatherapy, videos and overheads. She constantly requires her audience to be on their feet demonstrating through physical activity what they have just learned. Carol Ann feels everyone should go to clown college. Even if you are the world's worst clown you will have learned how to say more with fewer words.

e) Tell a Story

Another tool for improving the impact of your presentation is to read children's stories. Try to act out all the voices in the stories, making them as rich with feeling and imagination as you can. Tape record yourself. When you play it back, you will be amazed to hear that words you felt you were exaggerating while you were saying them still sound stifled and flat. Practice body language and tone of voice by reading stories aloud. It will bring expressiveness to your everyday conversation and increase the amount of attention and retention your communications receive. Besides, kids will love you. If you have no children to read to at home, try nieces or nephews (your siblings will love you) or the children's ward at the hospital (there's always someone there who needs a story).

f) Hire a Drama Coach

Hiring a drama coach (director) to come in and work one-on-one with you is inspirational and a surefire way to pep up your communicating skills. It's a very different process from that used at clown colleges. A good director can teach you how to communicate with your voice whereas the clown only shares his or her message through body language. Decide ahead of time where and by whom your message isn't understood (your teenagers, spouse, staff, a difficult customer). The drama coach will analyze your style and help you modify your body language and tone of voice in order to be more effective when speaking with them.

"Personal contact is important."
Tannis Ortynsky
CompuTemp's

The following is a list of phrases you can practice saying aloud to improve your voice control and body language while you tell your story:

As hard as flint—as soft as a mole;

As white as a lily—as black as coal;

As tight as a drum—as free as the air;

As red as a rose—as square as a box;

As bold as a thief—as sly as a fox.

Say **as sick as a dog.** Did your voice lower and weaken, taking on a whiney note? Did your shoulders sag, your neck fall forward, your eyes close? If you are really into it, you might weave with dizziness, or clasp an aching stomach. Note, however, that if you have the habit of waving your hands around to appear to be more expressive, you should try saying these phrases aloud without moving your hands. Monitor your body movements and sounds and determine if you're a hand flapper.

g) Understand Learning and Behavioral Styles

More than any other area of education, *Smart Women* are focusing their training dollars on improving their own and their staff's understanding of communication and of neurolinguistic programming (how the brain processes and uses language). They know improved communication is the fastest way to move the company forward to bigger profits and make the workplace fun.

• **Learning Styles:** We take in information in three ways: visually, aurally and kinesthetically. But each of us learns best through one of these methods. If I work for you, learn best visually and you *tell* me how to do a job, I am not likely to take in all the information correctly. If you, as my boss, learn best kinesthetically, that is, by doing (many entrepreneurs fall into this category) and I give you a ten-page memo on something, you're never going to read it. In order to communicate more effectively, it is wise to try to deliver the message in each person's preferred style. This may require delivering it three times, in three different ways, in order to have communicated with every person on the team. For example, an e-mail for your visual learners, a water-cooler staff meeting for your audio learners and a role play for your kinesthetics. Too much work, you say? What is the potential cost of someone on your team not knowing what you want?

• **Behavioral Styles:** There are a dozen varieties of behavioral characteristics profiles. You don't want to pigeonhole anyone, but understanding and being able to identify other people's communication styles and needs easily can help you avoid personality conflicts. The hair pricking up on the back of your neck may result from your inability to relate to their different style. Being able to identify and value different types of people will aid you in building a better, more balanced team. If you can learn to adapt to others'

> **"Remember that people have different personalities so that your version of reality is not theirs."**
> *Valerie Hussey*
> *Kids Can Press*

styles, when communicating with them, you will increase your rapport tenfold. *Smart Women*'s previously mentioned workbook, *A Shared Message: Your Communication Profile* focuses on behavior styles, allowing you to quickly identify your own style and your communication strengths and weakness, with the aid of a five-minute test. A companion audiotape helps you identify where your communication breaks down with different personality types. It also enables you to identify how to adjust your style to be more effective in communicating with others. The kit includes a Master Behavioral Profile and permission to copy it for use with family and staff.[3]

As a leader, you should invest time and dollars for communication

[3] Call toll-free 1-877-444-1940 to order *A Shared Message: Your Communication Profile.*

training for yourself annually. It will ensure your continued improvement in understanding people.

3. How can I encourage my employees to communicate better?

Information is power. If I know something you don't, I come from the stronger position. Having people share their information readily and happily takes a great deal of leadership effort. You must create a culture in which everyone on the team, inside and out, feels it's essential to let everyone else know what's happening. No one does this better than Barbara Housser, owner of Sam's Deli.

Barb Housser, a dynamic and highly expressive communicator, has created an atmosphere in which her customers and her staff provide feedback, kudos and information to improve her business on a daily basis. She has created this culture by implementing a hundred little things that clearly say "share." One tool is a communications book in which all activities are written down. Each person coming on shift is expected to read back to the last day they worked. Everyone on staff writes in the communications book. They note everything from customer comments, to broken equipment and crises. Management writes brief notes in response.

Barb saw how well a communications book can work when a drunk began bothering customers outside the restaurant. The staff handled the situation and wrote it up. The following day Barb read it and added some words of praise and some additional actions staff could take if the problem recurred. Even the newest staff member now knows how to react. Similarly, when a customer had a heart attack in the restaurant, it was recorded in the communications book and staff, from then on, knew how to react. In essence Barb is creating a policy manual in reverse. Barb also uses the same type of communications book at home, to keep her busy family tuned in to each other's activities and needs.

> "Be genuine. People know when you're not real."
> *Rhoda Herring*
> *Rhoda's... Elegance Again*

Throwing parties may not seem like a communication tool, but Barb says they are her most successful way of getting her staff comfortable with talking to each other. In bringing everyone together in a fun, informal way, she provides the opportunity for bonding, building trust and a sense of belonging.

Another way to improve communication is to create empathy among your staff members by promoting an understanding of each other's roles.

Perhaps the most important element in the culture she has built within her business, is Barb's use of cross-training. In recognizing each member of her team as human and vulnerable, she emphasizes the need for cross-training. Yes, everyone on the team takes a regular stint in the dishpit. How does this affect communication? Clearly, everyone comes from a level playing field and everyone understands the needs of the person doing that particular task. "In addition," Barb explains, "even the friendliest of us just wants to get away from people occasionally. By rotating my staff from front to back they can hide when they need to."

In your business you may need a particular skill for a particular task. In that case you may not be able to rotate your team. However, some responsibilities can always be shifted regularly from person to person, to give everyone a better understanding of the whole, thereby improving communication.

4. How can I communicate when I'm not there all the time?

a) Guidelines

One proven way to communicate in absentia is the old policy manual, with a new twist—called guidelines. Staff use common sense to customize behavior for given situations. If you want to lead your business to a more profitable future you must take your knowledge of the way you want things done out of your head and put it down on paper. If you expect your staff to be mind readers you are being unrealistic—even in this New Age world.

The bad news, as Michael Gerber[4] tells us, is you have to stop working *in* the business (worker) and start working *on* it (leader). But you can't use a policy manual successfully in your business if you don't first build up a communication-rich culture. Often your staff members' common sense will go out the window as they cast your policies in stone.

[4] Michael E. Gerber, *The E Myth*: HarperCollins

They must understand your policies are only guidelines and each situation must be handled on its own. When guidelines are linked to the vision and mission of your business, staff can use their own good judgement as they deal with an issue.

> This is of prime importance in Julie Tubman's business, Tubman Funeral Homes. Communicating with clients who are suffering from shock and grief requires exceptional care. All four of Julie's chapels are run with the same high standards. Because she can't be in four places at once, she has developed comprehensive guidelines that help her staff handle even the most difficult situation (the death of a newborn baby or a family fighting over what they think would have been the wishes of the deceased). "In our business you must take immediate action when the phone rings," Julie explains. "There is urgency in death. A mistake can cause a crisis. All our procedures are set up in systems that require double-checking. Because listening to our client's needs is critical, all our directors and managers take courses in building their listening skills and have training throughout their careers. In addition I give a manual of guidelines to every director. It contains my philosophy on how staff and clients should be treated. When they understand the guidelines, staff can make wise decisions around individual situations."

A further word about guidelines and manuals—people don't want to read them. You may have to make it part of your training policy for new staff to go through it one-on-one either with you or an experienced member of your staff.

b) Info Letters

Less than a newsletter, more than a memo, an info letter is a one-page (two-sided) read-at-a-glance update on what is happening. It works well for communicating both internally to staff and externally to customers. It has proven more effective than multipage newsletters, which tend to accumulate dust in the "in" basket. If you want to put out a top-notch info letter consider these formatting tips:

- Don't do it if you have nothing to say.
- Make it bold.
- Make it brief (no more than one two-sided page).

- Leave lots of white space.
- Grab attention with a headline, graphics, photo or cartoon.
- Edit, edit, edit. If it's sloppy, your staff and clients will think you do business the same way.
- Too much news? Send out an extra edition rather than adding a page.

Great idea, you say, but I have no time to publish one. Get out of worker mode and into leader mode. Choose the dates you want your info letters to come out. Have a designer create a template and then farm out all or part of the job. You can feed a writer the ideas. Finding someone to write for you can be as simple as phoning your local writers' guild (your library will know how to contact them). Interview a few of its members to ensure a writing style that reflects your taste. Many excellent writers are struggling to make a living and would welcome the opportunity to use their skills to help you, at an affordable rate. You may discover a good writer can help you with some of your other messages.

5. How much communication is enough?

a) Meeting at the Water Cooler

"Take twice as long as you think you need to communicate, so you include the listening portion."
Joy Hanley
Fine Food Investments Ltd.

Regular staff meetings are essential if you want your business to grow and profit. They provide the best venue for team building, by sharing the same basic information with everyone. The staff meeting is always an opportunity to focus on what business you are really in, and to continue to sell your vision and mission. Without regular reinforcement, people forget what their job entails.

Staff meetings must be brief: no more than an hour long—45 minutes is preferable. In some offices, a 10-minute "standing" meeting twice a week near the coffee pot or water cooler is the best solution. Staff meetings must have an agenda; move swiftly through it in order to model expected individual productivity and performance levels. They are also the perfect place to publicly reward and recognize individual performance. Staff meetings are a proven way of increasing productivity, raising morale and making the job more fun. Make sure that every department contributes regularly so it's clear that the whole team is important.

As the company grows you may find that mini water-cooler meetings work for teams involved in specific projects, but that the staff as a whole must come together in a slightly more formal way. You will need weekly meetings of small groups and monthly meetings of divisions. Annually, the whole company should be brought together.

> "Staff meetings should be a place for staff to talk, not you. When they come up with ideas, let them follow through, just attach guidelines for time and money."
> *Jacqui MacNeill*
> *escents Aromatherapy*

> Meredith DeGroat tells delightful stories of her company's successful staff retreats. Being bitten by a fish or finding accommodations misbooked just seems to increase staff communications.

When you get too rushed for staff meetings, you will experience the cost of increased staff turnover and lower productivity. When you function as a team with good leadership to pull you together, synergy happens. The sum becomes greater than the parts. This ensures more coins jingling in everyone's pockets at the end of the month.

b) Channels of Communication

As you grow, who tells what to whom becomes a bigger challenge. Job descriptions take on increasing importance. This facilitates communication by removing confusion around who needs to know in order to get the job done. "Need to know" can be ominous words in a small business. You must create a climate where information is openly shared, but where people are not bombarded with information that simply distracts them from their task. They should take responsibility for finding out what they need to know.

Again, a water-cooler meeting might be a good place to regularly announce "good news briefs" to keep your team feeling like they know what is going on. At Communicating Power we call it *"Four O'Clock Rock."* Everyone gathers informally to share information on Friday afternoons. It pays big dividends for the company. If you have a group of people who work their socks off all week, you need to provide them with a short time to celebrate and pat themselves on the back. It is a productive, creative, cross-fertilizing time.

c) Time and Place

Small businesses tend to handle communication on the run. While this is effective in the short term, as you grow it slows you down and becomes inefficient. "Open doors" can lead to constant interruptions. There are times when communication must take a back seat to other tasks. A closed door means don't interrupt unless the building's on fire. Have your staff take notes on conversations on a steno pad so they don't lose them and don't have to refer back to you as often for clarification. Open up the less productive time of your day for interruptions (e.g., after lunch when you're bottoming out). Voice mail and e-mail are great new tools that allow you and your staff to communicate quickly externally and internally. When using voice mail, do so courteously, respecting other's workloads by being as brief as possible. Formulate your message before you pick up the phone so you don't ramble on.

Operating a profitable business in a knowledge-based, global economy is increasingly about how well your company communicates. Can you get your message out? in how many languages? in how many learning styles? How close are you to being a **whole person** communicator? If you haven't mastered the necessary communication skills, you may find you're dealing with escalating conflict. Like many women, you may want to run and hide from it. Only when you can quickly and emphatically deal with conflict can you lead your business effectively.

The WHOLE PERSON
Action Plan for Communication

1. a) Where are your communication weak spots (a staff person, supplier, family member)? Why do misunderstandings tend to occur?

    _____

    _____

    b) Visualize yourself delivering various types of messages to these people. What is your tone of voice? What does your body language say?

    _____

    _____

    c) How well are you listening to them? What is their body language expressing? What is their tone of voice indicating to you? What do their words tell you?

    _____

2. a) Write a list of *who, what, where, why, when* and *how* questions you want to ask your (banker, child, staff member) to improve your understanding of your situation with them.

    _____

    b) Go and ask them the questions.

    c) What were some answers they gave back that you didn't want to hear?

    _____

3. a) Check the Yellow Pages for schools—drama, arts and speech. Call several of them. What training do they offer?

    _____

    b) Ask to audit a beginner drama class for a couple of hours. See if you can break through your comfort zone to be more expressive. How does it feel?

    _____

4. List four little things you could encourage your staff to do in your business next month that would give them more responsibility for communication and create a more caring culture.

    _____

CHAPTER 5

Conflict Resolution

What frustrations are you experiencing in trying to resolve conflict?

Frustration caused by conflict infringes on every aspect of a business owner's life. Chief amongst these is family-caused conflict. You may have a partner who feels threatened by your success and you are experiencing the inner conflict caused by dealing with his feelings. You may have external damage caused by his interference with your staff and how you run your business. It seems there is a subconscious need, on the part of some mates, to sabotage their wife's business. Partners who both work together and go home together experience conflict around keeping the marriage out of the business and the business out of the marriage. Are you going through conflict with young children who are angry because you are not there for them? Perhaps there is conflict between you and your teen? This causes stress that you have difficulty suppressing while at work. Frustration around expectations goes both ways. You may be concerned because your family expects more than you can give. Or, you may feel the family members aren't giving enough.

Staff is a fertile "host" for growing frustration. You deal daily with conflict caused by staff mistakes, by recalcitrant staff who fight change, by a constant attempt to balance individual needs with fairness to all, and with loss of your time and energy due to inter-staff conflict.

Poor communication causes conflict, such as misunderstanding your clients' needs and therefore making decisions about the needs that are incorrect, not knowing a client's dissatisfaction because they didn't tell you, or people who don't understand what they want, yet expect you to figure it out. Perhaps you are not expressing your needs out of a desire to avoid conflict. The opposite is also true. You may receive more communication than you want and be frustrated by everyone's need to have an opinion on the way you operate your business.

Conflict with customers is to be expected in people-driven businesses. What is identified instead, is your frustration at being ineffective in practicing conflict management. You may not pick the right time to deal with an issue, or have the patience to deal with it. Possibly, you procrastinate until a small conflict becomes a big one. Or do you try to be a peacemaker and put a bandage on an issue that needs a tourniquet?

Maybe you're just in over your head because of the type of people in your industry.

> Gladys Saren said her contract salespeople were so type-A competitive she couldn't handle them. Babe Warren laughs when she says the beekeepers she employs all act like aggressive orangutans because they get stung so often.

By far the most distressing issue around conflict for many of you will be the inner conflict created by your sense of inadequacy in failing to deal well with external conflict. Do you avoid it at all costs, even though you recognize you are being ineffectual? Do you take it too personally? Often your emotions may interfere with proper conflict management. Many women express discomfort in handling conflictive personal situations. Allowing criticism to hurt you can ruin a whole day. When you bring your logic instead of your heart into a conflict situation, you may be resented for your (alleged) lack of feeling.

If you avoid conflict in order to make people like you, you can wind up disliking yourself. If this describes you, you might want to ask yourself, "Who do I spend more time with, them or me?" You need to understand the pattern and try to understand why you sabotage yourself in these various ways. You must look yourself boldly in the eye and dig for the assertive, fair-minded side of your character (it's there somewhere). Examine how well you balance your conciliatory approach with a **whole person** attitude. Be true to yourself.

Test your ability to resolve conflict by checking the danger signals on the next page.

Are you sabotaging yourself?

Conflict: Danger Signals

(Circle the appropriate answer for each question. Add up your numbers and check the next page for your conflict resolution quotient.)

5 - always	4 - regularly	3 - occasionally	2 - rarely	1 - never

1. Do you assess criticism objectively?

5	4	3	2	1

2. Do you hold your own against a stronger personality?

5	4	3	2	1

3. Do you "tell it like it is"?

5	4	3	2	1

4. Do you allow others to vent without interruption when they are clearly upset?

5	4	3	2	1

5. Do you keep your emotions from interfering in conflict resolution?

5	4	3	2	1

6. Are you fair to all your employees—treating them all the same?

5	4	3	2	1

7. Do you deal with conflicts as soon as they arise?

5	4	3	2	1

8. Do you provide a forum or opportunity for your employees to express their feelings?

5	4	3	2	1

9. Do you run your business the way you want, even though it is against your spouse's/friend's advice?

5	4	3	2	1

10. Do you try to avoid conflict with clients by explaining exactly how work will be done and what it will cost up front?

5	4	3	2	1

Your conflict resolution score _____

41–50 Excellent. You are leading a peaceful life and creating a pleasant atmosphere for others. Your business will thrive under your assertive style.

31–40 Are you hesitating, trying to avoid a "fight"? If yes, listen to your inner voice and examine your fears. For a boost in self-esteem, choose an ongoing conflict and resolve it today.

21–30 You are wasting energy on unresolved conflict. Your employees may be caught in situations that are reducing their productivity, and you are probably procrastinating on several conflict issues. Make a list. Write down your resolutions, and implement them.

11–20 Serious work needs to be done in this area. Check out the **whole person** approach to conflict resolution and see how you can boost your weak areas by adopting new strengths. Take a workshop in conflict resolution. Bring in a speaker to do several short sessions with your employees. Try some role playing with your staff.

10 Your business is suffering because you are sabotaging yourself badly in this area. Carry out all of the above recommendations. Bring in a mediator to help you resolve long-term conflict. "Come from love." (See people from a non-judgemental, compassionate perspective.)

If your conflict resolution quotient is low, you will lose profits for the following reasons:

- You are wasting creative energy stewing about unresolved conflict.
- Your employees are focused on conflict, not work.
- You are not resolving conflict with customers and they are switching to competitors.
- You may be resolving conflict between you and your suppliers and customers by backing down.
- Too much infighting or waffling is giving your business a poor reputation that will keep customers away.

1. What is conflict resolution?

Conflict can be smoldering tension or a raging inferno scorching everyone in reach. Either way, it undermines productivity and destroys the harmony of the group. It may be personified by a prima donna top salesperson, who ignores your orders because they are convinced you wouldn't dare fire them. Sometimes it's a troublemaker disguised as a nice person who spreads gossip and shoots poison darts behind backs. Perhaps it's a long-time employee, who quietly, stubbornly resists change. At home, conflict might appear in the form of a rebellious teenager, or a best friend who is constantly dumping her problems on you.

Conflict resolution is the ability to "resolve" these problems, thereby improving behavior and removing tension.

Conflict, no matter how subtle, is the fight.
Resolution is the peace.

Whenever we face conflict, our survival instincts cut in, and we experience huge adrenaline surges. The adrenaline is there to help you fight or flee. Centuries of conditioning have taught women to flee! As a business owner, flight has serious flaws. Even if you run all the way to the Arctic Circle to hide, sooner or later you have to return to the business and face the conflict. The longer the conflict lasts, even when you're not directly dealing with it, the more adrenaline in your system. One of the aftereffects of an adrenaline surge is exhaustion. In order to utilize your energy more efficiently, you must end the conflict as quickly as possible. For most women this means learning to stand your ground rather than flee from anger or dissension.

> **"Inner conflict is self-destructive. You may need professional help to learn how to control it."**
> *Irene Pearson*
> *Robrene Company Ltd.*

"Most women cannot win," says Harriet Ruben, author of *The Princessa: Machiavelli For Women*. "Not because a woman cannot fight strategically, but because no one wants her to win and often neither does she. Both she and her opponents see to it that she fails. She herself may become consumed with guilt if she wins—guilt for having created another loss. Men hate losing to a woman; this can prompt a counter attack. And to another woman, a triumphant woman is a lifelong threat. But the princessa cannot cripple the enemy. She must make her opponent an unwitting ally."[1]

2. How do I handle conflict in a professional way?

a) Bitch Is Beautiful

Women who are adopting the **whole person** approach are no longer willing to lie down and be walked over. You probably find you're asserting yourself more. Smile and take pride in being a bitch.

A bitch is a female dog who is "bitchy" when she's in a protective mode. The minute you stand up for yourself, as a woman, you are labeled a "bitch"—suggesting you are being nasty, ill-tempered and rude, when in fact, you may have spoken politely and emphatically about something you have a reason to be displeased about. According to increasing numbers of *Smart Women*, it is a title you should aspire to win. They say, no matter which gender you are, standing up for yourself when you are right, feels good—really good!

"Go beyond right and wrong to focus on solutions."
Beverley Keating MacIntyre
BKM Research and Development

Zandra Bell, the stand-up comedian owner of at wit's end, uses her comedy routine to tell women the best way to overcome the stigma of the bitch label is to proudly take ownership of it, thereby neutralizing it. In her words "bitch" stands for: Being In Total Control of Herself

In other words redefine the label—don't use it as a cover for unprofessional behavior, Zandra cautions, but with laughter and with wit she shares the message "This is a state women should want to achieve. Don't hide from it, embrace it!"

Eveline Charles, of Bianco Nero, learned to accept the label "bitch" with a smile, while working her way through three major business expansions in the last few years. Each included extensive leasehold improvements. When things went wrong and she told contractors to correct their mistakes at their own expense, she was called a "bitch" and asked if she was suffering from PMS. She explains, "I am essentially a nice person and when someone calls me a bitch, I cringe. After a while you feel so abused, you have to let it go. I found myself

[1] Harriet Ruben, *The Princessa: Machiavelli For Women*

putting my shoulders back, sticking a big, sincere smile on my face and saying in my most pleasant tone of voice "Why thank you," as if they'd just paid me the nicest possible compliment. You could see the double take on their faces," she laughs, "and almost hear the slow grinding of gears as they realized they hadn't crushed me and forced me to back down."

Next time you're feeling stomped all over, just stand up, smile sweetly and say, "Excuse me, I'm a bitch and I don't want you to do that anymore." Then walk away, feeling beautiful.

b) Business Attitude

As a shrewd businessperson, you can no longer be concerned with people saying you're tough. A **whole person** will put peace ahead of passiveness. If conflict interferes with performance, your business's image, or steals energy from others affected by the conflict, you must remember your priorities. A business atti-

> "So much in life is style. Take the time to understand another person's style."
> **Valerie Hussey**
> **Kids Can Press**

tude comes first. Women are great at admitting when they are wrong and apologizing for it. They are not as good at asserting themselves. Often when they finally fight, it can be with words used as weapons. Many of the women over 40 whom we interviewed referred to their increasingly low tolerance for poor attitudes and service. They were told they were intimidating on occasion. Sometimes the pendulum swings too far: as we learn to stand up for ourselves, we become harsher than the situation warrants. Check the appropriateness and level of your displeasure and subsequent behavior.

> "Know the difference between being non confrontational versus avoiding confrontation."
> **Loretta Mahling**
> **Enchanted Forest Retail Group Inc.**

Don't get nasty and don't get personal. Get the job done. *Smart Women* are finding the courage, not only to stay and fight, but to play David to some pretty big Goliaths.

Val Petrich sued one of the largest mall owners in the country for copycatting her business after she relocated. She was perceived by the mall owners as harmless, both as a woman and small business owner, with neither the guts nor the money to take on a major player. "During the worst part of the lawsuit," she said, "when I just wanted to quit and walk away from all the ugliness, I read *The Art of War* by Sun Tzu. I learned to stand up for myself and understand my enemy. To speak up! And speak out!" It took her to the limit of her resources emotionally, mentally and financially, but she won!

"When partnerships don't work out, let go of the disappointment and get on with your life."
Elizabeth Noonan
Elizabeth Noonan & Associates

c) Beware Partnerships

We know statistically that in business the most damaging conflict usually erupts between partners. It destroys the partnership and often the business with it. For many women-owned businesses, the partner is their spouse. When this is the case, the conflict doesn't end at the office door. It carries on into the home and risks destroying the family. The potential for harm is great: 12% of the 100 women we interviewed have been sabotaged financially and personally by bringing their spouses or partners into their businesses. In almost every instance the marriage itself was shaky to begin with and the business partnership was an attempt to shore it up. At the same time, however, 11% of the women interviewed have strong marriages with husbands who work in the business with them. These relationships are mutually supportive and conflict is dealt with quickly and as soon as it arises.

If you are planning to bring a spouse or partner into your business, you must be as objective as possible. If the company is one you built yourself, you should never sell off more than 49% of it. Retain majority shares to retain control. Make sure there is a clear and written agreement with your spouse or partner regarding both his or her job description and the extent of his or her authority. Come at each issue from a business point of view. When necessary, use neutral outsiders (such as your advisory board members) to provide impartial advice on personal issues. Many women are tempted to split the business 50/50 because they believe this sends the right message to the significant other in their lives. This is a prime example of how we subconsciously sabotage our chance at success. An even split sets up the potential for conflict and leaves you extremely vulnerable. Who has the final vote?

Spouses are not the only partner problem. Many women seek to share the load by bringing in an outside partner, friend or relative. In the majority of cases these relationships do not work, proving to be a drain on both finances and energy. If you prefer to run from conflict rather than deal with it, you may want to think before you partner with anyone. You will lose every argument/difference with your partner. If you have learned to be assertive, query your potential partner. You may find the positions reversed and the partner storing pent-up hostility at what they see as your abrasive style and their inability to stand up to it. The same common-sense approach applies to all types of partnerships. Be cautious. Measure what you are giving up for what you are getting. Clearly define and document responsibilities and rewards.

3. When should I stand up for what I believe?

a) When It's Unethical

Standing up for yourself is required on many occasions. Collecting bad debts and reacting to disloyalty from staff members are two of them.

> "I've learned customers who won't pay their bills are unethical," Judy Harcourt says. "I no longer fold. I send a demand letter telling them they have 10 days to pay or they'll be taken to small claims court. Usually they'll settle out of court when they know you mean business. If you do end up in court, represent yourself (if you are capable). The judges like it and tend to feel you're in the right if you're willing to take it that far."

> "Recently," Eveline Charles said, "I was hurt badly by one of my senior managers in whom I had invested a lot of myself. She was planning to open a new salon and began recruiting my staff and customers on the sly. I have always supported staff who have gone out on their own—she's seen me do it over the years. By going behind my back, she undermined the entire team. I could feel morale dropping, watched sales plummet and didn't know why. When I discovered what was wrong I fired her on the spot. She was indignant and nasty. Later she phoned me, apologizing and asking if we could still be friends. In the past I would have said yes because I needed everyone to like me. This time I accepted her apology, but found the courage and confidence to refuse the friendship. Our values are so far apart, I don't want to be friends with someone like that."

b) When It's Unacceptable

Dealing with suppliers is another instance when standing up for yourself is mandatory.

> "I get forceful and let them feel my anger when it will make a difference to the outcome. I want them to take me seriously," states Monica Gross, who owns a unique retail gift shop that depends heavily on suppliers. "When I am in conflict with a supplier I tell them 'It is not acceptable.' It puts the ball back into their court and forces them to come up with a solution. I don't back down."

> "I have a reputation for being tough because I set high standards and insist they be met by my employees and suppliers," says Irene Pearson, who operates a Home Hardware store. "This image used to cause me a lot of emotional distress. Now I accept it as their problem and not mine."

c) When It Interferes with Your Company's Business

Staff comes in a close third in producing situations in which you must stand up for yourself.

> "When there is conflict between staff members," Anne Kramer says, "I make employees aware a staff position exists to meet the needs of the business not the other way around. I make my decisions based on the company's needs and not on those of my employees."

Smart Women know staff performance will be affected if staff are experiencing personal problems. Completely separating our life from our work is impossible. Look first to see if the conflict is coming from the workplace or from baggage the employee is dragging in each morning. If it is external, a counseling session with an outside counselor is essential. It may require a listening ear, or referring your employees to professional help. Deal with "out of sorts" behavior immediately or request the appropriate person on your staff do so. Delays spread the tension and erode the entire team performance.

Prepare for instances of conflict. Obtain the name of a good counselor

"Remember conflict is usually related to how people feel about themselves."
Nicole Beaudoin
Quebec Business Women's Network Inc.

and check them out before you refer a staff member to them. Have on hand the community service booklet published by most cities, so you can bring to the employee's attention a support or social service group that could help. Also, have available a list of clergy members from a variety of denominations who would be willing to counsel your troubled staff member.

4. How should I behave when conflict occurs?

a) Embrace Your Authority

Dr. Susan Vertefeuille has her own way of embracing power. "I keep the hierarchy loose so the staff can discuss problems. But it is in place securely enough that, if I have to, I can deal with conflict from a position of authority."

"I no longer allow myself to be intimidated," Anne Kramer says proudly, as she talks about her growth in dealing with conflict between her and the men she must work with in the technological field she is in. "If they get loud or angry, I just walk out of the meeting rather than giving into them."

According to Eveline Charles, "I've learned to fire people who are jealous troublemakers. Too often you hang onto top producers who are giving everyone on the team a hard time. It is tremendously freeing to know I don't need to tolerate anyone." Reassuringly, she adds, "When you let a troublemaker go, even a high producer, the relief on the rest of your staff is so great, they're energized to pick up the slack."

b) Control Your Body Language

So much of a person's perception of what is happening comes from observing and internalizing tone of voice and body language. Tension tightens your vocal cords and sends many women's voices up an octave. It also tightens your body muscles, giving you a more rigid, angry appearance. Stiff facial muscles make you look stern. When dealing with conflict, relax your body, breathe deeply and drop your voice

"Dealing with conflict takes courage because often you have to expose your vulnerabilities."
Karinna James
Catalyst Insights Ltd.

to normal range. Mastering these **whole person** skills will give you the authority a leader needs to bring people to the table to resolve their problems. Practice in front of a mirror until you're confident you have your anger on hold. Don't diminish yourself or the seriousness of the situation by smiling, shrugging, joking, avoiding eye contact and saying all those self-deprecating phrases women tend to use when they are trying to be conciliatory. Be aware, too, that if you are lifting your voice at the end of the sentence, it turns your statement into a question.

Coming from logic rather than emotion is difficult enough in your business. But, when it's family you have to get tough with, it's even harder.

> Elaine Donald went into the dairy business after years of working in the academic world. "I was in conflict with my husband over the type of business I started, who I employed, how they did their job. My husband interfered with my employees and my operations procedures. Every time I saw him I tightened up, expecting more criticism or another problem. Finally I said to myself, "I'm working in a man's world and in that world the guy with the checkbook is king … that's me! … I took a firm stand and was willing to live with the consequences. Things changed for the better."

c) Let the Anger Flow

A *Smart Woman* listens without interrupting. She recognizes that when a person in conflict feels they have been heard, they can generally resolve the situation themselves. When tension escalates to the point of outright conflict, it usually means a lot of anger has built up underneath. This anger must be vented before the individual can return to being logical enough to solve their own issues.

> Mary Dixon, who owns Peguis Press, intervenes immediately when conflict erupts. She listens to each side of the issue so that each person is heard without interruption from the other. Then she steps back and leaves them to resolve it. Mary recommends you use an impartial outsider as a sounding board when in conflictive situations. "They can help you be objective by letting you vent, and then they can apply their experience to the situation by giving you some good advice." Mary, who has two daughters working with her, doesn't hesitate to bring in a mediator to produce quick, amicable resolutions.

A mediator must be objective. Don't use a staff member or close friend, unless they are professionals. Use your network to obtain the name of a good mediator, then ask for a meeting to see if their philosophy and style mesh with your needs. An increasing number of mediators are available; the supply has been growing as the courts choose this means more and more to deal with many civil issues. If you are unable to afford the fees charged by a professional mediator, you may want to ask a businessperson, whom you respect for their wisdom and fairmindedness, to mediate a situation. An alternative is approaching a member of the clergy who has specialized in this field.

> Bea Harks says, "It is important to let them know you are listening. Repeating back a person's words shows them you are. They immediately become more willing to negotiate."

5. When is the best time to deal with conflict?

a) Don't Stall

Avoiding conflict doesn't make it go away. It tends to escalate when ignored. A **whole person** doesn't stall! More than 90% of the *Smart Women* we interviewed agreed the best way to deal with conflict is to handle it immediately. Both internal and external conflict inflicts the same penalties when you try to hide from it.

"Do the best you can at the time and don't regret the decision you made."
Diana Courtnier
. Starting Point

> "Indecision is the biggest internal conflict I face. It eats my guts," acknowledges Laurie Peck. "Once I've made a decision, the conflict goes away, even if later it turns out to be the wrong decision. The 12-Step Alanon program has helped me learn to act immediately. I don't always have to get it perfect the first time."

> Valerie Pusey started six small businesses out of her home in seven years and moved them out into the community as successful, viable companies. She chose to build her businesses this way to accommodate her role of single mom. She wanted harmony in her family. When her daughter started mixing with people about whom Valerie had considerable concerns, Valerie said

"Blame is a useless way of going about resolving anything."
Valerie Hussey
Kids Can Press

nothing. When marks started dropping, she let it slide. But when Valerie found herself on a Friday the 13th in a hurricane on the East Coast, receiving a phone call from police on the West Coast, who told her her house had been trashed, she decided to take action. She removed her daughter from school (and away from the influence of that particular group), hired a full-time tutor for her and arranged a classroom for her on the premises of her main business.

The price of procrastination is huge. A situation can become infected," *Smart Women* say. "Things [like relationships] start to rot," "People take sides," "Teams break down" and "The problem grows" were some of their observations. You lose good people—they move on and you're left with the stinking carcass.

> "I call myself confrontational in a positive way," says Kate Thrasher, who operates a public relations firm. "I won't waste time and energy suppressing conflict. In my experience a lot of women in conflict exhibit it through bad body language—slamming doors, going around in a snit. This is wasted energy and does nothing to improve the situation. I don't allow it to remain a covert problem. Instead I initiate discussion. Bringing it into the open forces resolution."

Dealing with conflict head on, as quickly as possible, allows everyone to work in peace and harmony.

> "Just stop long enough to move the conflict out of the range of customers and other employees," Beatrice Meili says. "Why should others be made uncomfortable?"

b) Set Timelines and Guidelines

Anne Miner, head of an international marketing firm, has her own whole-person method for resolving conflict within her marketing company. "When conflict arises between co-workers, I want it resolved," she declares. "If it is between me and senior staff, I recognize it, confront it and work to resolve it. If it is between two employees, I draw to their attention that it is visible. I talk with each one separately and help them to express what is bothering them; then I send them off-site together (for a walk around the block, or lunch). I tell them to take as much time as they need to resolve it and not to come back until they have. They are both still on the clock and if they take the rest of the day to work it out, it is fine with me."

Terry Chang says, "I recognize this is not my problem but theirs. If two staff members are in conflict, I speak to each of them immediately to show I have heard both points of view. However, they must resolve it themselves. If that doesn't happen, then I get tough. I tell them, 'This is what needs to be done. Here is my expectation ... I am empowering the two of you to resolve this now and to get on with getting the job done.' "

c) Avoid Meltdown

When you are about to go ballistic, you are not in any shape to deal with conflict. You need to step back for half an hour of deep breathing. The only time to delay dealing with conflict is when the people involved are so emotional that things might be said in the heat of the moment that cannot later be unsaid.

> **"Don't kill a mosquito with a sledgehammer."**
> *Mary Sutherland*
> *Sutherland Books*

Shirley Schwab suggests "Never deal with a hot issue. Let it cool off first."

Bea Harks agrees: "Walk away from it and tell them you'll get back to them. Give yourself time to think about it, or you'll end up saying things you'll regret."

Ashley Smith elaborates: "Learn to postpone it to the right place and the right time. This is called anger management. Don't dilute the issue in your mind while you've postponed it."

6. How much of this is my responsibility?

You can't stop conflict from affecting you. You **can** stop taking ownership of it.

Signa Gilchrist steps in when conflict with a client looms because one of her employees will miss a deadline, "I take over the job; see it is done immediately. Then I step out by giving my employee work I would have completed in that time. I take personal responsibility for maintaining the company's reputation; but the employee's consequences are clear and I don't get loaded with extra work, just other work."

Loretta Mahling operates three top retail stores and deals with her staff continuously. "Making people take responsibility for their actions is hard," she says. "But," she adds, "they have to understand there are consequences. I hired a manager who suddenly wasn't prepared to meet the commitment of working the five days designated in her job description. When I replaced her she was angry and stirred up all sorts of conflict with other employees. I had to communicate that it was her choice not to be a manager."

7. How can I stop staff conflict from happening in the first place?

You cannot eliminate staff conflict altogether. You can minimize it by looking for clues when you're hiring. Learn ahead of time how people deal with conflict.

Denise Bagley, owner of The Learning Edge, agrees: "I learned from early mistakes how much time and money can be lost from a poor choice. Now I put considerable emphasis on interviewing. I make certain this person is the right person before I ever say, 'you're hired.' "

Smart Women have developed measuring sticks. Three interesting ones are:

a) Get Clues from the Past

Phillipa Hudson digs for potential sources of conflict. "When I am interviewing I ask the person, 'What was the worst thing that happened at your last job?' Their answer shows me how they deal with conflict and how they would work on our team."

b) Observe Them in a Different Setting

Bev Durvin, whose thinking is always innovative, explains her method of weeding out possible troublemakers. "I have a 'litmus' test I use when considering someone for my company, whether it's staff or a new bank manager. I take them for lunch to a restaurant I know has a reputation for poor service. I watch first what they order to drink, then I watch how they react to the service, the situation and the people. The ones I want on my team handle the situation pleasantly and politely but are clear in verbalizing to staff that there are problems that need fixing.

"Check the alternative. Is it worth it?"
Beatrice Meili
Saskatoon Book Store Inc.

c) Check Out Your Own Behavior

Karinna James, owner of Catalyst Insights, recommends, "Before you 'step in' you better examine your own behavior. Often conflict exists because it directly relates to one of your own vulnerabilities. I am a compulsive tidier, obsessed with clean and neat. It helps me feel more in control. I was experiencing increasing conflict with my teenage daughter around how messy she was becoming. When confronted, my daughter refused to cooperate and the conflict escalated. Finally I realized she was telling me to ease up and not be so perfect. As soon as I did, she pitched in and started helping again."

Often your need to control your environment, in order to keep yourself feeling safe, puts you at cross-purposes with others. **Step back** and think before you **step in** to fix things.

Doris Tan agrees with Karinna. She says, "For many, dealing with conflict means examining yourself inside and experiencing the 'dis-ease.' Internal conflict is directly responsible for most illnesses and is often the source of our conflict with others. For example, if I don't like someone and we can't get along, I often discover by doing an internal check, it is something I dislike in myself that I don't like in them. The solution is to work on yourself, not try to change them."

"The customer is not always right, but is always worthy of respect."
Mary Ann S. Turnbull
Turnbull Learning Centre

Education that helps you to understand people better is a top priority in most **whole person** businesses. Isn't it nice to know that while we are trying to learn conflict resolution in the boardroom, Canadian school curriculums are now teaching it to our children on the school playground?

8. How do I handle a difficult customer?

a) Chronic or Situational?

As a *Smart Woman*, you need to understand the difference between chronically bad behavior and situationally bad behavior. You must ask yourself, "Does this person behave this way all the time, or is she justifiably upset about something?" You know one of the joys of owning your own business is the ability to choose with whom you want to spend time. This includes customers. Sometimes you have to tell customers you are not the right match for them and that they'd be happier (and so would you) if they took their business elsewhere. This is a far cry from "The customer is always right."

> While running my first retail business, I [Barbara] found it difficult to diagnose some conflictive situations accurately. In one instance, I had scheduled a customer for an hour-long session. Throughout, she was extremely difficult to deal with. I rescheduled her with a different adviser. This difficult person slowly worked her way through everyone on staff and ended up back with me. This was unusual; normally a customer would find a staff member she really liked and ask to stay with that individual for all subsequent appointments. Obviously, no one was getting along with her. After consulting the staff, I decided to terminate the client relationship at the next meeting. When she came in, I took her to a private area and expressed my regret in being unable to satisfy her. I asked her to return all the products she had purchased for a full refund and delivered the parting hope that she would be happier elsewhere.
>
> She burst into tears! Between wrenching sobs, she explained that she had been deaf until a few months ago when surgery had given her the ability to hear. "The noise is killing me," she sobbed. "My head is so full of sound I could scream! I'm sorry I was so hard to get along with." Indeed the studio was constantly full of energy, with music playing, and a dozen women chattering at once. It was an impossible environment in which to create quiet. The staff and I discussed the problem and we agreed to take turns coming in prior to opening for this client's appointments. This gave her a measure of the quiet she needed. She continued to be

"Be sensitive to your customers' needs. Sometimes you don't know what is behind them."
Beatrice Meili
Saskatoon Book Store Inc.

difficult, though not as abrasive as she had been. Everyone was able to stretch their patience a little further in order to cope.

"Leave people feeling expanded not diminished."
Valerie Pusey
Northern Passage Gallery

b) Laughter Is Still the Best Medicine

There's one other foolproof way to get people in conflict to move forward. Get them to laugh! Introducing humor into a situation has immediate positive results. A good laugh clears the tension, lowers the stress levels and increases the endorphins. It puts everyone in a better mind-set to negotiate.

c) Put It in Perspective

Bev Durvin, who grew a multimillion-dollar retail business in 18 years, sums up conflict resolution beautifully: "When things go wrong I tell myself and my staff 'We don't make AIDS serum or heart valves—we deal in details [kitchen accessories]. There will be no death over a wrong decision, just some discomfort."

Smart Women struggle with, and master their need to take ownership of, everyone's problems. They learn to handle conflict with their heads and not their hearts. They create an environment based on honesty and justice, allowing room for everyone to be heard. These are the skills of a leader. If your people are busy fighting with each other, they can't possibly help you win your battle to accumulate more wealth for everyone on the team.

**Resolve conflict so that you can move
forward to PROSPERITY**

Now your business plan is in place and smoothly delegated to a happy, productive team. It's time to temporarily change your hat and manage your business, ensuring your team has the systems to get the job done.

The WHOLE PERSON
Action Plan for Conflict Resolution

1. a) Describe the last time you backed down instead of standing up for yourself.

    _____
    _____

    b) Think of the last time you jumped on someone (staff, waiter, child) when you should have approached the issue a different way. Write down your new approach.

    _____
    _____

2. Identify any conflict in your personal life. How effectively are you dealing with it? Determine if you need help. Decide how you are going to come to grips with it.

    _____
    _____

3. a) Describe a person in your life who knows all your hot buttons. Identify these buttons.

    _____
    _____

    b) Determine how you can best handle a confrontation with this person (e.g., you might bring in a neutral third party or try sitting back to back so you can't see their facial expression and body language while you talk it out, or write a letter that you hang onto for three days and reread before you mail it).

    _____
    _____

    c) Make a decision on the best way you can change your reactions to the person to neutralize your interaction with him or her.

    _____
    _____

4. If there is a problem with staff, identify a similar problem you have had in the past. Are you fostering problems by not laying clear ground rules? Do you need some written guidelines to prevent a recurrence?

    _____
    _____

SECTION 2

MANAGEMENT

"**L**ead people" is only half of the equation. The other half is "manage things." As an entrepreneur you must wear both the leader and manager hats. The manager's job is to build. The shift today is from manager as order-giver to manager as coach. The manager's job used to be to know the answers. Now it consists of knowing the questions and involving others in finding the answers. Your management style requires all your skill to maximize your resources. You must oversee a **marketing system** that puts your product or service into your customers' hands. You must help your team create **operating systems** to maximize your resources. These resources include inventory, facilities, equipment and staff. You must also install and review **financial systems** that measure your company's progress, control your expenses and ensure the cash to feed your business growth.

Systems are important. They allow you to produce your products/ services consistently, day after endless day. Inconsistencies in quality, service or pricing infuriate your customers and waste everyone's time and energy. Provide a great experience and a customer rushes back for more of the same.

Most women new to entrepreneurship have gained the bulk of their experience from managing a home. If this is your only experience, you use a hands-on style of managing, which works well at home, but won't have taught you how to hand off to anyone else.

Take a look at how other businesses have taken most of the pain out of managing. They've documented what they want people to do, and how they expect them to do it and they get the results they want. McDonald's, for example, serves the same quality of hamburger, whether it is cooked by someone 16 or 60, and whether it is served in Paris or Saskatoon. You need to create mini McDonald's systems in your business. Great systems ensure you can move your product or service flawlessly into your customers' hands five seconds before they expect it.

Great managers have great reputations. Managing your resources by building great systems makes your business fast and dependable—an essential component of a great reputation. Your systems allow your business to do what you say it will do, when you say it will do it. As a result, you receive respect and trust from your suppliers, financiers and customers.

Wearing your leader hat, you determine what the final result or goal must be. Wearing your manager hat, you establish the most effective and efficient way to achieve that goal and you make it happen.

How do women sabotage their ability to manage?

A majority of women use systems they keep in their heads. They control the process, but because it's not written down, it is not easy to delegate the tasks to others. For your staff, trying to guess how you want something done is intimidating and risky. This can be a spin-off from a leader's inability to delegate—a failing that can cripple your business.

A large number of women are trying to slide around the systems issue by hiring others to create and implement their marketing, operating and financial systems. This is fine. But only you, as manager, know what resources you have and what results you want. It is you who must measure the efficiency of the system and the result it delivers.

Many women avoid formal marketing systems. You may not have developed the skills to make you a competent salesperson—you may find selling is outside your comfort zone. Many women are attracted to the creative aspect of promotions and try to do it themselves, despite lacking the necessary skills.

Another marketing danger is the reluctance to take risks. This reluctance stops you from buying those expensive television spots, paying for the right location or financing a special promotion at Christmas. Each has the potential to bring in bundles of cash, but you vote to play it safe.

The most critical thing to understand about modern operating systems is that technology, particularly computers, play a key role. Many women are not comfortable with machines, which means we may be slow to adopt technology. You may not have time for long learning curves. Only if you can see a fast practical application are you willing to take the time to learn how to use it.

Sometimes, you may simply be afraid—afraid the system will eliminate your flexibility, afraid it will steal your control. By learning, you regain control. In "owning" the system, you lose your fear.

Finance and financial systems are explosive areas for most women. Money is power and power corrupts. That's what scares us. Most women are accustomed to handling the dollars it takes to run a grocery budget. They are not prepared, however, for the hundreds of thousands that are turned over in profitable small businesses. Many women find themselves at a real disadvantage when they try to understand traditional, male-dominated financial systems. Women say it's an old system—a dinosaur that needs to be revamped. They want a new, more user-friendly "money lingo," with practical applications to their businesses that cut to the quick of their problems.

You must move past old thinking to a **whole person** attitude to managing. Women have many talents to bring to this area. Marketing is a more comfortable area for women than men, because it appeals to right-brain strengths of creativity, intuition and building relationships. You've probably spent more time in your life growing these skills than others that come more naturally to men—pricing right, closing the sale, refusing to take no personally. If you add these left- and right-brain functions together you get a whole brain approach to marketing.

Operating systems can be exciting if you approach them from a woman's strengths: the ability to ask questions, to organize, to research and shop wisely and to make the system user-friendly. Then you must draw on other talents you may have left untapped—left-brain areas such as logistics and the ability to give orders, to work at a computer and to operate and fix machines.

Finally, a **whole person** breaks finance and financial systems down into the more feminine skills of preparation (writing your business plan), networking (finding the right banker to approach) and handling the money (women are more cautious spenders and tend to take fewer risks).

Then you combine confidence (in your approach), a familiarity with the numbers pertaining to your business and an easy ability to talk about money.

A **whole person** approach to managing means you bring calm, reasoned thinking to the small crises that appear every day—it might be a sick receptionist, a bank loan that has been turned down or a bottleneck in your factory. You work through to a solution and see that the solution is implemented. Developing a strong management style takes years of experience. If you have the patience to learn from your mistakes and to work constantly for quality improvements you can turn management frustrations into next-time victories.

CHAPTER 6

Marketing Systems

What frustrations do women experience in trying to market their product or service?

Making sales is the primary task of your business. You can speak of providing a service with complete sincerity. You can speak of your love of the people, your passion for the product and your need to serve a higher purpose with complete truth. But unless your business is making sales, enough sales to cover the costs of running it with some left over, it won't exist for long.

In marketing, much frustration is caused by external factors, such as the economy, government and competition, over which the entrepreneur has no control. With the lifeblood of her business dependent on sales, these factors are of primary concern.

Have you done everything you can to create a solid foundation for your business (vision, mission and ethics statements and an SCA) only to find you can't get the attention of the public? A greater amount of frustration focuses on the need to identify, then understand your customer. It also seems impossible to move fast enough to keep up with your customers' demands. More time is required these days to know your customer, because increasingly, your customer is insisting you "customize" to meet his or her needs. And more time is needed to communicate information about your product, because increasingly, the customer is insisting on being educated before sliding her or his money across the counter.

Finding the money to promote is all too often the last expense on your list. Only after all the bills are paid do you check for anything left to promote with. We call this "the affordable budget" and it does not provide the return on investment (ROI) your promotions plan should.

Finally, women are frustrated by the amount of choice. Grandma could just put up a sign when she wanted to sell her honey. Now you have to delve into the mysterious word of multimedia and decide what will sell your product best. Marketing is a huge quagmire. You may have your rubber boots sucked off as you wade your way through its complexities.

Is marketing a tough area for you?
Test your marketing quotient on the opposite page.

 Are you sabotaging yourself?

(Circle the appropriate answer for each question. Add up your numbers and check the next page for your marketing systems quotient.)

5 - always   4 - regularly   3 - occasionally   2 - rarely   1 - never

1. Does your customer information go into a regularly updated database?

5	4	3	2	1

2. Do you cooperate with other businesses to pool your promotion costs?

5	4	3	2	1

3. Do you have at least three promotion activities that take place every month?

5	4	3	2	1

4. Do you plan a twelve-month promotions calendar?

5	4	3	2	1

5. Do you ensure your SCA (strategic customer advantage) is clear in every message you send out?

5	4	3	2	1

6. Do you track how your customers heard about you?

5	4	3	2	1

7. Do you ensure everyone on your team has sales training?

5	4	3	2	1

8. Do you focus special attention on the top 20% of your customers?

5	4	3	2	1

9. Do you set a total annual marketing budget based on projected sales?

5	4	3	2	1

10. Do you pay a referral fee to those who bring in new business?

5	4	3	2	1

Your marketing systems score _____

41–50 Your excellent score in this area means you have intuition and creativity. Your marketing dollars are well invested.

31–40 You will want to check your past promotions. Look with a fresh eye at all your printed pieces; do they look professional? Is your SCA immediately apparent? Order the *Smart Women's Annual Promotions Planner*[1] and get a proactive plan in place.

21–30 You need to take some marketing workshops. Try some new ideas even if it means taking a risk. Work through the **Whole Person** Action Plan for Marketing Systems on page 142.

11–20 Do all of the above. It's time to get some professional help. Find a marketing coach.

10 You must be frantically wondering how to get a little nibble of the market, let alone your share. You must push outside your comfort zone. Ask friends and business associates for referrals, and ask for recommendations from past clients. Make some sales calls. Try a new approach. Remember you must be able to tell your customers why your service or product is just the right one for them. Good luck!

If your marketing systems quotient is low, you will lose profits for the following reasons:

- You are not leveraging (using your purchasing power, e.g., buy three ads and get one free) to maximize your promotion dollars.
- You are wasting advertising dollars on ads that don't hit your target market.
- You have promotional material piled up in the storage room because you don't have a strategy on how to use it.
- You are not focused on your top customers who would like to do more business with you.
- You are spending too much of your profit dollars on charitable giveaways that bring little return.

---

[1] Call toll-free 1-877-444-1940 to order *Smart Women's Annual Promotions Planner*.

1. What is marketing?

Marketing is everything you do to make it *easy... easier... easiest* for your customers to do business with you. It means being easy to find, easy to understand, easy to use, easy to benefit from.

The Ps of marketing

• **Product:** Do you have the right product or service to satisfy your customers' needs? (see Chapter 1, "Planning")

• **Price:** Today, pricing means not just pricing competitively, but also packaging your services and throwing in value-added features. When today's customer has learned to trust you, they will want to do more business with you. By "packaging" services (translation, desktop publishing, audiotapes and a fulfilment house that does the shipping) combined with value-added features (e.g., three languages instead of two and shrink-wrapping the product), you will have a happy customer who is willing to pay more for the extras and convenience.

• **Place:** Are you located where your customer can easily find you and will they identify with the image your location projects? Are you on the right floor for your services? (Or are you a third floor maternity wear business with no elevators?) Do you have a distribution channel (a way of getting your product into your customers' hands)?

• **Personnel:** Do you have the right people to supply consistency no matter when your customer uses your service? (If you're not sure, re-read Chapter 2, "Finding and Keeping the Right People.")

• **Promotion:** Are you sending messages that ensure your target market is aware of your existence and what you have to offer?

2. What is promotion?

Promotion is every single way you can educate and inform your customer about your business and its products or services. It is a critical area that deserves your attention. The following is a list of tools for your promotion kit.

The first three are part of doing business and will tell the world about your business whether you plan them carefully or not. Your potential customer can be *unsold*—if they haven't been handled well—just as easily as *sold*.

• **Merchandising:** the impact and attractiveness of your visual presentation, including your and your staff's appearance and manner, your business and your displays. The overall impact of your business on the senses.

• **Customer Service:** personal contact allowing you to customize your product or service to each customer while building one-to-one relationships based on trust. It's also the special touches that are "free" to the customers but cost you plenty. (e.g. parking, coffee, alterations, estimates, time and caring).

• **Public Relations:** getting along with your neighbors and all the other people who are affected by your business.

• **Advertising:** messages creating awareness of your product or service that you pay for and have control over.

"Consider a long-term goal of a bigger market. Be a big bang instead of a bunch of small pops."
Dorothy Murray
crossXtrainers

• **Publicity:** "free" media attention (e.g., TV news interview, expert articles), more credible to your viewers because you didn't pay for it.

• **Sales Promotions:** the refrigerator magnets and coupons that act as ongoing reminders to your customers to come back.

Most small business owners use the promotional elements listed above one at a time. When you use only one of them without supporting it with several others, you get a little poof for your money instead of **POW**. Analysis shows that using one method and not supporting it is one reason why 80% of the dollars invested in promotion are wasted. So many small business owners say, "I used to put a sale ad in the local paper and people would come. That's all it took. Why doesn't it work anymore?"

3. How do I define my market?

It is essential to identify your customer profile and use it to work out your total market share in dollars. You need to go back to your plan (see Chapter 1, "Planning") where you determined which customers you want to attract.

A variety of measurements are used to find and count your total market share:

- **geographics:** where you do your business, where your customers live;
- **demographics:** the kind of customers you want to target—age, income, gender, education, marital status;
- **psychographics:** how your customers think, what's important to them, how they want to be perceived;
- **behavioristic:** how your customers behave, what media they connect with, how often they buy a product, where they like to buy a product or service like yours.

Tracking the information can be hard, but it is worth every minute. Statistics Canada and your local economic development office are good sources. Also, use the resource list in the back of this book. Surveying prospective clients will help you. Once you know who your customers are, how often and how much they will buy, their preferred price and who your competitors are, you can determine your market share and projected revenue.

4. How do I know what my customers really want?

Well, here's that old *"Listen to your customers"* line—as if we haven't heard that a thousand times before. But remember:

It isn't an old line—it's the only line!

You must actively demonstrate that you and your staff are constantly listening. Some *Smart Women* provide positive proof they are paying attention to what their customers want.

Terry Chang, an alert, insightful woman, shows she hears and cares when she takes the suggestions from her BIG suggestion box at her fitness centre. "If they are simple, easy and low-cost, they are implemented immediately. We post the suggestions and what has been done to meet them, giving recognition and thanks where possible. We also post explanations for why certain things can't be done or if doing them will just take longer." The instant response encourages the customer to tell all.

For 20 years, Lise Cantin has operated a popular restaurant in a rural area. "If we didn't listen to our customers we'd still be deep-frying everything in sight.

Our menu reflects a smarter, healthier consumer and our sales keep increasing," she says.

Survey your customers on an ongoing basis, through print, phone and focus groups. Empower your staff to create an atmosphere in which your clients feel not only able but also welcome to express their concerns, dissatisfaction and accolades.

Liz Wyman owns a service for office personnel. She feels so adamant about having customer input to shape the company's policy that she has her staff hand-deliver a questionnaire to their top 200 clients every year. They do a phone follow-up and collect the questionnaires in person. Their clients understand that when that much effort is expended, their feelings and ideas must be important to the company. Each client puts a great deal of thought into answering the questionnaire.

Start with ten surveys this year if that's all you have time for. Plan how to get more feedback next year. Building your business is easy if you are implementing information of that quality. It can also help you avoid costly misses along the way. This process is called being customer-driven, and it pays big dividends in customer loyalty. There is something intensely flattering in the thought that a business cares enough about you to change the way it does business.

5. How do I ensure good merchandising?

"Remember, you are promoting your business simply by walking down the street for coffee."
Lynne Sutton
Totally Pets

Our primitive brain responds to all sensory stimuli. Therefore, a strong visual message and the sense of smell, sound, taste and touch should, wherever possible, be involved in our contact with customers. This is obviously much easier for a retail business than for a service business. If your merchandising consists of you, your briefcase and perhaps your car, you're going to have to work very hard at making an impression. Professional merchandising sells. We're still seeing tacky window displays with bunched and dusty fabric. Handwritten signs with letters that droop. Merchandising is an art. Knowing little things like the importance of balance, that people shop most at eye level, that end units sell more and that lighting draws people to the back of the store are extremely helpful. Phone your local college and sign up for a course or hire a merchandising coach to come in and teach you how while you remerchandise your store together. It is money well spent. A talented professional merchandiser and I (Barbara) went in and redid a retail T-shirt store from end to end, working all night. The next morning sales increased. By the end of the week sales had doubled for that week compared with those of the previous week and, even better, the store had moved some slow inventory.

> Bev Durvin guarantees that if you take your slowest-moving merchandise and create a whimsical, brightly lit display, you will start to move it. She also cautions that if the merchandise will never be a fast mover regardless of what you do, you should not use a display area that could be used for higher-end merchandise that will sell. Put the slow mover on the "garage sale" table and get it out fast.

Speaking of garage sales, one way retailers are moving dead stock without downgrading their stores is by banding together and literally moving inventory to a garage sale location over a long weekend. They don't have to waste money advertising, word of mouth spreads the news quickly. By the way, they don't say it's from their store.

6. What is the key to good customer service?

a) Building a Sterling Reputation

Having found out all about your primary target in your planning phases, you can now determine the customer service strategies that will be most meaningful to them. It is within this window of opportunity that your reputation is built.

> Signa Gilchrist, of Gilchrist & Co., takes her accounting business seriously. On the premise that most people like to go where they are comfortable, she has created a welcoming warmth in her offices. She fosters an atmosphere that keeps staff smiling. She has unshakable values and a quiet professionalism that immediately put her clients at ease. She explains, "My industry is not allowed to do paid advertising, so I insist on the highest quality of work from my employees. Our

"When your reputation is on the line, be ruthless."
Linda Naiman
Linda Naiman and Associates Inc.

excellent reputation for being on time and saving clients money is what keeps our business growing."

Over and over *Smart Women* say, "Deal honestly with your customers." Many admit to prevaricating in the early days of their business, agreeing to deadlines they weren't sure they could meet, telling white lies when things went wrong. No more! "It gets you in such trouble," they declare. "Often your customer finds out, and even if they don't, you know. Being honest lets you sleep nights. Immediately owning up when you make a mistake allows you to move on. A good reputation is your single most important customer service tool to develop in the Information Age."

> "One of the joys of owning your own business is the fact that you get to spend time with nice people," Barb Housser says. "Sometimes you blow it and it's your fault. Don't hesitate to apologize and make amends."

b) Where Are Your Tissues?

A ski resort in the Sierra Nevadas attracts the best skiers year after year. These skiers appreciate being able to grab a tissue from the box at the bottom of the lift so they can wipe their goggles and mop up runny noses on the way up. This is such a simple thing, but it shows what is critically important to the hawk-like eyes of the vigilant consumer. Customer service today must be tailored to individual needs. It is composed of a thousand and one details that clearly demonstrate your joy in being of service.

7. How do I ensure good public relations?

Public relations is about getting along with the public or not getting along. It can be as simple as running a home-based business and ticking your neighbors off because you have 36 big delivery trucks showing up in your neighborhood every day. Or it can be as complex as lobbying the government to change a law that hurts your business. Great public relations means inviting everyone to the Christmas office party—customers, neighbors and influencers (people who have influence over your target market)—having fun together. Great public relations is having people

> "Write a monthly, newsworthy column for your local paper on your area of expertise. It will pay off more than all your advertising combined."
> **Laura Lauzon**
> **Lauzon Consulting Inc.**

(who aren't customers) praise your business because of the positive impact you have on the community. Great public relations is figuring out how to say no to the dozens of requests for donations you get each month without offending anyone.

Statistically, small businesses are being asked to donate an average of eight times per week to many worthy causes. While you want to be generous, you quickly feel besieged. If you try to meet everyone's need, you will cut your profit margin and affect your bottom line. Using your business as a vehicle for doing good should mean trying to donate to a cause that is identifiable with your business services and is of interest to your staff and customers. Consider making your donations part of the publicity and public relations component of your promotion plan. Some of the costs can be built into your promotion budget; you may also receive a charitable tax receipt for some of it and customers and suppliers can contribute the remainder.

Meg Herweier, of Dovetail Enterprises, gives a lot of people who like to volunteer the opportunity to tackle something challenging. She annually supervises the building of a house for charity. For her last house Meg had 55 women and 5 men volunteer to work with her. Twelve of the women volunteers were living on the streets at the time.

We could do an entire book on the charitable contributions the women we interviewed make. Next time you reach for your checkbook to make a donation, ask yourself if there is some special cause you could get everyone in your business behind. Instead of a $20 donation, you could be making one for $20,000. We can really enhance our public relations by putting money back into the community.

"Community involvement is very important. I really believe in it."
Carmel Cochrane
Town Textiles (Inc.) Timmins

Debi DeBelser, of Northwest Pipe Ltd., believes strongly that a portion of profits generated from a community should go back to it. Each of her division managers has a charitable budget based on that division's profits from the previous year. They donate pipe for playground equipment and trucks for local parades, as well as sponsoring scholarships for local students. They consider themselves part of every community from which they generate revenue.

When you just plain care about something, you put it out there and extraordinary things happen. There's that synchronicity again!

8. What type of advertising can I do?

a) Electronic and Print Media

Many small business owners say, "My ads don't work like they used to." Today's busy customer is harder to reach. When it comes to advertising examine the options available to reach *your target market*.

Before you pay for your next ad be sure you've placed it properly. What do your customers read? listen to? watch? For example, if your target market is professional women over 45 who earn over $50,000, you must know that they read few newspapers and watch little TV. Also, the time they spend listening to the radio is limited to the drive to and from work and is done at earlier and later hours than the norm—and this radio period can easily be preempted by listening to music on their CD players. Interacting with them, therefore, is extremely difficult. An ad in the symphony program may be a good way to reach them.

Once you know where to advertise, you'll be certain they get your message. Here are some simple guidelines for advertising:

- One message: keep copy simple and deliver one idea;
- Lots of white space: uncluttered sells. (If it's audio/radio, don't jam too many words in.);
- Repeat four times: if you don't get any calls after the first couple of times, try different days of the week, sections of the paper (print), or times of the day (electronic) before you decide it doesn't work for you.

b) Direct Mail

Direct mail can be the strongest communication channel to cut through the information bombarding your customers. Successful direct mail requires a person-to-person relationship.

Bea Harks, owner of Canada's most successful Merle Norman cosmetics outlets, uses direct mail to create one day of enormous sales, plus spinning off an extra 20% increase through the Christmas season. It works because she designed a promotion that is personal, benefit-laden and sensory. In

November of each year, Bea Harks mails an open house invitation to her Gold Key Customers (her top purchasers), who number in the hundreds. A follow-up call is made to confirm attendance and offer to prepackage any purchases the customer knows they need in advance (a time saver the customer greatly appreciates). Each client receives a lovely gift which Bea buys a year in advance at wholesale prices. By noon the premises are packed. She does more sales in one store that day than she would normally do in an entire month.

Knowing how to send a message directly to your customer is valuable. Be certain you track and update names, addresses and phone numbers so you can benefit from direct mail. Ask every customer, every time, for their name; ensure that it's in your database. After each mailing, follow up on returned mail pieces and update or delete your database.

c) Brochures

If you print a brochure, sometimes called a "leave-behind" or "collateral piece," you should determine ahead of time how you are going to use it to get business through your door. It is amazing how many entrepreneurs print brochures and leave them packed in boxes in the storeroom because they never had a strategy for how to use them.

Phillipa Hudson, who owns an adventure retail company on Vancouver Island, puts her brochure on the ferry, where she has a captive audience of people who have time to read and are making decisions about what they want to do on the island when they arrive.

Where will people who need your help be most likely to hear about you?

The image of your collateral materials is critical to your success. If you are targeting a high-end corporate client, you need photos, great graphics and full color to do the job right. On the other hand, that piece might scare smaller clients away with the immediate assumption that you'll cost too much.

d) Internet

Judy Harcourt, of Harcourt & Associates, has built her firm into the second largest company providing international job opportunities in Canada. She promoted their SCA by going on-line. Their Web site receives over 20,000 hits a month. They update their job list every week and receive e-mail from around the world.

While the Internet is a great communication channel for Judy, you must ask if your customer even has a computer, let alone knows how to access your Web page. A Web page that actually generates business for you costs many thousands of dollars. Traditional advertising media must still be used to guide your customer to your Web page.

e) CD-ROMs

Some high-tech businesses are using CD-ROMs to market their products. But, because paranoia about viruses has increased, many CD-ROMs go unplayed. A marketing CD-ROM often works best if your salesperson puts it in their own laptop as a demonstration sales tool. Be certain the potential buyer can get involved. Program a little game or something fun the customer can do on the marketing computer during the sales call.

9. How do I get publicity?

Publicity is "free" messages that are spread by media. They give your business credibility and attract customers. Getting publicity requires a story that is both interesting and newsworthy. While the end result might be "free" in terms of cash, the cost involved can be quite high in terms of time and effort. One of the best ways to gain publicity and build your business is to become an expert in a carefully selected area of your business. Every time issues arise in that area the media will think of calling you for a quote.

Maureen Wilson's company pops up on "best of" lists and in national features on the top studios in the country to get a workout. Seasonally, Maureen offers fitness tips on a television show. Because of her reputation as a trainer to the stars, she earns herself much free publicity.

"The best advertising is free. It just takes more effort. You pay for it in other ways."
Rhoda Herring
Rhoda's... Elegance Again

When you are building your "expert" reputation you may need to work with a publicity coach (see page 219). Choose a coach who can help you write your articles and get them accepted or who has excellent media contacts and can use them to create opportunities for you to appear on radio and TV for "expert" interviews. If you are trying to handle your own publicity, go to the library and look at the *Matthews Media Directory*. It lists all the TV and radio stations, daily newspapers and magazines in Canada and provides contact names. Once you have prepared a media contact list for your area, call each one and find out what subjects are timely and the format they prefer. Design an information letter to match their needs. Mail, fax or courier it to the contact people and follow up with a phone call a few days later. Be prepared to respond to questions asking for more in-depth information.

10. Will I benefit from participating in trade shows?

Trade shows are excellent means of directly targeting your customer, providing you get creative. If you're just going to do a flyer or sit behind a table in a booth, don't bother. You're not only wasting time and money, you are creating a bad impression.

Get customers involved and spending time inside your booth. Appeal to their senses as much as possible with sights, sounds, tastes, smells and ways to touch. Also appeal to their sense of curiosity and fun.

> Communicating Power Inc.'s client, Safety Concepts Inc., was attending its first American Correctional Trade Show. How could this little Canadian company with one product (a security air vent) compete against the big multinationals? We designed a want ad poster and a contest—win $50 if you could hook anything on or hide anything in the vent (you received a T-shirt just for trying). We set up a mini jail cell with a vent that had air flowing through it from a hidden fan. This helped us to physically demonstrate some of the vent's other benefits. We made up look-alike contraband (duplicates of confiscated weapons from a prison—everything from sharpened steak bones to melted tooth brushes). Attendees began accepting the challenge and within minutes of opening there was a lineup at the booth. We were told later by some of the large participating companies that if they ended a show with 24 good leads, they were happy. Safety Concepts walked away with over 400 hot prospects.

11. How can I maximize my sales?

a) Cultivate Referrals

Most service companies are built painstakingly on referral after referral. This is why it takes most service companies five years before they begin to pay off. Obtaining higher quality and more frequent referrals is the best way to speed up growth.

Learning to *underpromise* and *overdeliver* will get you over one of the largest hurdles to inspiring great referrals. The more recognized and the more prestigious the referral, the better. Often the most successful sales tool you can develop is great referrals from well-recognized firms or people. One way to achieve them is to provide a product or service, at no charge, to an influential potential client who then evaluates and endorses your good work after the job is completed. When you do work at no charge, always include a "no charge" invoice at the completion of the service. This ensures that the client understands the value of what they received, and will not expect further "freebies." After all that work, you may still have to write your own recommendation. Then your client only has to adjust it, photocopy it onto their company letterhead and sign it. Too pushy, you say? Just remember, it may be high on your priority list, but it's on the bottom of theirs, even when you've done a great job. Make it easy!

> Margo Almond, a composed, quiet woman, has lived all over the world. She has been involved in huge projects like the English Channel Tunnel. Margo's computer-training company provided team-building tools to a multinational firm at discount rates in return for an endorsement, which proved to be the deciding factor in landing her company a major contract with an international computer company.

People who refer new customers to you are your golden geese. Do you reward and thank them? Have a system in place for determining who referred each client to you. Send them a referral fee, a percentage of sales, a gift certificate for their favorite restaurant or, at the very least, a hand-written thank-you note. Build money for referral fees and dollars for spec work into your marketing budget. Referral fees can give you a bigger return on your investment than a dozen ads.

Another excellent source of referrals is influencers. These are people who have a contact point with your customer and who are capable of influencing their decisions. Build close connections with these influencers, educate them on what you do and how well you do it.

> Cindy Maloney ensures that all of the veterinarians, kennel owners and pet photographers in her area are aware of the quality of her dog-grooming business. Pet owners will often seek advice from these sources on where to take their pet for special grooming care.

b) Take Care of Existing Clients

While getting new customers from referrals is important, *Smart Women* focus first on enhancing their sales with existing clients. They know the adage "it costs five times more to get a new customer than to retain an old one" is true.

> Shirley Schwab owns Earl Beebe Trucking and has a stress-free attitude. She says, "I make an annual, personal visit to the head offices of all our major clients. I make certain they are happy with our service and listen for new ways we can meet their needs. Our continued growth comes from increasing our business with long-time customers."

c) Build Your Top 20%

Look at your existing clients and focus on the best of them. Use two rules of thumb to do this: Pareto's 80/20 rule and *The Strategic Coach's** "Top 20." Pareto's 80/20 rule appears over and over in different areas of your business. In this instance, the 80/20 rule says that 20% of your customers give you 80% of your sales. Analyze your customer sales and you will discover this is true. Strategic coach Dan Sullivan advises you to identify the top 20% of your customer base, know their names, addresses and phone numbers, and keep in touch by phone, mail and in person. Customize for them as much as possible; reward them with thoughtful gestures and show your appreciation in a hundred different ways. You will ensure their loyalty, their increased business and their referrals. The other 80% of your

> "Pace yourself and be thoughtful of the consequences of over selling."
> *Gaye Trombley*
> *The Avalon Group Ltd.*

customers don't go away, you just spend less time looking after them, which is a good thing, considering they're only bringing you 20% of your revenue.

> Laurie Peck operates a speakers' bureau and makes connecting people and opportunities look as easy as breathing. She has learned to place great importance on the 80/20 rule when dealing with her clients. "Almost 50% of our calls are for contracts under $1000. I can't break even on sales this small so we now refer these elsewhere. The $1000 ones are assigned to our junior salesperson. She looks after them with a minimum of time. This provides her with experience and keeps a happy client. It is good public relations more than a sales strategy."
>
> According to Laurie, these particular clients are rarely going to grow into larger, more profitable customers, no matter how much effort she puts into them. (She knows this just by the nature of the organizations they represent (e.g., nonprofit or school organizations). She focuses her attention on a $5000+ client. Sales that large usually mean the client is a national or international firm that can instantly provide her with $5000 referrals to 10 or 20 other similar opportunities in their branch offices. If she lives up to her reputation, they will continue to depend on her help on an annual basis. In the $1000 instance, she's lucky if she makes $500 doing 10 of them; and it takes more time than the $1500 she makes doing the one $5000 deal. "If I get 10 referrals, that is $15,000 in sales with next to no additional marketing costs," Laurie calculates. "At that rate, I can start passing some savings onto the client and give them a better deal."

Every business has its own $5000 level. Whether it's a $45 eye cream an older woman would use versus the $15 teen's moisturizer, or breeding queen bees for sale at $300 a queen versus $5 per jar of honey.

Dan Sullivan has proven many times over in almost every industry sector that if you want to quantum-leap your sales, just focus on your top 20%. Your top 20% consists of those people who bring you the bulk of your revenue. These people might not even be your customers. They might, for example, consist of a mix of the top 20% of your sales staff, a dynamite referral service, and even a broker, as well as the top customers you personally service. *Who is responsible for bringing the money through your doors?*

Remember, no matter how well you look after someone, you are always going to be replacing a small percentage of your top 20%. They move away, their interests change or their brother-in-law (who needs their support) starts selling for the competition. Learn to watch your 80% out of the corner of one eye and keep track of those positive individuals who keep coming back on their own. They are part of your future top 20%. You will know when the time is right to tell them they've been awarded VIP status in your business.

Smart Women each have their own unique way of building their top 20%.

Joan Macdonald has a great way of looking out for her customers while increasing business for her farm service operation. She calls it her Try Five method. She makes a list of five people or companies with whom she does business, phones them to say "Hi," share new information and ask how they are doing. She lists five more, phones them, and continues with as many as 50 people. By this time she has brought in new business from some of the people she's approached. The method works just as well for Joan's second company which supplies truck parts and maintenance, and for her commercial truck-driving school. "When you're done," she says, "you start at the top of your list again. Usually someone has new needs by then." Joan stresses the importance of making your customers your friends, particularly when your work is seasonal and the clock is putting tremendous pressure on you. "That way," she confides, "you can phone them at odd hours and they're not going to be upset, because they are pleased to hear from you." She guarantees that it works.

12. How can I be proactive in planning my promotions?

a) Share the Promo and the Cost

An annual promotion plan will help you maximize your promotion dollars. When you have an exciting plan, you can get someone else to pay part of the costs. Try:

• Co-op: Share costs with suppliers or strategic partners (e.g., a merchants' association) during a specific promotion.

- **Contra:** Barter service or product for promotional opportunities (donate a product for a draw on a radio contest).
- **Cross-promote:** Give your customers a coupon to another business, and have the other business give their customers a coupon to yours (e.g., fast food restaurant and a service station).
- **Leverage:** When you are tentatively booking a year's worth of advertising at a time, you can achieve considerable discounts. "Buy three, get one free" is an acceptable deal for many media spots (print or radio).

"Give out gift certificates (not coupons) to introduce and educate customers to a new product."
Shelley Stewart
A La Mode Fashions Inc.

b) Budget Your Resources

Budgets are usually planned as a percentage of sales. When you are new and growing you should be spending up to 20% of your projected sales for the year on promotion. Too many small businesses use the "affordable method" for calculating their promotion budget. That's everything they can afford after everything else is paid. Obviously this won't do anything to grow your business.

Rather than blowing your budget, run your promotions by a professional and have them help you fine-tune them. Check professional marketing associations to find help. They can provide you with some referrals. Ask for recommendations from other small business owners. Do your homework before you go to see a professional marketer. Write out: (1) what business you are in; (2) what your SCA is; (3) what other benefits you offer your customer besides your SCA; (4) who your target market is; and (5) what you want to accomplish with the promotion. Take in any image art work you have and any past promotion pieces. Preparing this information, sometimes called a marketing platform, can save you the hundreds of dollars an hour a marketing agency would charge you to pick it out of your brain.

Your promotion should be an investment, not an expense. To ensure a high return, all the elements of promotion need to be combined in a 12-month promotion plan. When you sit down with a 12-month calendar to talk to media sales representatives, you will stun them. The idea that you know that you want to make a 12-month media buy will ensure they are very receptive to negotiating price and value added with you. Become proactive instead of reactive.

c) Build a Calendar of Events

Design your own calendar, listing on it (1) statutory holidays; (2) community events (call your provincial public affairs office and get their annual calendar of events, which will have every provincial event listed on it from Girl Guide Cookie Day to major festivals); and (3) industry events (e.g., if you are in jewellery sales and Timex® always does a back-to-school promo).

Record your average monthly sales to determine your peak and slowest sales periods. Use this information to ensure that you:

- *always promote during your peak sales periods*—build on strengths, and
- *leave your slow times alone*—generally a good policy, or diversify into other products that move at your slow times.

• **Balance Daily Promos:** Identify your ongoing promotions (those messages you get out month after month in much the same way).

• **Create Impact with Special Events:** Schedule in three to four major promotional events. Do this for your peak sales periods throughout the year. The number of promotions will depend on available time and dollars. Schedule a special promo event first for your top sales-volume month. When that one is working well, add a second event for your next highest month.

See pages 138–139 for an annual promotion plan calendar. Using this or a similar tool will keep you on track, proactive, and ensure that your promotions are cost-effective.

The Fragrant Florist
Promotion Plan for 19___

Revenue Cycle	January	February	March	April	May	June
Projected Sales	$15,000	$60,000	$30,000	$50,000	$65,000	$30,000
Ongoing Promotion	Flower of the month; Sign 3 new corporate accounts	Flower of the month	Flower of the month; Sign 3 new corporate accounts	Flower of the month; Sign 3 new corporate accounts	Graduation ads; Flower of the month; Sign 3 new corporate accounts	Graduation ads; Flower of the month; Sign 3 new corporate accounts
Special Events Name	Heart Smart Valentine's contest	Heart Smart Valentine's promo cont'd	Easter Lily	School grad info sessions	Mother's Day gala	
Partners	Jewellery store Hotel Hairdresser	Chocolate shop	Church group		Restaurant Party shop Hallmark	
Components						
Advertising	Tags to regular ads; Radio	Direct mail to VIP customers; Radio—on-air chatter			Newspaper; Ticket sales; Radio—on-air chatter; Direct mail	
Publicity	Percentage of profits donated to Heart Fund	Percentage of profits donated to Heart Fund	Fundraiser		Contest on Great Moms	
Public Relations	Bulk mail drop —heart info	Involve men's nonprofits			Huge brunch for Great moms and their kids	Summer Solstice party for staff and customers
Customer Service	Free deliveries for VIP customers	1 hour service				
Sales	Hire extra staff	3-hour sales training session				
Sales Promotion	Prepare coupon	Heart pin with purchase;	Valentine's follow-up coupon		Flower fridge magnet	
Total Budget	$2,500	$18,000	$5,000	$10,000	$12,000	$6,000
Estimated Costs						
Future Action Plans Event _#1___ Event _____ Event _____ Event _____ Event _____	Activity Delegated to	Activity Delegated to	Activity Delegated to	Activity Delegated to	Activity Delegated to	Activity Delegated to

Note: A small amount of money is set aside for a slush fund.

Promotion Plan for 19__*

Revenue Cycle	January		February		March		April		May		June	
Projected Sales												
Ongoing Promotion												
Special Events Name												
Partners												
Components												
Advertising												
Publicity												
Public Relations												
Customer Service												
Sales												
Sales Promotion												
Total Budget												
Estimated Costs												
Future Action Plans	Activity	Delegated to	Activity	Delegated to	Activity	Delegated to	Activity	Delegated to	Activity	Delegated to	Activity	Delegated to
Event _#1__												
Event _____												
Event _____												
Event _____												
Event _____												

* Call toll-free 1-877-444-1940 to order your 12-month *Promotions Planning Program and Calendar.*

"Know your market, know the media available and pay to reach potential clients, rather than just anybody."
Susan Nicol
Lilyfield Communications

Judy Richards, of Davidson's Jewellers Limited, holds an annual, elite luncheon in which she focuses on a new feature. One year it was Fabergé eggs. Exclusive invitations were issued, making it a must-attend event. The eggs were priced at between $2500 and $4500 each and ten were sold at the luncheon. The lunch was a special promotion of an outstanding product that produced "golden" profits. This type of promotion works for an exciting high-end product. Judy reminds us of the importance of paying attention. "I believe in looking after existing clients. I listen when a woman says 'I always wanted a diamond bracelet,' then I relay the information to the appropriate person. To do that, I have to keep my database totally current. And always be ready to pick up the phone."

13. How do I evaluate my promotions?

Planning ways of measuring your promotion's results is essential today. Evaluate and write down the results so you'll remember for next year. Measure the resulting sales and calls from each promotion so you will know if it's worth repeating.

For example, we're inundated with ads and flyers begging us to take up a free 3-month trial at a fitness club and we throw them in the garbage. Can investing in a promotion that costs ten times the price of the useless flyer be worth it? Terry Chang thought so.

Terry Chang, owner of a fitness centre in Yellowknife, based her promotion on her belief that we focus too much on fitness and not enough on the *whole person*—the lifestyle, nutrition and esteem issues that cause people to be out of shape in the first place. She wanted real measurements of the benefits a fitness centre could provide and she decided to showcase two individuals as they used her program. She ran a newspaper ad headlined: "2 Overweight Individuals Needed" and received 80 responses! Her preset criteria screened the applicants down to 54. The applicants had to agree to work with their fitness coaches for six months and be featured monthly in the local paper with photos and progress reports. Two applicants were finally selected during personal interviews. Their success was measurable. The calls resulting from the newspaper articles were measurable. Meanwhile, Terry offered the 52 women who were turned down a free lifestyles workshop on self-esteem, nutrition and fitness. It was a lot of fun and resulted in around 50 new customers signing up for paid programs. Now that's measurable.

All too often, promotions that don't work are repeated, and ones that showed promise are forgotten. Ask, ask, ask, how your customers heard about you and document their answers. Create a system for compiling results and build in planning time to review.

At CPI we were doing simultaneous print and radio ads to attract people interested in our business startup programs. Each caller was tracked. As soon as an ad ran on the radio, the phone began to ring. Certainly the radio ad achieved more calls than the print ad. Other tracking that followed clearly showed, however, that the majority of radio respondents were not qualified for the program. In the end, the highest percentage accepted into the program came primarily from the print ads. If we hadn't done the extra tracking we would have concluded that radio was the better medium. We would then have put more of our budget into it, and, as a result, failed to fill future programs.

"Entrepreneurs have to be citizens of your community. If you are involved in international business, then the world becomes your community."
Beverley Keating MacIntyre
BKM Research and Development Inc.

Better marketing systems bring customers pouring through your doors, set your cash register ringing and make your bank deposits grow. As you get busier, you will need to perfect your operating systems to handle the increased volume of work. This will guarantee consistent service and happy, repeat customers.

The WHOLE PERSON
Action Plan for Marketing Systems

1. a) List your top 20 customers. Describe as much as you can about them (e.g., geographics, preferences, demographics, behavior).

    _____

    _____

    b) What 12 things can you do to support them and build your relationship with them? Prioritize so you can implement one idea a month for a year.

    _____

    _____

2. a) Write down three things your customers told you this week, that if followed up on would improve your business.

    _____

    _____

    b) If you don't remember any, phone them and ask.

    _____

    _____

3. Plan a special event. When is the best month for it (one of your best sales months)? Who could you partner with? (Give yourself a good four months to get organized the first time.)

    _____

    _____

4. What charity would satisfy your heart and excite your customers? How could you get behind their cause?

    _____

    _____

CHAPTER 7

Operating Systems

What frustrations do women experience in setting up and using systems?

Operating systems are the way we streamline work. By breaking down tasks to the smallest parts we find faster, cheaper, easier ways to do things. For many women the boring details involved in this process is drudgery that holds them back from the important jobs in their business. In a review done by the Organization for Economic Cooperation and Development (OECD), on *The Impact of Women Entrepreneurs on the World Economy*, presented in Paris in April of 1997, technology was identified as one of the key barriers holding women entrepreneurs back. Technology may be as outside your comfort zone as it is for many of the women we interviewed. However, if you refuse to embrace it, you are sabotaging your company's profitability.

You can't talk technology without talking big bucks. Women are struggling to finance the technology they need to stay on the leading edge and not be passed by competition. The frustration around finding the money for Web sites and photocopiers, fax machines and robots goes hand in hand with the pressure of keeping up. Are you staying compatible with your clients' or suppliers' software? If not, you may be missing an opportunity to create a huge loyalty link that could be your SCA. Does adjusting to the global impact on your business make you feel like you're on a speed curve? Perhaps you're too busy to do the research necessary to meet the next demand on your system. Money is also a factor around the need to set up a database and keep it current. Many women cannot afford trained staff and depend on untrained employees to input data. This often results in data files that are riddled with errors. Self sabotage indeed!

Surprisingly, one of the most limiting frustrations around systems is lack of space. Of the women we interviewed, 21% are struggling with lack of space in some way. You may lack space to manufacture inventory, store inventory or display inventory. You might not have enough offices for your administrative staff or enough room for your front-end people. Maybe you are concerned about the lack of parking space for your customers.

Perhaps you are frustrated by a bottleneck that occurs in your manufacturing system—a problem over which you have minimal control. We also heard about the frustrations of retailers when suppliers held up deliveries, which created cash-flow problems; creative systems that didn't work to meet deadlines; and delays in repairs to technical systems .

To operate excellent systems the team must function in specific ways. This means you must deal with the bad habits of: disorganization, procrastination in doing research, failure to follow through once the system is installed.

Once upon a time life was a whole lot simpler. Sigh!

**Check out your operating systems quotient on
the next page.**

Are you sabotaging yourself?

(Circle the appropriate answer for each question. Add up your numbers and check the next page for your operating systems quotient.)

| 5 - always | 4 - regularly | 3 - occasionally | 2 - rarely | 1 - never |

1. Do you have the ability to turn out consistent quality no matter who is on staff that day?

| 5 | 4 | 3 | 2 | 1 |

2. Do you have a backup person who knows each system?

| 5 | 4 | 3 | 2 | 1 |

3. Do you adopt the best technology possible for your business?

| 5 | 4 | 3 | 2 | 1 |

4. Do you design your systems to meet your goals/fulfill your mission?

| 5 | 4 | 3 | 2 | 1 |

5. Do you negotiate with suppliers for the best deals?

| 5 | 4 | 3 | 2 | 1 |

6. Do you save money by subcontracting work to companies who already have systems in place?

| 5 | 4 | 3 | 2 | 1 |

7. Do you purge your office files at regular intervals?

| 5 | 4 | 3 | 2 | 1 |

8. Do you color code and/or number code your filing systems?

| 5 | 4 | 3 | 2 | 1 |

9. Do you have a procedure manual for each system in your operation?

| 5 | 4 | 3 | 2 | 1 |

10. Do you set timelines for each stage in a system?

| 5 | 4 | 3 | 2 | 1 |

Your operating systems score _____

41–50 You are a well-organized manager. Congratulations on being far ahead of the field.

31–40 You need to make improvements—schedule time and assess your weaknesses in this area.

21–30 List the technology you need to make a profit. Analyze how it will save you money in other areas. Choose one, research it and calculate the cost. Consider who will operate it, who will train the operator(s) and if you should learn to use it. Implement your plan. Your self-esteem will increase along with your profits.

11–20 Your team is not being provided with the necessary systems to work to their potential. You are probably wasting much of your time doing jobs that technology or a commonsense system would accelerate. Begin to adopt the **whole person** attributes. Work hard at the **Whole Person** Action Plan on page 164.

10 Your business is in trouble. Read this chapter and then list three immediate changes you can make to improve your systems. Set timelines for: completion of research, training and implementation. Move on it within the next 90 days.

If your operating systems quotient is low, you are losing profits for the following reasons:

- You are not able to turn out consistent quality work, which is costing you "making-amends" time and money.
- The outside world cannot easily communicate or interact with you (e.g., fax, e-mail).
- Your staff is unable to do the job efficiently because there is no manual to tell them how.
- You have bottlenecks slowing production.
- You waste time hunting for things you can't find (e.g., invoices, receipts).
- Your productivity grinds to a halt every time a key person is away for the day.

1. Why are operating systems important?

Your operating systems detail all the activities necessary to move your product or service from your hands to your customer's. A well-thought-out operating system permits one person to do the work of five who are poorly organized. Systems also ensure important steps aren't over-looked—steps that could cause expensive problems later. Systems reduce conflict by communicating to everyone the process of what has to be done to achieve a specific goal. Systems add wealth to your business by helping you work more effectively. Systems give you a way to deliver your vision to the world consistently, on time, every time. Great systems come from constant fine-tuning. Put a system in place and then immediately look for ways to improve it.

2. When do I need a procedures manual?

Anytime you want to delegate a task or have someone else train staff for a specific task, you need a procedures manual. Procedures manuals ensure fairness because everyone works with the same information. Procedures manuals are the first step in quality control.

> **"Get the stuff out of your head and onto paper ASAP while you're small. You'll have it in place as you grow."**
> *Liz Wyman*
> *Office Compliments Ltd.*

A complete procedures manual:

- defines the task (e.g., the assembly of and preparation for shipping silk plants);
- identifies the tools needed for the task and the area to work in;
- lists the procedure step-by-step;
- lists the don'ts and do's—ending with the positive;
- explains how the process is evaluated (e.g., a successfully assembled silk plant looks like _____).

An appendix may be required with sample work sheets, labels and other necessary materials.

In the early years of the business, informal guidelines may be all you need to improve communication and work flow (See Chapter 4, "Communication.")

3. How do I evaluate my systems?

"A well-trained staff with extensive knowledge of your product is the best system you can have."
Judy Richards
Davidson's Jewellers Limited

Once you've defined the tasks, use value management criteria to determine if they are maximizing your efficiency. Whether it's a special form for tracking inventory or an assessment of work flow on an assembly line, teach everyone to regularly ask the following questions about any procedure or system tool: **What is it? What does it do? What does it cost? What else would do the same thing? What would that cost? What would happen if we didn't do it at all?**

4. What is the most important system to develop first?

Swap time management systems for activity management systems. *Time management* is an old management tool used to determine how efficiently you are getting things done. In today's world it's more important to measure our effectiveness. *Activity management* is the new tool *Smart Women* are using to get the important things done. Its assessment tool is Pareto's 80/20 rule. Pareto's rule appears again and again in business. As mentioned in Chapter 6, "Marketing Systems," 20% of your customers brings 80% of your sales revenue. You probably also know that 20% of your staff does 80% of the work that achieves end results. And 20% of what you do brings you 80% of the results you want. Planning your activities in blocks makes you more effective. You experience less overlap and you find others to involve in the task. It removes you from the hands-on rush and puts you back far enough to examine your options. Ask yourself, "Am I doing this for me? for them? for him? Who is calling the shots?" Activity management involves a personal assessment of the critical versus the important.

Time management organizes your day according to time slots and tasks which you grind away at. For example, you might have your day broken down in the following way: 9:00 to 9:15—return phone calls; 9:15 to 9:30—review incoming mail; 9:30 to 9:50—update with managers; 9:50 to 10:00—review previous day's sales. Activity management groups little tasks into bigger activities and then decides on the importance of doing them.

Smart Women are into activity management big time. Activity management blocks off an hour every day to stay on top of what's happening in your business. Instead of devoting 15 minutes every morning to returning unimportant phone calls, you might be talking to employees on the floor, taking more time to look at your financials or otherwise achieving that goal. At the end of the week, you can be confident that you know what happened and there will be fewer surprises.

If you move forcefully in this direction, learning to be proactive instead of fighting fires all day, it will be the most rewarding **whole person** tool you will have mastered. It will enable you to grow your peace of mind and your business in giant steps. It is, however, an ongoing process. You must assess daily the important things (the 20%) and be certain you are not just filling in time with more work. Often this means hiring others to lift some of the work and even roles from your shoulders. "I can't afford it," you say. Try bartering. Try begging. Try just not doing it and see what happens. Get creative. Dump the work that bogs you down without anything more worthwhile to show for it than one more task done.

5. How do I manage a paper-trail system?

Tracking your customers' contact with you from the first phone call to the last follow-up is critical. It requires a "paper trail" backup for when our memory fails. This paper trail is a part of your administrative office systems.

When PCs (personal computers) first began to land on office desks, we spoke brightly of a day in the future when we would enjoy a paper-free office. Instead, technology has multiplied the amount of paper in circulation. For example, how often do we do a rush fax and then follow it up by mailing the hard copy?

> **"Know the job. You can't develop a system unless you understand the end results."**
> *Barbara Hodges*
> *Spadina Industries Inc.*

a) Handle It Faster

Keeping in mind that a clean desk saves you an average of 20 minutes a day, start with an initial housecleaning. Everything on your desk goes into one of two folders: red for action or brown for reading/useful information. Train your staff to put everything they bring you into one of these two files. You will have to review the paper in your red folder a couple of times a day. Now your desk is clear and you are bringing a **whole person** approach to your working environment.

Next take your daily planner and book off 15 to 30 minutes each morning as red file time, and also block one 2- to 3-hour brown session each week for your brown folder.

The red file contains important correspondence and phone messages. Let's start with phone messages. Start by ensuring they are filled in accurately. Regardless of who takes the call, he or she needs to learn to spell the caller's name back to them, confirm the message and repeat their number. Everyone on your team must make it a rule never to take a phone message without a number, even if it's from your sister. It takes an additional 10 seconds to ask for and record a phone number. It takes 2 to 5 minutes to look it up if you don't have it on the message.

Some people keep phone logs, either in their day planner or on a sheet of paper on their desk. They record the details and necessary follow-up action. A quick version of this is to simply write the information on the phone message itself. Record necessary action in your day timer and staple all phone slips together at the end of the day and throw them in a monthly file that gets junked at the end of the year.

Now that you've dug through the phone messages in your red folder, start on your correspondence. For these items, the old rule "Handle only once" is still a good one. In some instances, image is critical and a beautiful desktop-published response is called for. However, many of us today just want a fast answer and a handwritten note on the corner of the letter and a fax back is excellent. It keeps everything in context.

b) File It Effectively

File management is about being able to find a document when you need it. Write on the document what file it should go in (e.g., file to CL Marketing) and place all papers to be filed in a blue folder. If you have an executive assistant (EA), the blue folder goes to this person. If you don't have an EA, the blue folder should wait for the student you have coming in twice a week to do office cleanup. Students in secretarial schools are happy to have part-time work in return for experience and a reference when they graduate.

Each set of files should have a standard format. Open your file folder and on the left inside cover write the pertinent details beside the following headings: Contact Name, Company Name, Address, Phone number, Fax number, e-mail address and other important client information (e.g., husband, John Smith, minor shareholder and company bookkeeper). The inside right cover has a two-hole punch clip to ensure each piece of paper is attached and can't go missing from the file.

> Liz Wyman's bookkeeping clients' information is held in separate loose-leaf binders. Each has dividers listed: GST, monthly balance, profits and losses, A/P, A/R. The client has a copy of the binder, which allows Liz backup to augment the computer disks, if needed. She asks each client to fill in a profile sheet for the front of the binder. Each month the client drops off his or her receivables, payables and so on. As work for each is completed, new pages are added to the binder. At the end of the year the client has a 12-month financial picture in one neat, easy-to-store book.

c) Reduce It

Getting rid of excess paper happens only if you schedule a spring and fall cleaning or—at the least—a day-before-New-Year's-Eve bonfire. Turn cleanup into a fun and very important grubby day. It should be marked on your staff calendar. Choose your quietest time—often the days between Christmas and New Year's are good (provided all the staff isn't on holiday). Leave your voice mail on.

Have everyone start with their files, working to their desks and finally heading to bookshelves and closets. These days purging your computer files has to be added as a significant piece of cleanup.

Another way to reduce the amount of paper you are shuffling is to eliminate it before it builds up.

When Susan Nicol decided to set up a home office specializing in communication, she created an efficient and effective business that allows her to do everything from her home via computer. Susan is able to move from first contact with her clients, through price quoting, drafting, completing the work and billing without ever meeting her clients. "Almost all of my work is done through e-mail which saves time for my clients and eliminates duplication of work."

When to Duplicate: Decide what information requires backup. For instance, a signed contract you must have in the client's file might also be needed in the financial files. The need for backup is determined by how critical the information is and how accessible it is from another source.

6. What do I need in my purchasing system?

Your purchasing system details who, what, when, where, why and how. This must be determined and written down to ensure everyone on the team understands.

"Work to get the best deal from your suppliers and pass it on to your customers."
Lillian Neaman
Paper Gallery Ltd.

• **Who** (1) has purchasing power (i.e., authorizes the purchase)? (2) physically makes the purchases? More complex purchases might be assigned to one expert who coordinates to ensure the best deal and so on.

• **What has to be purchased?** Break it into departments. Make a complete list of all supplies that are necessary to keep that department running smoothly.

• **Why?** Ask yourself why you need it. How important is it? Could you get along without it?

• **Where do we purchase it?**

• **When?** Timing is everything. How late can you delay the purchase without jeopardizing the task it is needed for? The answer depends on the speed of the supplier.

• **How** is the supplier chosen? Do you want to lease or purchase? Do you want a discount or secondhand supplier? Do you want to deal locally, by reputation, by price or by some combination?

Building a relationship with (i.e., getting to know) your suppliers is critical. They can help you in a crisis with servicing or a "loaner." They can share sale information with you. They can provide you with research on what's happening in your industry. Put them on your Christmas party list, invite them for coffee occasionally, have them into staff meetings for mini information sessions.

7. How can a phone service help me?

The consensus of *Smart Women* is, next to your computer, a telephone system ranks highest in getting more work done. Voice mail or a telephone answering system are the "must haves" in a small, growing company.

> **"If our fax went down, we'd lose our business."**
> *Deb Hagman*
> *Hog Wild Specialties*

> Anne Miner, president of The Dunvegan Group, used technology to allow her to change her base of operations from Toronto to Calgary. She put a communication systems in place and moved to a Calgary office. Clients in the East dialed the same number as always and their calls were forwarded to Anne's office in Calgary, where she or her staff were happy to be of service. Because it was an invisible service, her clients assumed they were talking to her in Toronto. Anne made certain that she personally delivered the study reports to her clients and then, having been thanked for her excellent work, she told them about having moved her headquarters to Calgary. Clients were often surprised to hear this, but happy to continue to work with The Dunvegan Group, despite the move. Anne successfully used innovative technology to meet her clients' needs. In doing so she kept loyal clients in the East while positioning her business to attract new ones in the West, increasing the profitability of her business.

There are a few important rules to remember about phone service. When choosing the equipment for your business, consider:
• People prefer a real, and a cheerful, person on the other end of the line. If the person answering your phone handles calls well and has plenty of product knowledge she or he can be your best investment, by greatly increasing your sales. Instruct everyone in your office who answers a phone to give their own name along with the company name. "Hello. Communicating Power. Leslie speaking." This reassures the caller that there is a "flesh and blood" person at the end of the line who wants to assist them.

• You need an answering system. Today's customer wants to be able to call at any time. If you are working from home, remember that machines are the poorest form of answering service, particularly if your children are picking up the phone messages. Most local telephone companies offer a voice mail service at a nominal price. If you opt for it, your business can have its own secure voice mail box.

• As soon as your company can afford it, install individual voice mail for each staff member. This speeds up business, as voice mail is capable of taking down far more information, more accurately than a receptionist can.

• Don't ever kid yourself. If you choose to install an extensive recording system for daytime office hours use that leads the caller from "Press 1 for X to Press * for the next ten options," you will lose business.

8. What can computers do for my business?

Computers are the driving force behind some of the best small business-friendly technology. Some experts are calling the computer "the equalizer." A small, home-based business with a sophisticated enough computer can turn out products faster than a big corporation. The applications your computers are used for dictate what software, what memory, what speed is necessary.

a) Tracking Your Business Activity

The most important use of your computer is tracking your business activity. Customer profile information can be linked to purchasing, goods sold are deducted from inventory, materials are tagged for ordering and the sale is transferred to cash-flow statements. The speed and accuracy of a computer allow you to do these jobs—that traditionally took five people working with paper and pen—much faster, with one staff member.

> Brenda Boernsen, of B's Fine Coffee & Teas, and her husband designed a dynamite system for tracking daily income, expenses and supplies. The system is so good that Amway purchased it for their use. It easily allows her to target hot sellers for reorder and slow movers for clearance. As well, it tracks special promotions and events through which Brenda has marketed her product.

It tells her to increase product for an upcoming event or to decrease it because it didn't do well last year. It keeps her in touch daily with the profitable areas of her business, showing her where prices need to be raised or lines eliminated.

Set up your customer database by deciding what you need to know about your customer. This information can be used to make the client feel special, make it easy for them to deal with you and keep them coming back. This readily accessible information ensures consistent service: different employees can serve your customer each time, they only have to read the file instead of asking your customer to tell them everything about his or her needs again.

Setting up simple databases on your computer system may seem like a complicated and time-consuming undertaking, but it doesn't have to be. Start by ensuring whatever system you buy can grow with your needs over the next five years. For more complex database needs that allow you to link your financial, inventory control and client information together, you may need to look at customized software, designed by professionals for that purpose. There are also several major off-the-shelf software titles available that specialize solely in database development and input, but the novice may find them difficult to work with.

b) Resource Systems

Destination Montreal's client base is composed of large companies who regularly move new staff into Montreal. Hélène Tremblay, the owner, is the most extraordinary connector. With staff and computers going full out, she maintains a resource base of diversified services in Montreal—from doctors to insurance agents, from available secretaries to the names of stores that sell winter clothes. Approximately 1200 listings are in her database. These are monitored and constantly updated. They note the client's satisfaction, or lack of it, in dealing with the recommended contact. The companies who hire Hélène recognize the faster their employees are settled in their new homes, the sooner they'll be productive at work. The employees use Hélène's team, not the Yellow Pages, when they need to deal with anything from government red tape to allergies. In one week alone Hélène's team worked with 40 new families. Destination Montreal organized 800 houses for viewing by realtor, sector and price for these families. You don't do that without the help of a computer.

c) Internal and External Communication

Internal networks in your organization hooking all your computers together to talk to each other is a technology system for a new form of communication. It can save unbelievable hours by sharing databases, templates, updates and so on with everyone in your organization. Unfortunately, companies are rushing to build extranets (Web pages) to talk to their external customers instead of starting by connecting their internal customers (staff). There is a major payoff in cost efficiencies, elimination of duplication and faster processing by having an intranet that will in turn mean the external customer is better served. Don't run to jump on the Web page craze. In very few instances does it generate extra revenues or improve customer service. An intranet, however, can do both. When you exceed four computer stations, find an expert to help you cost out your own intranet.

> "The more entrenched you become in efficiency, the less effective you become."
> *Anne Kramer*
> *Current Technology Corporation*

9. How can I find the right software for my business?

a) Custom-Designed Systems

Smart Women complete industry-specific tasks more efficiently by designing their own software when there is no off-the-shelf product to do the job efficiently. In an even smarter move, they increase revenues by selling their well-tested software to their competition.

Manon Pilon is a petite dynamo. She started her first business when she was 15. As the owner of Europe Cosmétiques, she developed a software package, Datavogue, for the beauty industry. It tracks a multi-million-dollar salon operation. Recognizing the majority of staff in the industry are not computer literate, Manon made the software as simple to operate as pressing two keys. "Datavogue tracks everything from who is spending how much on marketing, to existing and needed inventory and individual staff productivity," says Manon with considerable pride. "There have been 140 versions added to it. We have adopted it for our Asian market, our training school and for individual day spas. It has been one of our most exciting leaps forward."

b) Off-the-Shelf Software

Meredith DeGroat cautions: "Try to buy off-the-shelf software and then customize it. That way you'll protect yourself by always having external consultants who know your systems." Her company invested thousands of dollars in two computer programmers who designed in-house software for the business. Down the road the two programmers teamed up and quit, informing Meredith they could be hired back for a price—a highway robbery price! Meredith also reminds you to buy from a company with a long-standing business record for service and stability. Her final word on the subject is: train backup even if it's only an outside, "on-call" contract person.

> "Being able to use someone else's experience puts a lot of challenges in focus."
> *Peggyann Boudreau*
> *JDP Computer Systems Inc.*

When researching software, try calling out-of-province competitors or asking attendees at industry-related functions. They'll readily tell you what software they are using, or who's using something good. Don't re-invent the wheel if someone can sell you an industry package, with the bulk of the bugs worked out.

10. How important is a system to monitor my inventory?

A user-friendly inventory system is critical to the financial success of both retailers and manufacturers. Many retailers have strangled their businesses on years' worth of dead stock. Inventory that doesn't turn over regularly eats up your cash flow. Using the 80/20 rule, you know that 20% of your inventory will bring in 80% of your sales. That means it is turning over far more times than the 80%. If you get too many dollars tied up in stale-dated inventory and the rest going out in wages, rent and so on, you quickly find yourself unable to buy more of the 20% you need. Stale-dated inventory must be gone—be ruthless. After it has been on your shelf for half a season, it's not going anywhere without some

"Measure your buffer of inventory to a point where you are comfortable."
Arlaina Waisman
Nutrawise Enterprises Ltd.

dramatic sales. Pennies on the dollars are better than nothing if those pennies are put back into your 20%.

Total tracking systems are the road to sanity. As quickly as possible, get an inventory system on computer. If you are retailing, use a point-of-sale system (when the sale is rung into a computerized register, it immediately removes the item from inventory). It will make you money by saving you costly reordering errors. If finances are forcing you to go manual for now, make tracking a priority. Every day that you allow inventory to sit on your shelf, you are losing dollars. Before you take the manual route, check out leasing rates. Most computerized systems can be leased for very reasonable amounts. If you switch to a computerized system, the time saved will free you up to sell more.

> Meredith DeGroat of totally tropical interiors has a fully integrated computer system that allows her staff to keep track of ordering and billing, and of the raw material, work-in-progress and finished goods. In the process the system tracks picking, packing and shipping and the entire process is completed in 48 hours. The only thing not integrated is the software that calculates the commission on the sale. Meredith has installed compensation software that is downloaded every night, ensuring that her sales people are paid accurately and in a timely manner. This encourages them to be out there selling more.

Semiannually, do a manual inventory count to match the numbers in your computer to what's really on your shelf. Also, make a point of doing irregular, frequent spot checks to discourage staff theft.

11. What other systems are important to my operation?

"A training system is not a luxury, it is a necessity to ensure growth."
Karinna James
Catalyst Insights Ltd.

Go and examine your industry everywhere you can—globe trot! Look hard for the **best practices**—things that are done exceptionally well—not only in your own industry sector but also in industries where cross-pollination might be possible.

a) Training Systems

Develop every training system possible to help your staff quickly learn how to service your customers.

> Of the hundreds of manufacturing companies across the country none will spark your imagination and enthusiasm like Barbara Hodge's operation, Spadina Industries Inc. Barbara has developed systems to ensure that any job in her mattress factory can be completed to standard by a new employee within 24 hours of starting. Colorful laminated posters and visual tools hang in work areas to keep quality at the top of employees' minds. Charts and representative samples show quality standards and workmanship details.

b) Total Quality Control Systems

> Meredith DeGroat's policy at totally tropical interiors Ltd. is to ship within 48 hours. "This means our inventory of raw materials must be high," Meredith explains. "We have the first stage of our product manufactured off-shore and do final assembly here. If a product proves hot and we've guessed wrong, we have angry sales staff all across the country. We err on the high side hoping not to run out. If you make that choice, you must recognize the extra cash investment required. You keep more money tied up in inventory."

There are many total quality management (TQM) programs out there. In a larger manufacturing operation you may want to contact the Business Development Bank (BDC) (see the resource directory at the back of this book) and ask about ISO 9000, the internationally recognized symbol that says your company has mastered TQM. It is a very expensive and difficult process, one not to be undertaken lightly. Service and retail businesses need to focus their TQM training on their staff to ensure consistency. Communication and delegation are key issues for quality control, as it is essential to have clearly understood standards that may not be lowered under any circumstances. Whether your business is a service, retail or manufacturing business, examine your rejection rate. How many times does work have to be returned and redone in one way or another? Getting it right the first time is essential.

> Angela Bucaro, an exciting designer who specializes in knits, brings her Italian passion to her work. She reminds you that making a profit depends heavily on

your sixth sense—being able to predict the market—combined with good systems. "Quality is everything," Angela declares. "We use proforma forms that list the cost of everything for each sample garment (fabric, thread, labor). Everything is controlled by these cost sheets. We contract our sewing out, which makes quality even harder to monitor. The contractor inspects it first, then we do an inspection; finally, our shippers are trained to do one last check before it is packed.

When you see a Bucaro suit on the runway, you understand the passionate commitment to detail that goes into it.

c) Research and Development (R&D) Systems

How important is R&D? The answer to that lies in knowing how fast your industry is changing. Most businesses today face some new form of obsolescence daily. The means needed to serve your customer quickly today are considered ancient tomorrow. The psychographics of your customer (how they think and how they see themselves) are undergoing dramatic change every couple of years. The cross-impact of other industries can change your industry overnight. The diversity and speed of your competition alone demands a huge effort on your part to keep up. R&D means constantly researching better ways to serve your customers through both product and service development. R&D means never being satisfied with the status quo. R&D assures constant quality improvement.

Joy Hanley, owner of Fine Food Investments Ltd., combined her formal training (bachelor of arts and bachelor of education degrees) with a degree from the Culinary Institute of Canada. With a wide scope of expertise in the areas of research, new product development and human resources planning, she came up with a pizza product so good it won her a position as a finalist in 1995 in the Canadian Grand Prix New Products Awards.

Even the smallest business needs to devote time, budget and technology to R&D if it is to grow and especially grow more profitable. *Smart Women* constantly refined and redefined their product/service offering.

Beverley Keating MacIntyre focuses BKM, her training company, on continuous quality improvement. "BKM's approach was and is to ensure that our workforce is competent and capable of responding to change on a continual basis," she says. That means R&D to search out customized training programs, innovative learning tools and cultural concerns to deal with expanding international markets. According to Beverley, "What we knew yesterday just isn't going to be enough to get us through today." BKM creates strategic alliances with international companies, public and private schools and a telephone company, all committed to the electronic delivery of education and to helping Beverley find new and better delivery tools.

12. How can I handle growth?

Room to grow is always at a premium and in most Canadian markets becoming more so. Even two years ago the economy was slow enough to provide selection, negotiating opportunities and options to expand into empty space next door. As the economy improves, we find the landlord dictating to us rather than the preferred reverse.

Before you spend more on rent, take time to examine each one of your work steps. Is it being done in the most efficient way possible? Do you have to walk across the room many times a day for the same task? As the price of space continues to escalate, *Smart Women* are coming up with new ways to expand.

a) Hoteling

Hoteling reduces overhead by eliminating office space that sits empty most of the time. It is most suitable for the type of business where much of the workforce is out of the office a great deal of the time (e.g., sales reps). A few offices are available and must be pre-booked by the staff member if they need it for a meeting or to finish up reports, for example. It can be difficult for staff to remember to book ahead for space. It requires everyone to cooperate and be proactive.

A good space planner more than repays their cost in the efficiencies they create for you. Start by phoning some good office towers for referrals. Ask who they use when they have new tenants moving in who need office space built. Malls also employ space

> "Make your space ergonomically sound—raising filing cabinets (less bending), lowering counters (short staff), adding extra phones and so on. You'll have a happier team and less staff absenteeism."
> **Dr. Susan Vertefeuille**
> **Optometrist**

planners. Make an appointment to interview the recommended person. You can hire them to help you with some rough sketches, to provide you with finished floor plans or to guide the entire process through from overseeing contractors to selecting carpets for your approval.

Remember, expanding means greater efficiency only if you have planned carefully for it. Lots of businesses who think they'd give anything to have more space find their work flow actually slows down when there is elbow room.

b) Homeworkers

Staff who work at home are hooked into the office electronically. They come in once a week for staff meetings, the human connection and perhaps their paycheck. Paychecks, though, are usually automatically deposited into bank accounts by payroll systems. Payroll systems are themselves offered by most major banks and are the perfect way to handle deductions and Revenue Canada effectively and cheaply.

c) Strategic Alliances

Informal partnerships exist where businesses share space in each other's business premises for different purposes. For example, two manufacturers who must stockpile inventory (paddling pools and snow blowers) at different times of the year share the same warehouse.

d) Outsourcing Work Flow

A business contracts another business to handle a task beyond its capacity due to lack of time and money. Many businesses use fulfillment houses to handle parts of their service, such as filling and shipping orders or direct market mailings.

e) Longer Operating Hours

Two people share the job on two different shifts. This can be extremely cost-effective if an expensive piece of equipment is used that would be sitting idle without the second shift.

f) Pickup/Drop-Off Spots

This offers neighborhood customer convenience while keeping the costs of an entire new office at bay. Simply create mini multiple service centers that send the work into a central, lower-rent area to actually get done, then return it to the drop-off service for pickup. Examples of businesses using this strategy are dry-cleaning, photography and photocopying businesses. Your transportation costs could be handled more economically with a discount courier contract.

g) Open Space

Many service businesses are tearing down their office walls and creating central workstations that allow for the extra productivity that results from everyone working together. Open space obviously takes less room and allows for easier sharing of equipment.

h) Extra Storage

Rent a couple of monthly underground parking stalls in your building and throw up plywood walls with a padlocked door for extra storage.

i) User-based Space

Reassess each of the rooms you pay for. Do you need the big meeting room? How often is it used? Could you put up dividers and split it into three work spaces and convert a smaller office into a new, smaller meeting room? You'd end up with two more work spaces.

Operating systems are the skeleton of your company. The business can't grow without a structure. Now that you see how varied and complex they can be, let's look at how to finance your systems.

The WHOLE PERSON
Action Plan for Operating Systems

1. Track each activity you did in a one-week period. Write beside each how important it was in achieving your long-term goal. Add up how much of your time is
   spent on the 80% that doesn't bring results?

   _____

   _____

2. Determine what procedures manuals you need. Prioritize and outline how you
   would do the task. Brainstorm details with staff. Write up your rough brainstorm-
   ing notes into a simple, user-friendly guide.

   _____

   _____

3. Determine how you can better utilize your telephone system as a sales tool. What
   will make it more user friendly?

   _____

   _____

4. Phone three business owners in your industry who are operating in other
   provinces or countries. Talk to them about what quality control systems they have
   in place to ensure consistent service to clients.

   _____

   _____

CHAPTER 8

Financial Systems

What frustrations are you experiencing around your finances?

When it came time to discuss finances with us, 80% of the 100 women we interviewed said they have experienced discrimination when applying for start-up money or further financing for their business. Of those women interviewed, 55% obtained startup money through a financial institution and even then 63% of the 55 said they experienced gender discrimination. Have you been patted on the head, patted on the butt, patted into a cramped mold with most of your options eliminated? You're in good company. These women, with fiery eyes and clenched fists, described the indignities, inanities and idiocy they experienced while dealing with lending institutions. There is no doubt the old boys' network which, up until recently, held the reins of the financial establishment has raised the blood pressure of many women entrepreneurs.

Perhaps you, like so many, made the decision to find financial help from other sources (45% of the entrepreneurs interviewed self-financed their businesses). You may have told your friends, "I'll never deal with a bank again." Did a manager agree to give you a renovating loan for a healthy business you've run alone for 10 years, *if* your husband cosigned the loan? Were you given the money, but forced to pay higher interest, and with harder terms and more paperwork than most of the male entrepreneurs you know? Did you pitch your vision, back it up with a great business plan and have it rejected because the manager couldn't relate to a female-oriented service? Or perhaps you reacted in stunned amazement when the bank called your line of credit when you separated from your husband. If any of these things happened to you, you are almost certainly a victim of unfair lending practices.

Financial institutions are today, though, waking up to the fact that there is a huge market of women entrepreneurs who need services customized to their businesses. Most of the major banks have new policies in place and are training management to meet your needs.

So now you have the money. This provides a whole new area of frustration. Many women find they are victims of their social imprint. A great number of the women we interviewed are frustrated by the feeling of being seen as "money grubbing" if they raise their rates to a standard that will actually turn a profit. (Women also sabotage each other by asking for services at a discount rate, something they would be unlikely to do to a male entrepreneur.)

Another frustration comes with tracking your finances. Many of you do not like numbers. You might be frustrated by the need to learn financial systems and the need to learn the computer to facilitate faster systems. You may be irritated by the day-to-day paperwork your bank manager insists on. Perhaps you just have too many jobs and the books are one more—the one that comes in last and should be first. Or, do you feel you have to grovel every time you go to your bank manager with a request?

The women whose solution to their lack of rapport with numbers is to hire a bookkeeper or an accountant experience the final huge frustration. One woman is on her 13th. Yikes! Are you having trouble finding someone who will take the time to explain, who doesn't patronize you, works to deadline, uses a system you can understand and doesn't run off to South America with your money? There are many good accountants out there. It's worth persisting to find a great match for you.

Test your financial management quotient on the opposite page.

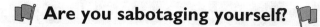 Are you sabotaging yourself?

Financial Systems: Danger Signals

(Circle the answer that best describes you. Add up your numbers and check the next page for your financial systems quotient.)

5 - always	4 - regularly	3 - occasionally	2 - rarely	1 - never

1. Do you have a comprehensive business plan with you when you go to the bank for a loan?

5	4	3	2	1

2. Do you shop for your lending institution by comparing terms?

5	4	3	2	1

3. Do you know all of your fixed and variable costs?

5	4	3	2	1

4. Do you read your sales figures weekly and understand what they mean?

5	4	3	2	1

5. Do you have fair margins in your product/service price with all your direct costs accounted for?

5	4	3	2	1

6. Do you prepare your bank manager ahead of time for bad news, such as late receivables and lower-than-projected sales?

5	4	3	2	1

7. Do you work at knowing your banker personally—building a relationship of mutual trust and respect?

5	4	3	2	1

8. Do you negotiate with your suppliers for such things as credit terms, co-op advertising, early payment terms and bulk-purchase discounts?

5	4	3	2	1

9. Do you generate a financial statement monthly and read it?

5	4	3	2	1

10. Do you have any extra cash in your business working for you, to gain interest?

5	4	3	2	1

Your financial systems score _____

41–50 Your excellent score in this area means you are challenged by financial problems rather than disheartened. You know exactly where your business stands financially. You're in a good position to solve any problems on the horizon and grow your business.

31–40 You will want to do the **Whole Person** Action Plan at the end of the chapter. Don't waste energy on frustration. Pull your account if the bank isn't making your life easier. Find the right financial adviser to help you. Take delight in learning to understand the financial end of your business.

21–30 You need to get help. Take a workshop on budgeting. Hire a professional to come into your business and set up financial systems. Make sure you take the time to learn them.

11–20 Do all of the above. Take your books to a reliable accountant and have him or her straighten them out and show you what you are doing wrong. Take advantage of seminars on financial matters. Implement what you learn. Measure your spending and savings—keep them in proportion.

10 EMERGENCY! You need to restructure fast. Sit down with an expert and, together, assess your financial situation, both business and personal. Check out your bad habits—start changing them. Question if your bank is giving you the help you need. Show them that you are taking concrete steps to change things. Follow up a good recommendation and find yourself a financial adviser who can help you deal with debt. Make certain you have rapport—she or he understands your vision and wants to help make it happen.

If your financial systems quotient is low, your business is losing money because:

- You don't know enough about your cash flow to anticipate financing needs.
- You are underfinanced and cannot grow.
- You are wasting energy on financial worries and frustration rather than being proactive.
- You don't know if you are on target at the end of the month, or the fiscal year.
- You may be using cheap labor to do your books and getting a poor job that will cost you big money in the future.
- You could be losing a bundle on expenses because you haven't negotiated better deals.

1. What is a financial system?

Your beautiful business has a "hungry monster" side to it that feeds on cash. This appetite is known as "expenses" and they include payments for rent, heat, light, insurance, business licenses and taxes, financing costs, business services (such as accounting or legal), office equipment and supplies, and some (or all) salaries and benefits (such as yours). These are "fixed costs" and the term indicates that no matter how many (or how few) widgets you make or widget cleaning services you provide, you will still have to pay for all of these expenses.

The hungry monster also has an appetite for money in the form of variable costs—these are additional expenses for the materials needed to make the widgets or perform the service. If your production staff varies with the number of orders you have, their salaries and benefits are a variable rather than a fixed cost, and so are any sales commissions.

> **"Have reporting systems that stop surprises."**
> *Meredith DeGroat*
> *totally tropical interiors Ltd.*

In order to make money, you must bring in revenue that is more than your fixed and variable costs put together. In order to make a profit you must know the direct (variable) costs for providing the goods or service, apply a percentage of your indirect (fixed) costs to every sale and add on a percentage for profit. You need to do this for every sale you make—these costs plus your desired profit are what make up the price you charge for your goods or services. If you don't know what your direct and indirect costs are, or you don't include all the costs (such as your own time), chances are that at the end of the year, you're not going to have a profit (and you'll also probably have trouble arranging financing). Just as you've planned everything else for your business, you need to plan the financial aspect, and your financial systems are what allow you to collect and monitor the information you need.

For most women, this is the toughest part of owning a business. Do you find it uncreative, uninspiring? The normal response to dealing with the financial side is to "hire a professional"—the right professional. All too often your financial people focus only on your "dead" numbers (those from your past, your company's financial history). Seldom do they look ahead to your "living" numbers (the ones happening today and in the future) and work creatively with them. So hiring a professional is part of the equation, but the fact is you still must understand what the accountant has done and why. If you find this aspect of business tedious, you need somehow to change your mind-set. You need to recognize that controlling your numbers is the key to making money in your business.

Bev Durvin reminds us: "The first step is to understand how important [financial systems are] to your business's survival and start learning what the numbers mean. The second is to get involved with your cash flow and project ahead for better control. The third step is to discover it gets sexy and exciting to play with your numbers."

2. How do I structure my business?

"You have to invest in yourself to be known."
Hermante Ayotte
Clinique De Médecine
Industrielle & Preventive
Du Quebec Inc.

There are three forms of business structure. The one you choose for your business is based on (1) the amount of personal exposure you have if something goes wrong; (2) the involvement of other people in the ownership of the business; and (3) reducing income tax.

Sole proprietorships are taxable as ordinary income to the proprietor. A sole proprietor has no liability protection. If your business is sued, you, as its proprietor, are sued. In the early years before the business is making a lot of money, sole proprietorship is the best and least costly way to go, provided you have so little exposure to causing your client harm you could cover it with insurance.

Partnerships are also taxable as ordinary income to the partners. The only real difference between a partnership and a sole proprietorship is that it has two or more owners, each of whom owns a given percentage of the company. In the absence of a written agreement to the contrary, all partners share equally in the profits or losses of the company. Having a business life insurance policy to pay off the estate of a partner in the event of death is necessary; otherwise you could find yourself in business with their heir—a spoiled son or ditsy aunt. In a partnership, the partner with the deepest pockets continues to pay if there is trouble. All the partners are personally liable for any damages.

Corporations are legal entities. A corporation is recognized as a "legal person" that exists independently from its owners under the law. Personal assets of the corporate owners cannot be seized to settle claims against the corporation. The owners enjoy limited liability. Capital can be raised in the corporation's name. Stock shares are transferable among owners, and the corporation continues independently of stock sales or stockholder deaths. These features make this form of organization almost mandatory for businesses that have passed the $500,000 mark in sales. A salary is paid to the employees who are shareholders (this includes you, the boss). Shareholders receive dividends in relationship to the number of shares they own and the profitability of the company. Dividends are declared by the director(s), not the shareholders. In small companies the director(s), shareholders(s) and employee(s) are often the same person/people. Corporate profits are taxed at the corporate rate, regardless of the individual income levels of the owners. Shareholders' dividends are taxed at a different rate as well, and you may choose to receive your income as a combination of director's fees, salary and dividends to minimize your taxes. If no dividend is declared, the money remains in the company and can be removed later or on retirement when the individual's personal income is in a lower tax bracket.

• **Year-End:** In a sole proprietorship your year-end is automatically December 31, as is your personal year-end. Corporations get to choose their year-end and should have their accountants' input on the tax ramifications of their timing. Losses of the company can be carried backward against past tax paid or forward against future earnings. You will want to ensure your year-end falls at one of the quieter times of your business cycle, regardless of tax issues, for your sanity's sake. Once your year-end is chosen, it is difficult to change it. Revenue Canada has to be informed as to why the change is needed and approve it.

3. How do I know how much money I need?

Zoom back to Chapter 1, "Planning." In your plan you will have determined what you want to do, how much it will cost you (expenses), what you project you can make from it (revenue) and what the difference between the two will be (profits or losses). In simpler terms you might call this a budget. You need a short-term budget for one month that focuses on cash flow, and a long-term budget for one year that focuses on future growth and the financing for this growth. Your three-year budget also deals with future growth.

Your budget provides you with a guideline for how much you can spend each month against what you earned last month and how much you have to earn this month to meet next month's expenses. When financial controls break down, you are earning this month's revenue to pay last month's bills (aged 30 days) or—shudder—the bills for the month prior to that (aged 45 days). That's being cash-flow challenged and when you get there, you are in trouble. There are only two ways to climb out of that hole. The first is for some good "angel" to lend you enough not only to get current but also to get, at a minimum, one month ahead. The second way is for you to cut your expenses to the bone and beg your suppliers to give you time to pay off in installments.

Your first indication that financial controls are not your strong point might be the number of unpaid invoices you have at the end of the month, or the threatening call from your banker regarding your overdrawn account. These will be your first real clues as to why people keep telling you—"Cash is king."

4. How do I understand my financial statements?

"Speculating happens. Cash flow is not a fail-safe tool."
Barbara Hodges
Spadina Industries Inc.

The *cash flow statement* shows when cash moves in and out of the company. For example, your insurance premium covers an expense that is 12 months long, but you must put 100% of the cash out for it at one time of the year. Or, you sell the contract now, but you won't actually see the cash from the client for 30 days when they pay your invoice.

The *income statement* may be thought of as a "moving picture" representing the flow of revenues and expenses through the firm each month or over the course of a given year. Most of us have a hard time grasping that our income statement can look great while our cash flow is busy putting us under. If these aren't concepts you've come to grips with... do so now. Hard to believe, but it can get interesting.

Balance sheets provide a "snapshot" of the financial condition of a firm at a given date and list the assets, liabilities and equities of the firm. By definition, assets must equal the total of liabilities plus equities. This is because the company's assets are the things it has that are of value including cash, receivables, buildings, equipment, investment and stock on hand. The other side of the balance sheet shows how the company paid for them—payables and loans (liabilities) or money the business earned (equities).

Understand your financial statements. Keep them current and close by so you can ensure timely decision making, so essential to your sanity and your business growth. If this is not happening now, make it your number one priority to call your accountant and determine how you can get your systems and your personal knowledge up to speed. Only then will you know how much money you have, and how much money you're going to make.

> "I pull up my spreadsheets every day before I leave, until the numbers begin to stick," says Phillipa Hudson, owner of Mineral World & Scratch Patch. "You get so you can recognize trends by checking actuals against projected and past performance."

According to CPI financial specialist Helen Webster, the most commonly used tool to analyze financial statements is ratio analysis. Bankers just love ratio analysis. "If they're going to plug ratios in to make decisions about your financial well-being, you'd better be able to do it too," Helen cautions.

According to Helen, key financial ratios are commonly grouped into the following four major categories:

- Liquidity: measurement of the company's ability to meet its short-term obligations as they become due:

  Example: $\dfrac{\textbf{total current assets}}{\textbf{total current liabilities}}$

  expressed as follows—1.2; 1.0.

- Leverage: measurement of the relationship between capital contributed by creditors and that contributed by owners.

Example: Debt to equity:

$$\frac{\text{total amount of debt (current + long-term liabilities)}}{\text{total amount of equity (tangible net worth)}}$$

- Efficiency: measure of the overall ability of the firm to produce a profit. Example: Return on owner's investment:

$$\frac{\text{annual net profit (after taxes) x 100\%}}{\text{total owner's equity}}$$

- *Profitability*: measurement of the number of (gross profit) dollars produced for every $1 of sales
  Example: gross margin

$$\frac{\text{gross margin x 100\%}}{\text{sales}}$$

Expressed as a percentage (a gross margin of 5.2% means that for every $1 of sales the company produces 5.2 cents of gross margin).

If you are not using any ratio analysis, make an appointment with your accountant or your banker (if your statements and relationship are good enough) and get them to teach you how to use them.

5. How do I price my product/service properly?

a) Undervalued and All Alone

Many small business owners grossly underprice their product or service. Your competition loses because you put them out of business if you undercut them all the time. Your customer loses because you'll have to cut value to supply the goods at that price. You lose because you haven't taken all your costs into consideration, leaving no room for profit margin in the contract and therefore no reinvestment dollars to pay yourself or to go after the next deal.

"Toughen up about how much you do for free. Now I set out my fees for speaking and articles. I only commit to two freebies a month."
Lara Lauzon
Lauzon Consulting Inc.

Just because you are home-based, with a low fixed overhead, and you are doing the work with no out-of-pocket labor costs, doesn't mean you don't have to add both of those items into your selling price. But, you wail, "My customer won't pay it." If this is the case, the unpalatable truth is that you aren't running a business, you're running a charity as a volunteer. Reevaluate. Would they pay more? If not, is there another customer group you could target that has more money and more need? No? Then it's time to look into some new products that will attract customers who will pay a fair price. As the new product lines build, gradually eliminate the ones that don't make you money.

> Monica Gross affirms, "I target customers who want quality and are willing to pay for it. I don't apologize for my prices. I give them exactly what they want and bring in new lines every month to keep things exhilarating. My customers are loyal and happy."

b) Focus

As a *Smart Woman* you must ruthlessly use the 80/20 rule to assess performance of your product or service offering. Just as 80% of your sales come from 20% of your customers so too does 80% of your revenue come from 20% of your products or services. It is essential to know what the latter 20% is and focus on selling more of it. No matter how much you personally love Product X, and we all have our favorites, you must put a drop-dead performance date on it.

> "By offering unique merchandise with fair margins I make as much money staying small as I would if I lowered prices and grew. It means I work *smart*," says Lillian Neaman, owner of the Paper Gallery.

6. What financial systems do I need to have in place?

Accounts receivable is a tough area for women who don't like asking for money. Start by minimizing your risk. Have a simple credit policy in place. Have the customer fill in a credit application form. If you don't have one, phone a supplier or a large business and ask them to fax you an application. Using it as a guideline, adapt it to your needs. Do check the references the new client gives you. Give a letter to the client clearly stating the terms of the account. Charge interest for late payment, offer discounts for early payment.

Accounts receivable can become easy if you adopt Mary Ann Turnbull's system. "I get my cash up front," she says. "My clients pay month by month in advance for the services they receive. This makes cash flow a breeze."

Collecting overdue receivables can be hard. Most small businesses know their customers well and don't have a problem. When it does occur, don't hide behind impersonal letters—pick up the phone and call. If the client says there are cash-flow problems, make an immediate deal to collect some now and put the balance on payments. Hang up the phone and drive over and pick up the preliminary payment.

The accounts payable is the same situation in reverse. As cash flow improves, you look hard at who needs to be paid first to avoid interest for late penalties, who needs to be paid early to enjoy discounts and who owes you credit for supplies or work you've returned. Looking after nickels in these areas can save dollars by the end of the month. That can really help small business margins.

Karinna James uses Quicken software to create a weekly budget. "Then I track weekly expenses and match them to my plan. At first it was hard work. Now it's like a computer game to see if I am winning."

Signa Gilchrist offers this great tip (as a CMA, she definitely knows her money issues). "I deposit my tax money (GST, PST) into a separate interest-bearing account. This way I don't risk spending it and I earn a little interest to pay for the expense of collecting it."

Payroll systems are available through most major banks today. Once you pass 10 employees, they are a cost-effective, simple way to ensure staff are paid on time and the government remittance (a time-consuming pain) is done correctly. They are a great solution to lightening your and/or your bookkeeper's load so you can focus on preparing cash flows instead. The banks will do payroll for you even if it's a matter of only one employee.

7. How can I control my costs?

There is a well-worn saying: It's not what you make that counts, **it's what you keep.**

Many of the *Smart Women* found cutting costs was a very satisfying way of making more money without working harder. Ask yourself the following questions:

- **Where is the waste in my business?**

   Barbara Hodges teaches her staff that everyone can have an impact on the financial well-being of the company. "I ask people to consider their feelings about losing a $20 bill out of their pocket," she says. "Most would feel a sense of waste. I point out how easy it is to lose $20 around the factory (freight damage, inefficient cutting, counting errors). When that idea sinks in, I ask about finding a $20 bill. Most would feel a sense of gain. Making good decisions to avoid waste and being relentless about damage claims is like finding money."

- **Who is helping me cut costs?**

   Angela Bucaro says, "I watch how I spend. I set aside regular time to track down better prices. I used courier X and found out courier Y is a fraction of the price. I tracked down pattern paper for $40 less a roll—a huge saving over a year. If I can use a contractor so I don't have to purchase a $10,000 piece of equipment, I do it."

   > **"You need to be flexible, determined and work hard to keep out of debt."**
   > *Brenda Boernsen*
   > *B's Fine Coffee &Teas.*

- **How could I cut back on spending?**

   Monica Gross suggests, "Work with neighboring businesses to help each other out with bulk collective purchasing, to get discount prices." (This works for anything from joint advertising to toilet paper.)

   "Don't be afraid to retrench fast," says Dulcie Price, of Optimum Agra Services Ltd., "When the industry went through a bad time, I cut overhead, stopped travel, downsized my house, sold the car, stopped using credit and ran the company *smart*. The payoff was survival when most of my competitors went under. Now I'm doing well and have a reputation of longevity in the industry."

- **Who could pick up part of my costs?**

   "When I began, I formed strategic alliances and worked out of my clients' offices," explains Kate Thrasher. "This covered my overhead and cut my expenses. The clients were happy because they could actually see me working on their projects."

- **What could I rent out?**

  Mary Ann Turnbull says, "I make money on a portion of my premises by renting out classrooms during downtime. I also negotiate depreciation for wear and tear on the furnishings and equipment."

- **How could I cut costs and still get the best?**

  Judy Harcourt says, "I can't afford a full-time controller so I contract an accountant for two days a week. He comes into our office and does receivables, payables and keeps us on track with cash flow.

- **What would it cost me to lease instead of buy?**

  "I price out leasing and buying. Sometimes leasing is cheaper, sometimes it helps your cash flow. Both are good reasons to go that route," says Kate Thrasher.

8. How do I find the right financial expert to help me?

"The proper accountant or financial adviser will open up the road map of success to you."
Lise Cantin
Fishbowl Restaurant

An *absolute must* investment in your business is a great financial adviser. You may not need them to do your day-to-day numbers. You may only be able to afford to contract them to "advise" you on a monthly basis. Understand that two hours of a wise person's time can save you more grief than 10 hours with a basic number cruncher.

I fired four accountants in three years until I found one who could track my business and show me what banks wanted," Kate Thrasher explains. "Someone who can only produce financial statements is useless. You need to understand banking ratios, 'How fat should I be for my height?' (What should be the debt-to-equity ratio for my industry?) You need to know what reports your banker needs every month and how to respond to questions regarding them when the bank calls."

Ask yourself, "What do I need from my financial help?" The usual things are basic bookkeeping, business management, help with my bank, and financials for my business plan.

• **The Rule of Three:** As woman after woman shared her horror stories of experiences with accountants, a surprising formula started to emerge. It was so identifiable we call it the Rule of Three. Ugly as it may seem, most women entrepreneurs go through two accountants before finding the right one. The formula looks like this:

Accountant #1: You don't understand the numbers they're showing, but you know things don't look right.

Accountant #2: You're starting to understand the numbers enough to realize that the accountant doesn't understand your business.

Accountant #3: You're understanding the numbers well enough to start asking for specific information; the accountant understands the business well enough to pull the information you need.

> Dulcie Price talks of the Rule of Three as "hellish." "My first accountant was bad—no accountability and all the books had to be redone. My second accountant went out of business. My third accounting firm is more service-oriented, with values like mine. They care about my business and I know I can trust them."

Can you avoid the Rule of Three? We're not sure. Try getting more quality referrals before you hire. Make sure the accountant or bookkeeper has experience with similar types of businesses—ask for references. What industries do they serve?

"Don't cut corners when it comes to the skills of finance. Hire professionals."
Mary Ann S. Turnbull
Turnbull Learning Centre Ltd.

During your interview, show them your spreadsheets (if you have some) and ask them for feedback on what your numbers mean to them. They may comment, "Labor costs seem too high, margins too low. Why so much on advertising?" This is the kind of thing you want to hear. If you have no spreadsheets, share some of your financial concerns and see how they respond. Can you understand them? Are they talking about ways to save you money? Do they make you feel stupid? If one of them can stimulate you enough to make you a little excited about your numbers she or he may be the right one. A final word of caution, it's not enough for them to be competent at what they do, they must also be able to teach you to be competent at understanding the impact of the numbers on your business.

9. How do I find the money I need?

"Sign all the checks
yourself, then you know
what is going out."
Maureen Wilson
Sweat Co. Studios Ltd.

Even if you finance your startup yourself (which most women do), you will need to be able to borrow to grow your company. Having borrowed once, you will go back again and again to feed your little monster. Finding sources of money for continued growth ranks high on the manager's Important Activity List.

a) Banks

It will take at least another decade of new banking behavior to convince the majority of women that banks have, in truth, changed their attitudes. We were scorched by the passion with which women shared their negative experiences and staggered by the numbers of women and businesses involved. To its credit the one bank that emerged with accolades was the Business Development Bank of Canada (BDC, formerly FBDB), which received high praise from the Yukon to Nova Scotia from women who had used its training services. This didn't pertain as much to their lending policy.

The Big Banks are waking up to the economic power of women. They are recognizing the impact you are going to have on their bottom line over the next 10 years. Old attitudes at the top have changed and gradually the effects of the new attitude and training are trickling down to the front lines. As a small business owner, you need to put past anger aside and meet them halfway. Your banker can be your most important management strength.

Smart Women have learned from past mistakes. They go before their banker prepared. As business owners they know exactly how much money they want and can explain satisfactorily how it will be repaid. When you're prepared, you can approach the challenge with confidence.

"Be prepared and don't feel shot down if you are refused financing. It is not something wrong with you. Be clear and confident about where you are heading and what is right for you. If the banker gets in the way, he is an obstacle you must overcome. Setbacks are just a rehearsal for the real performance," encourages Mary Ann Turnbull, of Turnbull Learning Centre Ltd. "When I built my school, there were all sorts of problems in getting the land," she says. "Several acquisitions I worked hard on fell through. But when the right site came along I sensed it was the way to go. I recognized it was right because I could compare it to the past obstacles. I acquired all the skills and knowledge I needed from my past efforts. I knew what kind of a banker I was looking for. I moved forward with confidence. They backed me all the way."

"An outstanding banker is someone you learn from."
Bev Durvin
Benkris & Co.

Start by getting a personal introduction, from the most prestigious person you know, to your potential banker. Check out first if this is a banker familiar with small business, your industry sector and women business owners. Give your banker your business plan to read (see Chapter 1, "Planning") in advance. Ask how you can improve it to ensure a stronger picture. Pick his or her brains clean on the ratios that will be required. As the two of you talk, you'll get a clear idea of personality, interest and energy, and know if this is a banker with whom you would like to do business.

Don't forget to ask the banks about small-business, government-backed loans. They are handled by regular banks. They can offer terms that are more flexible than regular business loans and have better rates of interest. They are also a fallback if the bank is thinking of turning you down.

Smart Women told us emphatically that their banking relationship was with the banker (the person) and not the institution. Intensely loyal relationships had developed with bankers who had faith in the business and went the extra mile in service, ideas and support. As do many women, I [Barbara] went through a very rough financial period after my divorce. My newest business was in its infancy and I had dependent children. My banker at CIBC was understanding, helpful and found innovative solutions for me. Without her my business would not have survived to help thousands of other businesses, many of whom are CIBC customers. I know firsthand that what goes around comes around.

In addition, this past year we have taken many clients to Royal Bank representatives who are focused on helping women entrepreneurs. We have found them extremely helpful, particularly in their willingness to share information on what the business has to do in order to secure the money it needs.

b) Government

In spite of government cutbacks, many women have received help through government programs that provide education, subsidies and a variety of loans and grants.

Call your federal and provincial economic development offices. They can direct you to whatever help is available. Check the resource list in the back of this book for contact names and numbers.

c) Angels

In the past, much small business financing came from "angels," that is, family and friends who cared enough to risk a little on you. Angels should be given the same professional courtesy with which you would treat bankers or outside investors. Send your business plan ahead to the angel, set up an appointment, wear your suit, discuss the plan, how much you need and repayment terms. Pay your angels better interest than they would make at the bank. Why should they risk otherwise? Treating them well will make them happy to reinvest in you next time and believe me there will be a next time if you continue to grow.

While angels are still the best first step, investment money and venture capital are going to become increasingly accessible. Low interest rates elsewhere entice healthy and wealthy retirees to take an extra risk on small businesses with interesting potential. Not only can they be persuaded to provide startup and growth loans, but you also might get lucky enough to get top expertise on your advisory board. Many of these retired risk-takers are willing to be involved in order to protect their investment. In the meantime, try phoning the heads of your local financial planning companies. They know people with money who are interested in dabbling. Junior investment funds are investing in many up-and-coming small businesses. There is a lot of money out there if you're patient and persistent. Here's a story to inspire the most cynical of you.

> "Aromatherapy is not seen as an asset by the banks," Jacqui MacNeill states with a crooked smile. "I started with my own money and then used profits to keep expanding my stock. I was selling from a table in the mall and had all my Christmas stock on display. The table collapsed. In the midst of the breaking glass and overpowering aromas I realized I had lost everything. An angel came to my rescue and co-signed a $10,000 loan.

In just 5½ years Jacqui's business has expanded to three retail outlets, a warehouse, manufacturing and wholesale outlet and a mail-order business. "My angel indirectly created dozens of great jobs, added to our economy and enabled our clients to enjoy a healthier lifestyle, in addition to getting her money back with interest. That's a 200% return on her investment," says Jacqui with justifiable pride.

Advertising in the local paper, using a heading such as "Excellent Investment Opportunity," can achieve worthwhile results. Many financial investment groups have clients who, besides buying mutual funds, might like a small-business challenge. It's worth giving them a call.

The Internet has a multitude of Web sites to explore for investment possibilities. (Several are listed in the resource directory at the back of this book).

There is money out there. Get a good plan on paper, have something of value to offer the private investor and keep knocking on doors.

d) New Partners

Women are forming new temporary and permanent legal structures as a way of finding the resources they need to grow their companies. What follows are descriptions of methods of sharing resources. The appropriateness of each will depend on the type and duration of the project.

• **Co-op:** In this method you join forces with other entrepreneurs who have similar products and needs. For instance, several women who manufacture crafts or gift items may join forces: a potter, a florist, an artist and a quilter can share the overhead cost of retail space and stock it with their merchandise. They draw up a schedule that allows each woman to spend so many hours per week selling in the store, so many hours on child care (i.e., looking after everyone's children) and so many on manufacturing the goods. Individual strengths determine who should be in charge of bookkeeping, merchandising, promoting and so on. It permits all the women to be available for their children while growing a lucrative business. Cooperatives should always have legal agreements in place. Talk to a lawyer.

"If you are small, don't partner with small."
Danielle Medina
Medina Foods Inc.

• **Strategic Alliances:** Many women are finding temporary partners in order to tackle larger projects.

Partners are chosen on the basis of strengths needed to successfully land and fulfill contracts. You get a piece of the action you wouldn't have been able to land on your own, your partner enjoys his or her share, and the customer gets better and more expert service. Strategic alliances should always have legal agreements in place that include areas of responsibilities, resources and payouts, as well as clearly setting out who owns what part of the intellectual property (e.g., Are you both free to go off on your own to provide the same service to other clients?).

• **Teams:** Rather than competing, try teaming up to win new opportunities. Competitors can do much to support each other by focusing on their individual strengths. Right now both of you bid for the same contract, one of you loses it and the other wins. But, if you are the winner, you win with such low margins that you ask yourself if you won after all. By teaming up, you create a stronger bid that offers the client more value. Women have high levels of trust that make forming partnerships easy. Look around for opportunities to share that will make you twice the money for half the work. Now that's *smart*.

Now that you have systems in place to keep this business running smoothly, you are in a position to back up and take a look at you. How have you fared over the last few years—exhausted, cranky, blue-deviled? It's time to tune up your body, mind and spirit.

The WHOLE PERSON
Action Plan for Financial Systems

1. a) Check your costs on every product and service you offer. Identify your profit margins. Are you working for nothing?

   _____

   _____

   b) What prices could be increased? Can costs be cut to improve your profitability? What product/service lines should you eliminate?

   _____

   _____

2. What four things could you do to better control your cash flow?

   _____

   _____

3. Prepare an up-to-date set of financial statements: income, cash flow and balance sheet. Make an appointment with your banker. Discuss your financial statements. Ask for input on where you might improve. Follow up with a thank-you note and an action plan for implementing the ideas. If you didn't get any help or didn't understand the suggestions, look for a new banker.

   _____

   _____

4. Do you have a great financial adviser for your business and one for your personal finances? If not, make it a top priority to find one. Ask everyone for referrals, follow up with interviews and continue to look until you have found the right person, someone who makes numbers easy and exciting for you.

   _____

   _____

SECTION 3

SELF-DEVELOPMENT

During the first four or five years of owning your own business your stamina must be unending and your energy inexhaustible. The greatest danger occurs in years three and four. The drive and passion pushing you through the early years is crushed beneath exhaustion, repetition and frustration. You begin to take shortcuts and dismiss important details. You operate your business like your tired body: on automatic, coasting in order to survive. Almost all women arrive at the five-year mark close to burnout. They are either forced to change their habits or collapse.

> Doris Tan says, "Women have to change their poverty consciousness [a way of thinking that is based on being accustomed to doing without and feeling you are unworthy of more]. When you need money, you say, "How dare I ask for more for myself or take more for myself? If paying someone else to do this job would cost me, for example, $65,000 per year, why do I not think I'm worth the same amount?"

Before you and your business collapse, you must develop a personal plan, just as you have a plan for your business. One of the best ways to start is to *write your own obituary*. Once you have written down what you would like to have said about you, each accomplishment credited to you becomes a goal in your long-term personal plan. A *Smart Woman* recognizes she can't achieve the goals if she doesn't look after the equipment needed to get the job done—her **body**, **mind** and **spirit**. A personal plan is essential for maintenance and development.

Your personal plan must carry you successfully through the landmark year, year five. When you secure your personal growth you will have the skills to ensure the continued growth of your business. In our surveys, *Smart Women* across the nation prioritized four procedures they use to facilitate their personalized plans. They have re-examined balance of body, mind and spirit; placed a greater emphasis on healthy living; turned up their learning radar; and started simplifying everything in sight. This has helped them to attain the high-energy, proactive, peaceful lifestyle that will lead to the longevity and quality of life they have set as a personal goal.

Why do some women sabotage their need for self-development?

The attitude that **everybody else comes first** floods through us. While we can justify long hours for work, domestic chores, child care and even the odd moment for our husband or mate, the choice to take time for ourselves produces endless guilt.

Many of us compulsively put ourselves last. Consequently, we are the last ones to benefit from any of the advantages of working for ourselves. Only when we have looked after everyone else do we permit ourselves to put energy into meeting our own needs. Women, we're doing a lot of hard time!

This deficiency is compounded because it is not just time we're talking about. Money plays a huge factor in self-development, whether it is the fee for a seminar, paying a babysitter or the price of a massage. Your time, money and energy go into everything but *you*. Can you judge wisely where your cutoff line should be, in your response to the never-ending flow of others' needs?

"I'm not sabotaging myself," you reiterate. "What would be the purpose?" "Why *would* I bother to squeeze myself from a plump grape into a dried-up raisin?" The underlying reason is fear. Yes, again it rears its ugly head and makes ugly faces at our attempts to justify our behavior. Putting everyone else first gives us the excuse we need to avoid challenging ourselves. We don't have to face the room full of strangers at the conference if our top salesperson is on holiday. No indeedy! We need to stay here and cover for her. We don't have to look like a dummy at the computer night-school class if our best friend is going through a messy divorce; she might need a shoulder to cry on. As certainly as there is something out there we need in the way of self-development—as certainly will we find an excuse to prevent ourselves from obtaining it.

Finally, women are frustrated by the amount of choice. How do you fit it all in? Your grandmother was happy to work in her garden and visit with her friends. You have the Internet and television, easy access to wilderness spots and cultural events. You are exposed to more places where you are needed, more people in crisis, more opportunities to learn than you can handle.

You are probably feeling a lot of conflict as you read this, identifying with many of the examples, but feeling you are past making many of these mistakes. *Smart Women*, on their journey to becoming a **whole person,** have long since sized up their martyr quotient and make good choices to balance their lives and arrive at a new sense of freedom and self-worth. A *Smart Woman* says no to the superwoman complex and creates a new definition of the word "balance." Then she sculpts her life to fit this new definition.

> Karinna James bemoans how she used to have little mental boxes for all the roles she played. "I would be constantly asking myself how well I was doing in each area. The results were a very thin me—thin physically from stress, and thin emotionally from being so spread out." As the owner of a voice dialogue studio, Karinna has developed the skills to stay centered, rather than fragmented. "Listen to your inner voice," she suggests, "and do whatever it takes to keep it peaceful. Balance is balancing your inner world with your outer world."

> Doris Tan suggests, "Make choices. If you can't fit it in today, maybe you can fit it in this week or this month or this year. By making intelligent choices to fit some activities into a future time in your life you always have something enticing to look forward to."

So, the new definition of balance is to determine what is important to you at a particular time in your life and go after it, confident there will be a right time for other things in the future.

Gladys Sinclair says she doesn't need a lot of leisure. She has met the demands of raising a family while running a home-based business. Her studio is in her home, so she is where she wants to be, doing something she loves (weaving and customizing clothes). She admits to working 60- to 70-hour weeks now that her children are grown, but says she sees much of her work as her leisure.

Many women who are over 40 and whose children have left home define balance as working a 12-hour day and a 6-day week. They are concentrating on what they want to do and discovering how well they do it.

These women are aware that their business needs to support them financially into their retirement; this is the time to ensure future quality of life. They know the importance of their goal and their inner voice is at peace. Contrast their lifestyle choices with those of a single, working mom, or a veteran businesswoman.

Val Petrich chose to limit the growth of her business for five years until her daughter was in school. She sacrificed some of her income to pay a manager, in order to free up time as a mom. She was fairly certain her daughter wouldn't remember whether she owned Air Jordan sneakers later on but would not forget that Mom was there to watch her race. Val kept her inner voice quiet by temporarily rearranging her priorities. She also used some of this "downtime" to do major, detailed long-term planning. When she returned to her business full time, she grew it at twice the normal rate, opening a new business and branching into multimedia in what appeared to be an overnight success.

Vivian Reid has been in business for more than 17 years. She is at a stage in her life when her body and her increased wisdom are telling her to slow down. She is taking more time for herself in daily increments, enjoying two days off per week and planning larger chunks of holiday time.

Ten percent of the women we interviewed are moving into this stage and preparing to sell their profitable businesses or hand them over to family members.

Other women like Mary Dixon and Lillian Neaman came to business late. They took time to raise a family first, and then explored their options, deciding finally to own their own business. They created successful businesses by thriving on the creative challenge of being entrepreneurs.

A *Smart Woman* realizes balance will shift with each new stage of life. Do mini assessments often. Ask yourself: Where am I now? What are the demands on my time? What are my needs for the future? Then write down your present definition of balance.

Learning to become a **whole person** starts with an honest assessment of how well we are developing our body, mind and spirit now. It follows with a decision to rekindle old activities we once felt passionately about (the yang we gave up in trying to fill our societal roles) and start a few new ones (to balance our strengths with added strengths). The bottom line is, the women who do take time for themselves are more interesting to be around, less antagonistic and resentful, and have more energy and more joy to give back.

CHAPTER 9

Body

What frustrations are you experiencing in the area of physical wellness?

Looking after your body is about physical wellness. It is listening to your body, learning to do what is right for it. When you do what is right for your body, you destress and detoxify yourself emotionally. This allows you to function at your best mentally. A big part of physical health is taking some time for leisure activities. Having a "master's degree" in wellness fine-tunes you, keeps you humming and your energy level high. Unfortunately, most of us are still in kindergarten or we play hooky from leisure, as we forever hide ourselves in work.

When asked to identify the frustration factors preventing them from indulging in a little leisure activity and paying attention to their wellness needs, women entrepreneurs said there is no competition: time, or in this case lack of it, is the big winner. Of the women we interviewed, 45%, when questioned about the leisure in their life, said they didn't take time for it, that is, they allowed no time for friends, exercise, or creativity. Another 17% said they didn't have enough time for leisure activities.

Are you feeling the frustration of not having enough free time because of demands of your family? not having time for relaxation? losing friends because you don't have time for them? Are you running a home-based business and losing personal time to drop-in visitors? These are some of the frustrations we heard about.

Not taking enough time away from work may be causing you to skip meals, which results in poor nutrition, and you may be developing a tendency to store food as fat when you do eat. Poor eating habits can also result in dry skin, hair loss and cavities. A can of soda pop and a chocolate bar may give you a quick energy fix, but this sort of fix will send you crashing back to earth later.

Lack of energy can be a major frustration. Some of you are overworking at home on your day off and showing up for work the next day exhausted. Family responsibilities may be draining the last of your reserves, leaving you nothing with which to pursue your own interests. Re-evaluate how you are using your energy. Maybe you're at burnout level. One woman described it perfectly. "I stopped mid sentence one day," she said, "and realized I was done with carrying everybody on my back. I announced, 'I'm not taking any more of this crap!'" As female boomers shake the load from their backs, and as younger women refuse to pick it up, we are finding a new way to cope with physical problems. An artist spoke of the huge amounts of energy devoted to the day-to-day running of the business, which left her none with which to be creative, the one thing that fed her energy. Is this happening to you?

Finally, you must measure the cost of the emotional strains affecting your physical health, such as lack of support from your spouse; the drain of supporting troubled employees; and the physical and emotional debilitation caused by the stress and guilt of not being there for your children, your parents and/or your friends. Possibly you are at an age when menopause may be affecting your ability to concentrate, remember and make decisions, and you are afraid because of these losses.

Are you just now realizing you have been worn down for months, but have not known it? If you are facing the devastation of burnout, you must now begin the long trek back to recovery—back to health. Join some *Smart Women* in finding new ways to look after yourself.

Do you feel you are caring for your body?
Test yourself on the next page.

 # Are you sabotaging yourself?

Physical Wellness: Danger Signals

(Circle the appropriate answer for each question. Add up your numbers and check the next page for your physical wellness quotient.)

	5 - always	4 - regularly	3 - occasionally	2 - rarely	1 - never

1. Do you deal with health worries promptly?

5	4	3	2	1

2. Do you get the hours of sleep you need to replenish your energy?

5	4	3	2	1

3. Do you do exercise of some type three times a week?

5	4	3	2	1

4. Do you eat lunch?

5	4	3	2	1

5. Do you schedule one activity a week to pamper your body?

5	4	3	2	1

6. Do you have regular medical and dental checkups?

5	4	3	2	1

7. Do you eat nourishing, well-balanced meals?

5	4	3	2	1

8. Do you find time for outdoor activity at least once a week?

5	4	3	2	1

9. Do you fall asleep easily, free from anxiety?

5	4	3	2	1

10. Do you schedule more than one week of holidays consecutively?

5	4	3	2	1

Your physical wellness score _____

41–50 A *Smart Woman*. Congratulations!

31–40 As a *Smart Woman* in this area, you may want to check on your **whole person** approach to the body (see Introduction to Self-Development).

21–30 No need to panic. Work through the **Whole Person** Action Plan on page 212 for a balanced lifestyle. Make a conscious effort to be more fair to yourself (everyone will benefit).

11–20 You need some serious work in this area. Take someone to lunch who has known you a long time. Ask them for constructive criticism. Don't make excuses. Just say thank you after each of their comments. You may want to make a few notes if you have a poor memory. Review them as soon as possible and adjust some of your attitudes and actions.

10 Give yourself a free day in a totally isolated place. Wind down, focus inward. Under four headings (e.g., family, community, work, social) list all of the activities you take part in over a period of a month. Then assign a number between 1 and 5 (1 being least, 5 most) to the level of stress each activity causes you. Add up the numbers under each heading. You may be surprised. I [Madelon] found I experienced more stress socializing than at work. Identify the areas causing you high levels of stress.

Decide how you can take action (eliminate, delegate, compromise) in this area to lighten your load. Also think about how you can change your attitude toward things you can't change in order to reduce your stress. You will be delighted by the results (such as a renewed sense of well-being) a *truthful* self-examination can bring in your life.

If your physical wellness quotient is low, you are sabotaging yourself:

- by not giving your body the exercise it needs to build strength and energy;
- by not taking time to relax and enjoy life so that you are vital and fun;
- by spreading yourself so thin you endanger your health and risk leaving your company with no leadership;
- by not scheduling regular care and maintenance of your body to stay healthy; and
- by not providing the necessary fuel, sunlight and rest your body needs.

1. How will owning my own business affect my health?

As an entrepreneur you may be worried about how being in business will affect your health. Great news! If you want to live forever, work for yourself. This was the consensus from one of the personal questions we asked entrepreneurs in our

> "When you own your own business, work follows you everywhere."
> *Gaetanne Riopel*
> *Party & Masquerade*

interviews. The response was interesting. Over 33% said yes, owning a business has affected their health in a positive way. Many *Smart Women* say they are seldom ill, adding that they feel they don't have time to be sick. Their good health can partly be explained by the many who conclude that owning their own business means being more health-conscious. When you do something you love, your energy is high and you are vital and healthy.

Of the 37% who said business has affected their health negatively, many added that they might well have had similar health problems working for someone else. For example, they cited foot problems, leg cramps and/or back problems caused by standing all day in a store.

The one negative directly related to business ownership is stress, though it is described as a different kind of stress. Owners speak of anxiety and fear, insomnia, mental exhaustion and high blood pressure. The flip side of this is that some entrepreneurs feel stress gives them a supercharge they thrive on.

The general consensus of the women interviewed is that sleep is the first to go. They eventually accept that it is worry (usually money-related), not lack of sleep, that wears them down. When they are dealing with problems effectively they said they can function well on five to six hours of sleep for long periods of time.

Most of the *Smart Women* are using many forms of alternative health care. They are listening to the needs of their body. They are determined to stay away from "the knife" and chemicals. Massage, reiki, reflexology, natural products, exercise and nutrition are a few of the tools they choose, to stay physically well.

Ashley Smith, of Charles Ben Studios, suggests, "When an idea is presented that might make you stronger physically or emotionally, do a feasibility study.

Ask yourself: Is it attainable? What resources do I need to make it happen? What connections do I have? How much money, time and skill will it take? Then, if it is really important, open a file and start to make it happen."

2. How do I find time to exercise?

All of you know a big part of mental well-being comes from physical exercise. But how many of you follow through? The best way to make it happen is to change your mind-set from "Exercise is just another job" to "Exercise is a way to play and I enjoy it!" You might try combining it with social time with friends, or quality time with your children and/or your spouse. You may use it to network.

"If you are a hockey parent, you are sitting on a bench watching your kid play. If you are a skiing parent, you are sitting on a chairlift talking to your kid, all for about the same cost."
Meredith DeGroat
totally tropical interiors Ltd.

Tannis Ortynsky schedules morning exercise with her children. Each child gets to pick the exercise and have a day's worth of one-on-one time with their mom. It keeps variety in her exercise program and ensures the follow-through because she can't let her kids down, even if she would rather roll over and sleep another hour.

Denise Bagley uses multitasking to combine socializing and exercise. She books regular golf games with her friends. In addition she has a business membership in a golf club and uses golfing to network with clients. Building business contacts in a relaxed setting is something men have been doing for years. Now, *Smart Women* are realizing how nice it can be to combine work with leisure. They are hitting the links in record numbers.

Phillipa A. Hudson: "We do a great deal of global traveling. Though primarily we go to hike a new area of the world, we integrate research and purchasing for our businesses with personal time and exercise."

You may want to multitask exercising and learning, for example, by using a treadmill or bike in your home or office to combine the priority of exercise with reading, listening to motivational cassettes, watching a documentary about your industry or listening to music that stimulates your creativity.

Even though she owns a fitness club, Terry Chang bought a treadmill for her home office. In a global economy, she felt she was getting increasingly out of touch with the world because of her isolation in the far North. At 5:45 a.m. every day she runs while listening to world events on the news channel. She feels it is one of the smartest Smart Women applications she has made. She feels better and more in control; meanwhile she's aware of global influences on her business and has her radar tuned into opportunities.

> "Set up your monthly schedule by booking active time with your family and/or friends first."
> Jane Cotter
> Heavenly Bodies

3. What kind of exercise should I do?

a) Building Strength and Stamina

Women are often pictured as slim and soft at the same time. But this duality is virtually an impossibility unless you were born with an overactive thyroid. Activity builds muscle and burns fat. If you want to stay slim and active, you are going to have to build muscle. You may want to hire a personal fitness coach to do this. They are listed in the Yellow Pages and most gyms have coaches on staff. Even if your budget is too tight to have a regular coach, hire one for one class to show you what weights to work out with at home and how to use them. Check in with your coach periodically to ensure you are doing the workout properly and receiving the full benefit from the exercise.

Bea Harks schedules a step-aerobics session and weight routine three to four times a week, and meets once a week with her fitness coach. "I know it is essential to maintain my energy levels and bone mass to prevent osteoporosis. Once in a while I cancel the session and it's the most wonderful, decadent sensation. Go with it. Don't feel guilty. When you get beat, you'll drag yourself back to the steps again to renew your energy."

> "Check daily to make sure you have spread your time over at least three areas."
> Denise Bagley
> The Learning Edge Inc.

Even the Smart Women who depend on exercise to assist them in maintaining the energy needed to complete other tasks, accept that it can't always be done—life gets in the way. However, they no longer see a missed workout as lack of discipline or a failure. They no longer let it paralyze them.

Of paramount importance to Mary Sutherland is being strong and safeguarding her body from injury. "Much of my business involves lugging heavy boxes of books up and down stairs," she acknowledges. "I have to be physically strong and have good stamina, so I go to the gym first thing every morning, every day. Discipline is important." However, if one of Mary's young sons becomes sick and she misses her session, she runs up and down the stairs with glasses of juice and comic books and works out with weights at home.

Babe Warren participates in aqua-fit classes three times a week. When she was 54 she earned her 25-mile swim medal. "It means more to me," she exclaims, "than the many awards and the recognition I have won in business." Three times a week she meets her friends at the local pool. Yes, she gets her exercise, but, more importantly, this time is necessary downtime for Babe, time to escape from the pressures of work and refresh herself.

Several of the *Smart Women* are marathon runners. Eveline Charles started out by running half an hour every morning at 6 a.m. with a few friends. She wanted to combine exercise with socializing, but instead she became hooked on testing her limits. She completed her first marathon, alternately running and vomiting, determined that if others could do it she could do it too. When she crossed the finish line she said, "I know now I can do anything!" Her running has eliminated her weight problem. No more need to starve herself. It gives her the energy and vitality to get through a long day.

> "Talk to the dog. They listen to everything. If you don't have a dog, phone the neighbors and offer to walk theirs."
> *Norene Gilletz*
> *Gourmania Inc.*

Most of us are not into that kind of brutal workout. Your fitness coach will assure you, however, that a good aerobic walk (throw in a few hills if you can) combined with a few minutes of strength-building exercises will achieve the same results for you.

b) Moving into Nature

It is hard to find inner peace in the midst of the concrete jungle. You may be fortunate enough to live and work close to nature, but for most of us nature is a trip down the highway. If we want to turn our creativity up high and renew ourselves, we can do it much faster if we are closer to nature. For a few, walking is a part of a hardcore exercise program, but for most *Smart Women* it is their preferred way to commune with nature—slow enough to smell the roses, fast enough to clear the cobwebs. We all know walking is one of the best forms of exercise.

> Renate Geier lives on the rugged and beautiful West Coast. She prescribes walking outdoors as much as possible. "There is no expense," she says. And, she adds, "It soothes the soul and energizes the spirit."

> Susan Vertefeuille walks 3½ miles every night. After she tucks her children in to bed, she enjoys the darkness and the quiet of the streets in the small city where she lives.

Susan ignores the messages the media has given us, messages about the dangers of walking alone at night. If you check the statistics, though, you will find it is no more dangerous to walk in the evening (before 11 p.m.) than it is to walk at noon.

> Mary Dixon's publishing business is a lengthy hike from her house. She often drives home with her son and has him drop her off halfway, so that she walks a fair distance. She takes the time, while walking, to breathe deeply and relax, enjoying the green of the foliage and the colors of the flowers along the way.

> Like Helen Read, you may operate a home-based business. She schedules a daily walk with a neighbor to force her to stop working at a decent time. The fresh air revitalizes her creativity and straightens her up after hours of bending over her sewing machine.

Would this work for you?

Mary Ann Turnbull says, "Getting back to nature is the way I feed my spirit. I plan special outdoor activities." "On New Year's Eve," she says, "instead of going to a crowded ball, my husband and I cross-country ski into a chalet in the Gatineau Hills. We lay new tracks under a star-filled sky, reconnecting with the basic elements of life at this important time of renewal."

One hundred percent of the women interviewed said that, while any walking, jogging or hiking was good, the more you could get away from the concrete (into a park or along a river bank) the more you would benefit. To connect spiritually while walking, seek a natural setting and take enough time (a minimum of two to three hours) to walk past your cares into a peaceful inner space.

A secondary benefit of walking is the breathing. In order to thoroughly benefit from the exercise, you must be conscious of your breathing. Feel cleansing air flooding in, filling you, renewing you, then blow it out gently.

> Try combining meditation and walking, as does Jocelyna Dubuc. "First you bring your attention to your feet and you visualize the ground is massaging them as you walk," she instructs. "You work up to your ankles, calves, knees, the sun and breeze caressing and relaxing each joint. Finally you work up to your head. Your head is your house, open the doors and windows and let the light in. Feel the flood of warmth, feel the fresh air breezing in. Move forward lightly."

Use walking to "move beyond." Let nature energize you and help you hear your inner voice more clearly. It will be soul-cleansing.

4. What else do I have to do to keep my body healthy?

a) Fuel It

Gwen Shamblin (M.S., R.D.), creator of the Weigh Down workshops for weight reduction puts forward the "opposite world theory." She says that so much of what we do in life is the opposite of what we should be doing. An excellent example of this is a woman who cancels her exercise class because she's tired and stressed then sits down and eats a chocolate-covered donut. She believes she is treating herself because she's had a hard day. What she is really doing is causing herself more harm. Her thinking is "opposite world."

> "I'm careful about what I eat and limit my alcohol consumption, to keep my body healthy and to produce the energy I need."
> *Maureen Wilson*
> *Sweat Co. Studios Ltd.*

We cannot pretend to care for our body without looking at what we are doing to fuel it. Yes, exercise and fresh air are part of the solution because they help us to burn our fuel more efficiently. However, if you are not putting in the right fuel or enough fuel or putting in too much fuel you will soon spiral into poor health. The Canada's Food Guide to Healthy Eating—a balanced way to eat—has been around far longer than any fad diet plans. It is a credible plan to follow if you want to boost your physical health with good eating. One other thing to consider is the old adage "all things in moderation."

North Americans have so much food that the great majority of us overeat. Gwen Shamblin's healthy eating workshops are based on two premises that make a lot of sense and will go a long way to helping you to a **whole person** attitude about your body. She tells us to simply listen to our inner voice and identify true physical hunger before we eat and not to listen to "head hunger"—that voice tempting us to eat when we don't need it for fuel. The other rule is to always stop eating the minute you feel full. This requires eating slowly enough to allow 10 minutes for the food to enter your bloodstream. Once you get the signal (again, this requires careful attention to your inner voice), leave whatever is on your plate. You will be surprised at how quickly you reduce the amount you eat, while feeling better than ever. Following these two rules faithfully will benefit you by: increasing your energy, decreasing the amount of time you need to sleep, and eliminating the heartburn caused by overeating. Adherence to them should also result in your body finding its best weight and maintaining it.

b) Nurture It

Many of the women we spoke with mentioned massage and holistic therapies as tools they are using either to improve their health or to stay healthy. These therapies include aromatherapy, natural-herb dietary supplements, massage, steam

> "Achieving balance takes discipline."
> *Monica Gross*
> *Sarah's Corner Ltd.*

baths, cleansing programs and salon treatments. In conducting the interviews, it became apparent to us that the women who were operating companies with profits in the millions were the ones who put the greatest emphasis on "wellness." "Sure," you may say, "it's because they can now afford the time and money." There is some truth in this statement. However, it's the chicken-and-egg theory: the fact that they are investing in themselves is allowing them to bring more energy, creativity and productivity to increasing their business profits. They are not at home sick, or working at a snail's pace because they've depleted their surplus energy. Rather, these women exude vitality and radiate good health.

c) Check Your Hormone Levels

One of the areas that will be of growing concern as this generation of women entrepreneurs age is the issue of menopausal symptoms. We cannot avoid the fact that when our hormones are out of whack our memory, energy, concentration and health are affected. Val Petrich, owner of the Yoga Studio, has produced an excellent videotape called *Yoga for Women*,[1] which deals with the relief of premenstrual and menopausal symptoms. On the videotape, a set of nine postures that help to stimulate women's glands and balance our hormones are demonstrated. We recommend it to all women who are looking for ways to improve their sense of well-being.

"When you start working too hard you work dumb, you don't work smart."
Jacqui MacNeill
escents Aromatherapy

d) Get Enough Sunlight

Seasonal Affective Disorder (SAD) is a form of depression that affects people in the winter. Eighty-three percent of sufferers are women. SAD is thought to have a genetic-makeup factor. The age of onset for women is usually around 30. SAD brings loss of energy and productivity. Symptoms vary from a craving for carbohydrates—usually consumed in large quantities—mood swings and a desire for more sleep.

"Beware! Fatigue from work can influence your ability to deal with conflict at home."
Joy Hanley
Fine Food Investments Ltd.

It is vital that the body get natural sunlight. During the winter months, when there are less hours of daylight, this is hard to do. Light therapy, the goal of which is to ease back the production of melatonin, is available for those who have been diagnosed with SAD. A woman suffering from SAD, and who works late at night, will have enough melatonin circulating through her system that her level of alertness will be equivalent to that of a person who is legally drunk. Driving home, therefore, could be lethal.

[1] To order Val Petrich's *Yoga for Women* call (403) 228-5808.

e) Be Aware of the Double Shift

Recent studies have redefined shift workers as people who work extended hours (that's every woman we know). The impact of shift work is devastating to your body, according to wellness instructor Kristina White, of Illuminate Solutions. Kristina is highly knowledgeable about the effects of extended hours on the body. These include negative stress, sleep deprivation, unhealthy eating habits and irritability. For example, neuropsychologist Stan Coren of the University of British Columbia has found that 70% more car accidents than normal occur on the day after the spring time change just because we've lost one hour of sleep. In fact, accidents from over-tired drivers are quickly catching up with the rate of those caused by drunk drivers. If you can't get out of doing a double shift, Kristina advises that you:

- Eat well. Focus on lower-fat, high-fibre foods.
- Try to get a minimum of six hours of sleep each night (or day).
- Avoid alcohol and caffeine (caffeine circulates for up to six hours in the system).
- Become physically active. Exercise helps "burn off" the chemicals (e.g., adrenaline) we produce when we are stressed.

5. What does how I look have to do with it?

The old "30 seconds to make a first impression and 30 days to undo it" requires 30 days you are seldom awarded in a business situation. Appearance can build instant rapport, increase trust and create a springboard for the relationship. Conversely, it can generate instant antagonism, distrust and a desire on the part of the person to avoid you.

> "There is an order in the universe and things work out in the end. Relax and enjoy the ride."
> *Gail Spencer Lamm*
> *crossXtrainers*

The way you look must be consistent with your industry. For example, I won't truly believe you're an artsy graphic designer if your clothes aren't a little flamboyant, and you'll never convince me you're a great financial planner if you aren't wearing a coordinated suit. People also have weird perceptions. Studies show a woman wearing a skirt is perceived to be more trustworthy than a woman wearing slacks. For men, the perception is that the one wearing the tie is more trustworthy than the one in the open-necked shirt. This is utter nonsense, of course, but impossible to ignore if you want the first impression to work for you.

> Bev McMaster admits she has strong views on appearance. As an employer of 4000, her opinion matters. "Dangling earrings and low-cut dresses have no place in business," she says. "I don't want to see them in the office, the boardroom or even at a luncheon. If a woman does choose to dress like that, I assume she's trading on her female attributes rather than bringing real skills to the table."

In communication, as we have told you, over 50% of the message is delivered through body language. Our clothing and grooming have a very real impact on the message we're delivering. For many entrepreneurs in the service business, personal image is an important part of merchandising. Your banged-up briefcase, your photocopied brochure and your missing button all advertise that you are going to do my work as sloppily as you present yourself.

> I [Barbara] was interviewing a woman for a bookkeeper position for several of my small business clients. The credentials of the candidate were excellent, her manner pleasant and her understanding of the small businesses' needs comprehensive. As she sat before me giving all the right answers, my eyes were drawn again and again to the middle of her blouse where a large safety pin replaced a missing button. We're not talking discreetly tucked inside after a last-minute crisis. It was blatantly out there. It seemed to grow as the interview progressed until all I could see was the safety pin. The interview deteriorated into a complete fiasco. I kept telling myself not to judge someone on something so trivial; but the safety pin took on the shape of missing zeros on a balance sheet. I continued to interview until I found a woman equally (not better) qualified, but neatly groomed. I often wonder if the first woman realized she lost out on an excellent position, all because she lacked a button.

a) Posture

We're back to that first 30 seconds—your one chance to land a $100,000 account. The name-brand suit, 14-carat gold jewelry and Gucci briefcase and shoes won't do it. Neither will the new manicure or your $125 visit to the hair salon. Making the best first impression doesn't cost you a cent, because posture comes for free. Standing tall, sitting straight, bringing your food to your mouth—not vice versa. It's so simple to present a composite of poise and confidence. It's so easy to blow it by slumping (she's too tired to do a good job) or slouching (she's too laid-back to really care). The best way to find out what type of impression you are making is to see it for yourself. The best tool to give you an objective view of yourself is the Camcorder. Have someone video you, or watch videos of yourself being interviewed, or at social events, even family get-togethers. How are you sitting? How tall do you walk? Is good posture helping your clothes hang properly, adding to the professional concept you wish to build? It's better than a mirror because there are no illusions. The cold, hard facts unfold before you. *Smart Women* learn from them and make changes.

b) The Cost of Image

The military is the best example of how you can dress someone in $20 slacks and a $10 shirt and have them look like a million dollars. Their secrets are simple: (1) well-groomed hair, (2) highly polished shoes and (3) precisely pressed clothes with knife pleats.

If you are in the printing business, where you have to work around inky presses all day, you need comfort and the ability to still look like the boss to the client coming through the door. Military policy combined with washable clothes and good leather shoes will give you just the right image.

Investing $100 in a wardrobe consultant is a good move if you want to avoid costly mistakes with your wardrobe. A wardrobe consultant will ruthlessly eliminate from your wardrobe all but the few things that really work for you. She or he will suggest changes to skirt lengths, jacket lengths and your shade of hosiery. They are simple solutions, but they make a huge difference to your silhouette and create a well-groomed appearance that will long outlast the appeal of the new sweater you might have bought with that $100.

6. What does how I behave have to do with it?

a) Manners Are Important

For some women entrepreneurs, rudeness and thoughtlessness stem from being in a constant rush, augmented by mental overload—not from hardness of the heart. We barge through the door without realizing someone is there, concentrating on the boxes we are balancing, not the people around us. We may hang up the phone without saying goodbye because our minds are on the next or the last thought. If this sounds all too much like you, it's time to ask those around you for a reality check. Ask them to point out shortcomings in your behavior when they occur, with a little humor or a secret signal (if you're around others). Give them permission to speak up when you're acting like a steamroller about to run someone down. **Manners are important. They make those around you feel respected and valued.** Improving them is a fast track to a better image.

"**Learn to change behaviors that don't serve you well.**"
Bea Harks
Visions of Beauty

Table etiquette became a dying art for the baby boomers who grew up in front of their TV sets. A large percentage of the population has been influenced by this style of eating. If you are one of them and you find yourself constantly in a rush, then you need a manners checkup. Families on the run, with only rare opportunities to sit down and eat together, have forgotten the little courtesies that make breaking bread together a special kind of bonding. Interestingly, the emerging sector of women entrepreneurs have begun to put back the emphasis on etiquette. However, many businesswomen today need a basic training manual. Ignorance is acceptable and correctable, but discourtesy and a lack of awareness of others' needs is appalling.

I [Barbara] recently attended a high-profile business luncheon and chose a seat at a table where I could meet a new group of women. The woman on my left appropriated my bread-and-butter plate and my napkin, while the woman on my right took my water glass. I could justify their actions in all sorts of ways—the woman on the right was lefthanded and accustomed to setting her table in reverse; or the woman on my left just didn't know any better. What I couldn't find an excuse for was that both of them were totally oblivious to the quandary in which I was left. I used humor to regain my place setting, but the inconsiderate behavior continued. Someone would start the salt and pepper around the table, the next woman would set it down without passing it on.

Too many women at that table were indifferent to the needs of those dining with them. Heads up! *Smart Women* mind their manners. One fast way to bring your table etiquette up to scratch is to talk to the maitre d' at the best restaurant in town. Ask if she or he would be willing to give you a private lesson during their quiet time at work. Most will be flattered and pleased. Some will charge $50 per hour, some won't charge at all. Be sure you send their boss a thank-you note. You may choose to organize a small luncheon or dinner for four to six friends who also want to learn. Have the maitre d' check on you with each course. Have him determine the menu so you get some tricky dishes to tackle—the ones that slip, drip and drop, and need special cutlery to control.

It's not enough for you as owner of your business to be up to snuff on etiquette. You also have to check your employees' manners, since their behavior affects your business's image. Do you have salespeople going after top accounts who have never learned how to choose a wine, or who don't know what to tip? They need training, too.

Make a point of using a meal as one of the steps in your interview program, so you can assess how much work has to be done in this area. One of the best ways to teach others is to consistently set a good example.

> "Relax. It's not always going to happen the way you see it."
> **Ashley Smith**
> *Charles Ben Studio*

b) A Quality that Attracts

Charm, according to *Webster's New World Dictionary*, is "a quality that attracts or delights." Charm is the warmth radiating from a sincere smile, expressed when you take a genuine interest in others. A charming person is someone who asks you about yourself and listens with interest to your answer. Next time you enter a crowded room, don't let your mind scramble frantically for what you want to tell others about yourself. Center yourself. Think of questions you would like answers to instead.

7. What are those little things that count?

"Play some
Work some
Talk some
Be quiet some
And it will all work out.”
Joan Macdonald
J.V.I. Commercial Driving
School

Several small details can make or break an interview or a first impression with a client. Right after the first 30-second look, for example, comes the handshake. Practice with friends and colleagues until you get an A+ for a firm, brief but warm handshake. Eye contact works in conjunction with both the handshake and the assessment. If you cannot look directly into the other person's eyes without staring them down, or without appearing to be shifty or ill at ease, you are going to lose points on his or her mental scoreboard. If we look someone directly in the eyes for five seconds, we have an effect on them. If it is 10 seconds, though, it becomes intimate, and after 15 seconds the look becomes intimidating. Time it with someone at home and see how the interaction changes as the clock ticks.

Another important detail is your energy level. Throughout the book we have emphasized how important it is for a **whole person** to have high energy levels. Keep up with the other person if you are following them down a hallway or into a building—don't make them wait for you. They'll conclude you will always be two minutes behind.

Personal space is an important issue. If you stand too close to your client or employee, you cause discomfort. If you do it enough times, they begin to anticipate it and tension builds. Soon they are focused more on creating distance between you and them than in concentrating on the business at hand. When their discomfort reaches a certain level, they will take their business elsewhere or look for a new job.

Entire TV talk shows have been devoted to the issues of bad breath and body odor. An enormous amount of energy is spent as people try to communicate a need for mouthwash or deodorant to someone they work with. Needless to say, you don't ever want to be on the receiving end of a roll of breath mints left subtly on your desk, or of someone holding their nose when you walk on the elevator. Little details left unchecked can destroy the entire concept of self you have been working so hard to create. A **whole person** has it all together, because they come from a position of consideration for others.

If you are on top of your physical wellness, we applaud you. A healthy body gives you the energy to concentrate your mind on all the new things you need to learn in order to grow your business.

The WHOLE PERSON
Action Plan for Physical Wellness

1. a) List one physical activity you would enjoy doing.

    _____
    _____

    b) What day can you do it this week?

    _____
    _____

2. a) Identify the three personal activities you would like to do this year (e.g., learn to meditate, learn to sail, knit a sweater, buy a concert subscription).

    _____
    _____

    b) Schedule at least one.

    _____
    _____

3. a) Identify four activities that are eating up your time and energy without giving you any satisfaction (e.g., negative friend, volunteer committee, ironing, annual reunion).

    _____
    _____

    b) How can you get rid of them (e.g., barter, bribe or leave undone)?

    _____
    _____

4. Write a full description of something or someone you need in your life right now (e.g., massage therapist, cleaner, exercise instructor). Put the word out.

    _____
    _____

5. Take out your day timer and schedule regular small meals into it. (Pick the time of the day when you experience your lowest energy for a lunch break.) Follow through for a week and measure whether or not you feel better.

    _____
    _____

CHAPTER 10

Mind

What frustrations are you experiencing keeping yourself up-to-date?

Once again, lack of time is the main culprit when women describe the frustrations they experience in trying to obtain the skills, training and knowledge they need to grow their businesses. One *Smart Woman* identified the paradox: "The smaller the operation, the more you are trapped. And, of course, the smaller your business, the greater the need for time to learn."

A similar paradox holds true for financing their education. The women that have the most to learn in order to grow their fledgling businesses have the fewest resources to put into their own education.

Hard on the heels of lack of time and money is another problem of equal concern. Existing systems, governments and businesses are falling short in meeting the educational demands of women entrepreneurs. The women we interviewed told us emphatically: "They are not providing courses we need"; "They schedule courses and workshops for our heaviest seasons"; and "They locate them in major centers, which discriminates against those of us in smaller centers and rural areas." Another potential source of information that is not meeting the entrepreneur's need for education is the Canadian publishing industry. Much of the business material available is written in the United States, and is based on American practices, laws and statistics.

The quality of the courses, workshops, seminars and published material available is a sore spot with many of you. Some of you have spent many hard-earned dollars in the hope of attaining applicable information only to find that many workshops are heavily motivational and give little practical advice. You also mentioned that some seminars misrepresent themselves, by not providing what their organizers had promised the seminars would provide.

One of the surprises on the list of frustrations was the women's recognition of their own limitations. Are you holding yourself back because you are too impatient to learn or have never stopped to analyze the way you absorb information best? Do you lack the inclination to sit in a classroom? One woman said she finally realized that before she could further her self-development, she needed to learn to ask questions. Possibly you can absorb the material you gather, but have not been able to apply it to your business. Some women were so tired and stressed they were no longer able to make decisions about what information to adopt. You must be able to recognize your business's need and move at the right moment to add to your skills.

In our surveys, gender was noted as a barrier to both self-development and company growth by an unacceptable 20% of the respondents. Women who own businesses in fields that are still heavily male-dominated, such as technology, oil, agriculture and funeral services, feel they are hindered by an attitude of exclusion that keeps them out of information sharing. You may find much of the material in these fields is slanted toward the male style of learning and that women are paying for advice, counseling and information in these fields to which they cannot relate.

Test your education quotient on the next page.

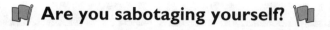 Are you sabotaging yourself?

(Circle the appropriate answer for each question. Add up your numbers and check the next page for your education quotient.)

5 - always   4 - regularly   3 - occasionally   2 - rarely   1 - never

1. Do you spend time just "thinking"?

5	4	3	2	1

2. Do you seek out highly successful people and spend time with them?

5	4	3	2	1

3. Do you put money into your budget for your own professional development?

5	4	3	2	1

4. Do you have a membership in a women business owners' group or industry association?

5	4	3	2	1

5. Do you have a subscription to one or more industry magazines?

5	4	3	2	1

6. Do you follow regional, national and international news?

5	4	3	2	1

7. Do you know as much about key aspects of your industry as your staff does?

5	4	3	2	1

8. Do you seek out the competition and learn from them?

5	4	3	2	1

9. Do you ask other business owners for recommendations on good coaches?

5	4	3	2	1

10. Do you attend industry-related conferences?

5	4	3	2	1

Your education score_____

41–50   You are up-to-date on your industry. You appreciate the advantages experience and education offer.

31–40   Build on your strengths and rearrange your schedule to create more time to learn. Step out of your comfort zone and sit with someone new at the next luncheon. Take a class in the area you have targeted as a weakness; or order one of the *Smart Women* programs listed in this book. Go into work one hour earlier each morning in order to work through it.

21–30   You need to take a self-development workshop. Try some new ideas like clown school, or a class in facing your fear by tightrope walking. Do something outside your comfort zone to give you a new perspective.

11–20   Make some phone calls. Find out what's out there that can help. What good coaches are available to book for a one-on-one session for some fast help?

10   Evaluate your **whole person** attributes in the area of education and training and see where you are weak. Make a list of the areas you need to strengthen, find a means to do this and schedule it into the coming year. Connect with a businessperson you admire. Spend as much time as you can with them. Ask questions to get the answers you need. Model your behavior on their strong points.

If you are not taking time to educate yourself, you are sabotaging yourself:

- by not finding time for the continual learning that will increase your knowledge;
- by not keeping up with the news so you know what is happening in the world;
- by not finding experts, coaches, mentors and networks to answer your questions; and
- by not joining a group that will provide opportunities for synchronicity and support.

1. What are the three Cs of learning?

With a stack of "I'm-going-to-get-to-it" reading on your shelf and an ignored correspondence course in your mail box, the last thing you may feel like doing is discussing how important it is for you to learn more. "Do you think I don't know?" you flare. "When do I get time? I'm working a 14-hour day. By the time I get done, I'm too brain-dead to learn."

Smart Women identify with this overwhelming problem and have struggled to discover easier ways to learn. You know that if you are not constantly building your skills and knowledge you stagnate and your business declines. The business cycle is your cycle. Ten years ago the business cycle might be 20 years from startup to decline. Today, with the speed of change and especially if you are in an industry that uses or produces technology, the cycle can be as short as two years.

> **"I'll be learning until I move on to the next stage—for as long as I live!"**
> **Elizabeth Noonan**
> *Elizabeth Noonan & Associates*

Today, you feel like you have about 5½ minutes to sit still before you start rolling backwards. This sensation isn't going to go away. The pressure is going to grow over the next few years as the rate of change accelerates.

The expression is "Green and growing, or ripe and rotting."

The **whole person** approach is: invest in yourself first. Only then will you be clear enough about the needs of those around you to make decisions that will increase the profits of your business year after year.

> **"Ask yourself—what knowledge do I need? At what level? Where can I buy it?"**
> **Deb Hagman**
> *Hog Wild Specialties*

Smart Women have three ways to fast-track learning.

COACHES
COMPETITION
CONFERENCES

2. How can I learn faster?

While all *Smart Women* were involved in lifelong learning, they were cautious about recommending business courses as a way to learn. As Danielle Medina says, "By the time you finish the course, the problem you need to solve may have already put you under." By nature, courses tend to be broad and theoretical, rather than directly applicable. Some courses have a certain status because they are needed to move up the ladder in the corporate world.

> Anne Miner described the reluctance of the Argentinean men to deal with her. As Chief of Business Development for her marketing and research company she has developed a strategy to deal with the resistance she has met with in trying to do business in Argentina. By obtaining a master's degree (something Argentine businessmen do respect) and focusing prospective customer attention on her business's agricultural expertise and away from herself, Anne expects to get all the business she wants.

If you don't need a degree and just need the knowledge, the most convenient and fastest way to learn may be through a customized coach.

3. What is the difference between a coach and a consultant?

Smart Women tend to shy away from the word *consultant*. Many have been burned bringing in highly paid specialists who gave them general information, then walked away without offering a plan for implementation. Without a practical process to apply to their business, the women were left feeling they had not received their money's worth. Busy with the day-to-day operations, they had little time or energy to start developing new ideas from scratch. Often, adapting them was so slow that it happened in bits and pieces or gradually went by the way. Outraged cries over the money wasted on consultants resounded in our ears.

"A willingness to always keep trying new methods is the biggest aid to self-development."
Gladys Sinclair
Naturals Handwoven
Clothing

A common story was, "I hired a consultant at $100 per hour and spent three precious hours explaining my business to him, for which he billed me. He came back with a 20-page document full of all the things I had told him and an invoice for another $1000. I was furious! If I looked after my customers like that I would not have any."

The difference between a coach and a consultant is a coach always works to improve *your* game. The coach helps with implementation, cheers you on and ensures you gain the skills to keep going. Coaches customize everything to your game plan and look for the best ways for you to soar.

a) Finding a Good Coach

So, how do you find a good coach? One hundred percent of the time we were told by the women we interviewed: "Through your network or synchronicity." In order to make this an efficient process that will net you fast results, you need to have a clear idea of what type of person and style you can best learn from. This relates back to knowing your own learning style (discussed in Chapter 4, "Communications").

Once you have a coach in mind, talk to someone you trust who has previously hired this person and can vouch for the fact that the relationship worked! In many instances coaches with industry-specific knowledge are known to that industry association. If you phone your association, they could provide a referral.

The main questions to ask a potential coach are:

- Will you allow me a "free" initial session to ensure a good personality match?
- Will I have to pay for your business education curve or do you already have a sound knowledge of my industry?
- Will you bill me on a pre-agreed-outcomes basis rather than an hourly fee, for a win-win for both of us? For example, I will pay $X for a marketing plan. If I get the 20% sales increase we set as an objective, I will pay $Y more.
- Will you help me assess and focus my learning needs?

b) Finding the Right Coach for You

You know you have the right match if you feel comfortable with your coach. You should be able to ask any questions without feeling ignorant. You should get answers that make sense to you and that paint the kind of word pictures that help relate the information to your business. You want a coach who communicates freely, but who also knows the value of your dollar and remains focused. You don't want to pay for "chitchat about the weather." The true test of whether you have found the right coach for you is determining whether this is someone who can define your concern, when you can't. For example, you may think you need help creating ads to move product, but the coach will show you an underlying problem that is causing you to lose sales.

> **"If you sacrifice time, effort and money to pay for it [learning] you will succeed."**
> *Donna LaChappelle*
> *Coldwell Banker Accord Realty*

Coaches introduce an emotional side to their interaction with you that consultants do not. Good coaches cheerlead and kick butt when you need it. They should play an ongoing role in your business.

Because they have committed themselves in some measure to your success, coaches are sometimes confused with mentors. However, unlike mentors who help free of charge, coaches are paid experts, hired to provide advice and to assist you with implementation. (The free ones are often family members with significant business experience.) Don't forget your advisory board (see Chapter 1, "Planning"). These people all act as free coaches to you.

> **"Insist on [learning]. Don't say, 'I don't have to do that.' You owe it to yourself."**
> *Barbara Balfour*
> *The Gallery*

Bev McMaster uses her brother as a mentor. "Sometimes when I am complaining, my brother just looks at me and says, 'If you can't take the strain maybe you had better get out of the game.' He loves me, but he plays hardball. It makes me ask, 'Do I have the strength?' Don't ask someone. Ask yourself. This is a reality check."

Karen Farkas uses her grocery-store-owner dad as a major adviser to her wholesale health-food business. She feels she gathers more immediate useful advice with one phone call to him than she gets from her master's degree in business. She put so much time and money into getting it she assumed she'd have all the answers when she graduated, but all she really had to do was "call home."

Many entrepreneurial individuals are not good classroom students. As previously stated, they tend to be action-oriented, kinesthetic learners. Coaches can tailor your information to on-the-job learning, rather than teaching generic theory. Often they help you implement as you go, so you have a double win. Both the business education and the task are completed simultaneously.

Alandra McLaren says, "I learn best by doing. I earned my captain's license by sailing under other captains all over the world."

"I love to learn," Carol Ann Fried says. "I often travel with my job, so courses just don't work for me. I identify an area I am interested in and look for an expert in the field. For example, I was being asked to do more 'Humor in the Workplace' presentations and read Matt Weinstein's book *Managing to Have Fun*. I called him and obtained his coaching services for my business for free by contracting him to do a college event for new students on campus."

4. How can I learn from my competition?

a) Pick Their Brain

One of the fastest ways to learn is to find someone who is doing it well and learn from them. This, technically, is your competition and obviously if they are right on your doorstep they won't be willing to share. Competition located farther away geographically may be willing to give you on-the-job training. Your association can quickly point you to the best in the business. If you don't have an association, head for your local library and look at the Yellow Pages for other cities. Let your fingers do the walking and choose one competitor whose ad you like. Call them and explain who you are. Say that you're trying to track down some of the best in the business. Things will escalate naturally from there. You may want to specifically target a city you would like to holiday in so you can make arrangements to combine business and pleasure, to the chagrin of the tax department.

"In the early days of setting up my business I took a lot of trips to other cities to look at what was happening elsewhere in my field," said Karinna James. "It gave me an opportunity to talk with owners of other training centers. I did not take formal courses but what I learned was far more valuable and practical to me."

According to Leslie Campbell, "When you first start a business the learning curve is immense if you are new to the industry and have to learn it too. Ask indirect competitors. My experience as a reporter taught me people are always willing to give you advice, when asked, and your competition is not an exception."

b) Volunteer to Learn

For Barbara Hodges learning from the competition took on a whole new direction. "When I started my mattress factory I found it helpful to tour factories that manufacture other products. I was able to observe a successful business's new technology and clean environment, and make good choices for my company based on what I learned. In the first year, I discovered my employees lacked confidence in the manufacturing process because they hadn't observed me or anybody else actually performing the work. I was no show and all tell. I persuaded a colleague in the United States to let my husband, oldest son and I train in his factory. Each of us trained in a different specialty. When we returned 10 days later, we became the "models" our staff needed. The decision helped me build competence and confidence in our small organization."

"Self-development can be like putting on a new set of glasses."
Mary Ann S. Turnbull
Turnbull Learning Centre Ltd.

Competition, far from your back doorstep, can provide much more than business education. Your competition offers the opportunity to create buying power with suppliers, codevelop marketing materials (you only need customizing for specific location information and company name), split industry software-development costs, share hotel rooms at conferences, jointly publish newsletters. Many of these ideas not only cut costs, but also help your business appear larger and more credible in the early years.

5. Why are conferences one of the best methods of growing my mind?

The joy of conferences is the opportunity to soak up energy and ideas for a few days, like a hummingbird flitting from flower to flower to get the best of the nectar. Eventually, you will flit back home bringing new insights and renewed energy to your business. You will have the enthusiasm to implement new ideas rapidly, before once more becoming caught up in day-to-day work.

"Choose a workshop opposite to your interests to challenge yourself and reduce your tunnel vision."
Barbara Balfour
The Gallery

The peer support gained at conferences does wonders for esteem. Discovering others are experiencing exactly the same business problems as you are is self-affirming. Being able to share your solutions is rewarding.

If you can't find a national conference in your industry, look for an international one. If one doesn't exist, find one in the next closest industry sector and attend it. You can cross-pollinate their ideas into your industry.

Meredith DeGroat shook her head in disgust when she said in the first two years of owning her business she did not attend a conference. She felt she wouldn't get value for her money. Then she joined the US Association for Direct Sellers. "I learned more in their first conference than I had in the past two years running the business. If I'd attended sooner it would have saved me dozens of costly errors," she lamented. "One of the best parts of a conference is meeting the best business owners in the world and benchmarking yourself against them. There is nothing more exciting than realizing how much you can grow," Meredith says.

"Attend as many trade shows as possible, it is a fast way to scope the competition."
Donna
The Art Mart

Maureen Wilson, a personal trainer/dancer with an international reputation, attends two conferences a year. Usually she is a guest speaker at one, which means, she says, "At the very least, you get your expenses paid, and you receive further business education."

Women have good brains and most of us come equipped with more than our fair share of common sense. We have the ability to apply knowledge for practical purposes.

Barb Housser enthuses, "My children and husband were all brilliant while I felt pretty dumb. It wasn't until I started running the company that I realized I had my area of genius too."

Smart Women know if they want to take home bags of money and change the world, they had better first spend a little on developing their minds.

6. How can I find the money for learning?

a) Applying Your Dollar in the Right Place

"Cross-train yourself enough to be able to understand other jobs connected with your own."
Pauline Melnyk
Les Portes Auto Magique Inc.

Liz Wyman, who owns an office service business, warns: "I used to put money into training staff in an area such as computer networking and then I would be left high and dry when they quit. I took 10 days out to attend the training myself. I now train the staff and have the comfort of knowing if someone leaves I can 'sit in' and keep things running smoothly." If this isn't possible, then have staff train an outside contract source, whom you can bring in to keep things going and train replacement staff in-house, on the job.

Conversely, if you pay for the training of one staff member, have them repay their tuition by training you and the rest of your staff. Knowing they have to teach it will ensure your representative attends every minute of the training and assimilates all of the material in order to pass it on. This is a sure way to guarantee a return on your investment.

Loretta Mahling, of Enchanted Kitchens, uses this method effectively. "I pay two of my staff to attend the SIRUS retail program at the university," she says. "They come back and train everyone else. That way I get more value for my dollar and everyone benefits from the more advanced knowledge."

b) Get Paid to Learn

Some *Smart Women* are getting paid to learn by teaching in areas related to their expertise. Sharing your own knowledge forces you to learn more as you develop your reputation as an expert. Several of the women participate in the Business Development Bank of Canada's "Step Up" programs and find several benefits in their mentoring role with new entrepreneurs. They enhance their communication skills, and the research they do helps them keep up with what is happening in the marketplace.

c) Co-op Education

Co-op education for both staff and customers is another inexpensive solution to learning. The expense becomes part of your promotional budget and you share the cost with someone else (e.g., suppliers/manufacturers/sponsor).

> Doris Tan, whose company distributes wholesale beauty salon supplies, chooses a subject she is interested in learning and then pays for an expert in the field to give a seminar on it (cost-shared with her manufacturers). She offers the seminar to her clients at Christmas time, as a gift of knowledge and empowerment. The admission fee is a donation of food for the Christmas Food Bank Hampers, a contribution that makes everyone feel good. She usually has 100 to 200 attendees. "All my staff attend and learn as an ongoing part of their life. Although I am doing it for my own business, in sharing the experience with others, everyone benefits."

d) Subsidization

Look for programs that are partially subsidized by government to help you out financially with your training. Many *Smart Women* said their best investments were programs that helped them to develop business plans at little or no cost, through the YMCA Enterprise Centres, Business Development Bank of Canada (BDC) and private companies such as Communicating Power Inc. Unfortunately, most government programs subsidized by Human Resources Development Canada and the provinces are available only for startup. Some *Smart Women* are involved in the BDC's Import and Export Programs or a Step-Up Program; some took business courses available through Industry Canada and the local Department of Agriculture (see the Resource Directory at the back of this book).

7. What should I be learning?

"In a competitive world education is equated to an access to success."
Doris Tan
International Beauty Services

Only you can make the list and prioritize the urgency. Obviously, financial management and technology will be right up there, followed by business planning and presentation styles. Don't forget in the process of learning that a dance class can turn on your creativity as well as exercise your body, and a golf lesson can be an investment in future one-on-one selling. A pottery class might reduce stress while providing beautiful office accent pieces or next Christmas's clients' gifts. In developing your mind in areas other than business, you can cross-pollinate for extra richness and bloom.

Everyone talks today about the importance of lifelong learning and the need to keep abreast of continuous change, but it's time to remind ourselves learning is fun, it feels good. You expand who you are and as your mind grows your business grows. Now it's time to grow your spirit.

The WHOLE PERSON
Action Plan for Your Education

1. a) What was the most helpful thing you learned this past year and what difference did it make in your life?

    _____

    _____

    b) List three key things you need to learn to move forward this year.

    _____

    _____

2. Identify how you would find a coach for one of the learning areas you listed above.

    _____

    _____

3. a) List some of the national and international associations you could belong to (e.g., industry associations, Women Entrepreneurs of Canada, etc.). Go to the library and pull the *Directory of Associations* for contact names and numbers.

    _____

    _____

    b) Phone each of the associations and ask that membership information be mailed to you. Review and select the one you feel would be most valuable.

    _____

    _____

4. Phone two businesses in your industry sector that are outside your target market's geographical area. Introduce yourself to the owner and ask for input on something in the business you want a new perspective on.

    _____

    _____

CHAPTER 11

Spirit

What frustrations are you experiencing in nurturing your spirit?

You may choose to concentrate singlemindedly on your business in the first five years, while making huge sacrifices in all other areas of your life, because you see it is the only way your business will survive. During this time you may make the decision not to have children in order to focus on your business; you may be neglecting your spouse/boyfriend/partner and expecting him or her to make many sacrifices. You may have lost friends because they don't understand the demands of your business and, so, stop calling. Or, you may have sacrificed personal time to hold positions open for staff on maternity leave. Over 38% of the women we questioned had previously confronted, or were now battling these issues.

All of them speak to a greater underlying loss—the spirit within. When we are too rushed, too tired, too caught up in worldly concerns, it is difficult to find our center, to find the source that fires our passion and cements our beliefs. When we do not take the time to get in touch with our inner voice, we begin to sabotage our business. Without a set of values to draw on we make inconsistent decisions and poor choices that hurt our business. As Marianne Williamson says in *A Return to Love*,[1] if we are not drawing on our spirit, ego gets in the way. Ego causes us to make all sorts of mistakes. By excluding our Creator we come from an autonomous position and believe we can accomplish everything alone. Of course, it is not possible. But ego is part of the reason we fail to delegate, fail to communicate and fail to profit.

[1] Marianne Williamson, *A Return to Love*; Harper Paperback (1992)

When it comes to balancing body, mind and spirit, the latter is most often the part of us left undeveloped. Again this is "opposite-world thinking" (what we do or how we act is the opposite of what is really best for us). Our spirit is the inner core that drives our emotions and connects us with our soul (the seat of our conscience). If it is not developed first, we have no values upon which to build our personal philosophy. Without a personal set of guidelines, we cannot care for our body or develop our mind. Many women are frustrated, feeling they are spinning out of control. Are you caught in the trap of never taking quiet time to get in touch with your inner voice, of not coming from love, or of not asking your Creator to strengthen and support you? If this is the case, you have really sabotaged your efforts to become a **whole person.**

Test your ability to nurture your spirit on the following page.

Are you sabotaging yourself?

Spiritual Wellness: Danger Signals

(Circle the appropriate answer for each question. Add up your numbers and check the next page for your spiritual development quotient.)

5 - always	4 - regularly	3 - occasionally	2 - rarely	1 - never

1. Do you take two hours a week just to be quiet?

5	4	3	2	1

2. Do you book a "date" with your partner?

5	4	3	2	1

3. Do you plan one-on-one time with your child?

5	4	3	2	1

4. Do you spend time with friends every month?

5	4	3	2	1

5. Do you have a daily activity that nourishes your spirit?

5	4	3	2	1

6. Do you listen to your inner voice?

5	4	3	2	1

7. Do you work to fulfill the vision of the person you want to be?

5	4	3	2	1

8. Do you take time to put your feelings down on paper?

5	4	3	2	1

9. Do you still laugh?

5	4	3	2	1

10. Do you find yourself singing, humming, skipping or just feeling good?

5	4	3	2	1

Your spiritual wellness score _____

41–50   Excellent. You are developing a **whole person** philosophy that begins with being centered on your spiritual wellness.

31-40   Look at your personal plan for developing your spirituality. Add some quiet time, try meditating or writing in a journal to get in touch with your inner voice. Be more aware—look for moments of synchronicity in your life and write them down until recognizing them becomes a habit.

21-30   You need some emotional nurturing. Look at your relationships. Plan some quality family time and make it happen. Read the books recommended throughout this book. Check out spiritual organizations and look for a spiritual support group to help nurture your soul.

11–20   Write down the *Smart Women* tips for nurturing your spirit and post them where you can see them. Implement as many as possible. Book a holiday at a retreat, or in the wilderness, that allows you a lot of quiet time. Take time every day to feed your spirit, absorb the beauty of creation—stop and pay attention to the details. Listen to music that soothes your spirit.

10   Put serious effort into the **Whole Person** Action Plan for nurturing your spirit. When you are floundering this badly, it is good to bring some light into your life. The most effective way to deal with low spirits (depression) is to do something for someone else. Pick three things you can do to reach out to others in need and implement them. You will feel good about yourself, happy for them and more centered.

If your spiritual wellness quotient is low, you are sabotaging yourself:

- by coming from ego instead of love;
- by not giving enough time to the important people in your life, and not giving them the opportunity to spend time with you;
- by not filling your life with beauty through nature, art, music, literature;
- by not allowing yourself the time to be quiet;
- by not following the guidance of your inner voice; and
- by not using synchronicity to improve your life.

1. How can I simplify my life?

a) From Accumulation to Clean-Up

Not so long ago we were acquiring "stuff" like crazy. We ended up with so much stuff we had to have garage sales to make room for new stuff. Because the majority of us were raising families it was necessary to accumulate and then it was common sense to get rid of what our families had grown out of. This is a Western consumer pattern. And, as fast as we were filling our homes, cottages and garages with stuff, we were filling our minds with the equivalent in information. We are in danger of getting buried by "our stuff."

Simplify. "Clean-up" is the call of *Smart Women* today. Simplifying is about restoring your energy; when your life is uncluttered you are free to focus on important things.

"Simplify your life. Downsize. Eliminate."
Dr. Devon Joy Mark Psychologist

> Mary Sutherland downsized her home from a large traditional house that required a great deal of cleaning and upkeep to a new contemporary home. In the process she went through the house and identified her family's needs and eliminated everything extra. Now she has more energy for the physical demands of running her bookstore, and more time to play with her family—rather than cleaning up after them.

> When Madelon Smid chose to move her home business because of her husband's job, she decided to rent a country bungalow rather than buy another large house in the city. Her life is much simpler now, with fewer people sapping her energy and little maintenance required. The beauty of her rural surroundings provides the energy and inspiration she needs to write.

b) 90-day Clean-up

Several of the women we interviewed were using a 90-day clean-up formula devised by Dan Sullivan, owner of *The Strategic Coach*. He recommends you make a short list of three things in your life that are stealing your energy (waking you in the middle of the night with an "I should have").

"Life is a real juggling act, sometimes there are too many balls in the air. Be good at picking the balls you want and dropping the ones you don't."
Gail Spencer Lamm CrossXtrainers

These tasks must be completed in the next 90 days. Then you start another 90-day list. One of the fastest ways to write your clean-up list is to identify areas in which you procrastinate. It might include an apology to Aunt Marg, cleaning out your cupboards or having a garage sale to get rid of some "stuff." Anything put on the list must be done.

> Bea Harks, a multiple franchise owner and long-time winner of top sales volume awards says, "When I get paralyzed from tiredness or fear, I just keep doing clean-up until finally I've cleaned myself right past the thing that was holding me back. The more I clean up, the more energy I free up—energy that was going into worrying about the unfinished jobs."

Clean-up includes cleaning up yourself, perhaps losing weight or having your teeth fixed. It includes emotional issues such as the anger you are feeling towards your daughter, or conflict that must be resolved with a customer.

The more you do clean up those things that are bothering you and simplify your life, the more you can focus on making your business more profitable. With the money you make, you can hire a personal fitness coach, housekeeper and handyman, all of whom will help you clean up more.

2. How do I find a little peace and quiet?

a) Spirituality

Some of you are finding yourselves searching for spirituality in new ways and new places; while others are finding renewal in the traditional church in which they were raised. You might be applying spirituality to your life with newly discovered tools—tools that are as old as creation. Through the processes of seeking wisdom, creativity and rediscovering the energy of nature, you can explore a new freedom to "be." Adopt the practices of meditation, yoga or journaling (i.e., writing in a journal) in order to find peace and learn to recognize and listen to your inner voice.

> **"When we feel 'God driven' our spiritualism is a strength we bring to business. If it is what we are gifted to do we love it and it is has meaning and we are connected."**
> *Valerie Pusey*
> ***Northern Passage Gallery***

Spirituality is identified by 73% of the *Smart Women* we interviewed as the grounding force in their life and in their business. Most talk openly of values, religion and personal philosophies. You may discuss the strength that your spiritual life gives you and the rich dimension it brings to your business. You may also insist it is the good your business does that attracts the staff and customers to it. A great number of you believe spirituality nourishes the creativity that grows your business. Spirituality makes it worth getting up in the morning. Long before motivational speakers started talking vision or mission statements, women were building businesses that inspired others who came in contact with this new style.

> Some built on the values of their religious upbringing, like Karen Farkas, who says, "My background of Judaism guides my business philosophy of integrity and honesty. I try to live every day with the principle of Lasher Hora, which means, 'It is worse to bring blood to a person's face [embarrass them] than to cut them physically.' I apply this philosophy to staff, customers and loved ones alike."

> Joan Macdonald takes her membership in a traditional church seriously. For over 30 years, she and her husband have taught, led groups and conducted Bible studies. Her faith is a constant in her day. She lives at peace because she lives what she believes.

> Carol Ann Fried observes Yom Kippur (the Day of Atonement) by participating in a group in which the members anonymously write out the sins that are weighing on their minds on small pieces of paper. The papers are then put in a basket that goes around the circle, with others picking one at random and reading what it says aloud. When all the sins have been read, they are burned.

You can do this as an exercise by yourself. Write them out, read them aloud to yourself and decide what you're going to do to atone for them. Then burn the scraps of paper and be free.

Many *Smart Women* build their values into their business by making them a core of their plans (see the section called "Can I bring my personal values to the business?" in Chapter 1).

Many of us are exploring our spirituality daily. The three primary tools women are using successfully to develop their spirituality and enhance creativity are meditation, journaling and moving closer to nature.

b) Meditation

Meditation is the quiet time you take to draw inward. If you are exhausted and anxious it may take an hour to quiet your mind. If you meditate regularly, you will find you can reach a peaceful plateau within minutes. There are as many ways to meditate as there are *Smart Women* meditating. We recommend that you try several to see what works best for your schedule and energy levels.

"Meditation is crucial to me to stay connected with what is important in my life."
Dr. Devon Joy Mark
Psychologist

Gladys Sinclair says, "I take 15 minutes after I get the kids off to school for a quiet time of prayer in order to get the day off to a good start."

Linda Maul meditates to music every morning.

Linda Naiman hiked past a Zen Buddhist retreat in California when she was a teenager. She knocked on the door and asked if she could stay a few days and learn their ways. She still uses the meditation technique picked up in that serendipitous way.

Dr. Devon Mark meditates for one hour once a week. She starts by reading something that calls to her and then sits quietly as images form in her mind. Often she focuses on her concern around a certain question by saying "I have a concern around X. What direction should I take for my highest good?" Sometimes the answer won't come right away and in that case she delays the decision until she connects with her inner wise voice and hears the answer. She recommends *Women's Bodies, Women's Minds* by Christina Northrup to anyone wanting to develop these skills.

"I am spiritually sound because of the morals and ethics I was raised with. These are applied to my business."
Gladys Sarens
Sunshade Products Ltd.

Find a quiet place, close your eyes, cut off as much outside stimuli as possible. Consciously relax the body, muscle by muscle, as you breathe deeply. You may have a mantra (a special phrase) you repeat over and over to focus your mind and to stop it from darting off to other problems.

> Madelon focuses until she can see herself surrounded by bright light. She draws it inward, asking God to show her his will and give her the strength to do it. The light is a healing light and her inner voice (spirit) often provides her with direction.

Meditation gives your brain a little time off. Fifteen minutes of meditation can prove more beneficial than one hour of sleep. In the quietness you create, you hear your inner voice clearly.

c) Journaling

Another way your inner voice can speak to you is through your writing. Putting thoughts and feelings on paper can be very cathartic. It helps you pull back and see yourself from a new perspective. You may journal on a regular basis, others do it sporadically. You can use the process in myriad ways.

> Laurie Peck spoke of a personal awakening that came from a decision to work through the journaling process as outlined by Laurie Beth Jones in The Path.[2] Two days and 60 pages later she emerged with a totally new knowledge of herself, and this knowledge completely changed her direction on a number of key personal and business issues.

> Linda Maul journals every day, writing 1 to 10 pages of everything that is in her head—everything that happened that day from an emotional, rather than a factual viewpoint. "I use it for stress release. I file it and sometimes go back and read it to find out if I see a pattern forming (something that is working or not working in my life)."

> Charlotte Semple practices a different kind of journaling. She created a collage with images and words cut from magazines and mounted on bristol board. The collage depicted where she wanted her life to go. She experienced a revelation as she pasted some pictures to the front and some to the back of her sheet of paper. The front held serious pictures of a dedicated woman in her

[2] Laurie Beth Jones, The Path; Hyperion (1996)

roles of mother, business owner, community supporter. On the back, out of sight, she allowed pictures of people having fun and enjoying themselves. Her message—*only after she had done all her work was she allowed to play.* She is now consciously working to integrate the two. She is learning how to relax and take time to have fun as a part of her other roles, and she is creating an environment where her family and staff can have fun too.

An exercise to search your inner self by creating a collage is also presented in *The Artist's Way* by Julia Cameron and Mark Bryan.[3] They offer a day-to-day program of journaling, self-analysis and inspiration to assist the user in finding and expressing his or her creative spirit. It is an excellent vehicle to help you examine your "positions," identify your needs and focus on the messages you want to put out there.

3. What else will enrich my life?

"Spiritualism is helping people."
Maureen Wilson
Sweat Co. Studios Ltd.

Rhoda Herring spends time with several elderly friends who inspire her. She finds the simplicity of their lives, and their wisdom and humor make them wonderful role models. She uses her time with them to reinvigorate herself.

Many *Smart Women* use volunteer work in personal areas of interest to keep them in contact with a broader world.

Barbara Housser is heavily into the arts, has chaired several boards and has made a significant contribution to her city through her volunteer work. She says, "You can't tell board members what to do the way you can your staff. You must learn to lead with vision and by example in order to get volunteers to perform. Those lessons pay off for both my staff and me back at the restaurant."

Learning to say no is a big part of the process.

Bea Harks counsels: "Learn to say no by understanding what you're saying no to and what saying no means to you and other people. For example, I would tell my staff not to phone me at home, but they would anyway. I would take the call and be angry with them when I was really angry at myself for accepting the call."

[3] Julia Cameron and Mark Bryan, *The Artist's Way*; Archer Putnam (1992)

A solution to Bea's dilemma is to have her staff contact her by voice mail or e-mail. Then it is up to her to choose when she responds. By constantly adjusting your own attitudes, you will stay focused on bringing positive reinforcement into the lives of everyone around you. Keep the door of your local card shop open by sending hundreds of thoughtful messages annually. Be extremely generous with little gifts that recognize achievements and special occasions in the lives of your staff, peers, customers and family.

Our favorite "pass the positives on" came from Carol Ann Fried who uses candy bars to say what she wants. She has been known to go so far as to tape real chocolate bars to heavy paper cards to send humorous and tasty messages.

4. Where will I find the money to look after me?

In the early years of business a much-repeated phrase is "I can't afford it/to." Not looking after yourself is even more costly. You must believe time and money are readily available for anything you identify as important. Believe in the power of **synchronicity**—there is a universal power you can tune in to find what you seek.

> You feel the prick of goose bumps on your arms when Eveline Charles tells you: "All my early years I heard there isn't enough. Stretching things was a way of life. Then I began to discover the power I have to make things happen. I started testing it on little things that were important to me, then on getting my own business and growing it. I reached the point where I built a new home and put $50,000 worth of extras in it. I put it out to the universe that I needed $50,000 by closing date. I knew I would have it. Sure enough, I had a surge of new customers and some unexpected windfalls. I opened myself to every opportunity. On closing day I handed the contractor a certified check for $50 grand and have never doubted for a moment since that if I need something I can get it."

If you really want something, clearly define what it is and send a mental message out. You are activating that special radar in your brain that homes in on information you tell it you need. The great majority of the women interviewed have no formal training nor have they read any books on synchronicity. Yet they practice it all the time. They learned the same way Eveline did, first by discovering little victories, and then opening themselves to recognize moments of synchronicity. Whether you are in search of cash or child care, you have only to clearly define what you need, unclutter your mind of the thousands of distractions and focus your energy. Awesome things start happening.

Ask and you shall receive (2 Corinthians 8:8). God is able to give you more than you need for yourself and more than enough for every good cause. Words *Smart Women* live by. Repeat them every day.

5. How can I get the emotional support I need?

a) Build Support Teams

"When your family has no faith in your decisions—have faith in yourself."
Rhoda Herring
Rhoda's... Elegance Again

Make sure you have good support structures in place. No matter how busy your life is, put time and effort into valuing, building and maintaining your emotional nurturers. The supporting team members have a variety of roles, including cheerleaders, advisers, companions, resources, referrals, helping hands, fellow adventurers, confidants and, the odd time, a shoulder to cry on.

• **Will my children feel angry and neglected?** Guilt... you expect tons of guilt! And certainly there is a lot of it to go around. This applies to any working mom's feelings about her children. It's tough for any child to go without the extra attention provided by an at-home mom or dad. But if a parent has to work, an entrepreneur has advantages over an employee, when it comes to meeting the needs of the children. The flexibility to come and go from the business is a start. In addition, 85% of the *Smart Women* we interviewed acknowledged their children are proud of them. The kids state emphatically that they like the fact that their mom owns her own business. You might find your children's attitudes boost your self-esteem and help you be a better role model for them.

"It is good for any child to see his/her mother using her time the way she chooses—not sacrificing herself to work for others."
Alandra McLaren
Sea Sisters Charters

Renate Wowchuk, of Renate's Hair Design, said her children were less selfish because of her work. She felt she had set an example that taught them to serve others.

Smart Woman after *Smart Woman* said she felt the ethics she practiced in her business taught her children to live values, not just give lip service to them.

The women suggested that an entrepreneurial mother can, in most cases, better equip her children to deal with today's job market than can a nonentrepreneurial mom. "My kids picked up people skills and business sense in my womb," said one owner/mom. Your children may also be more focused, more decisive and more goal-oriented. Actively involve your children in the creative process, run ideas by them and use them as sounding boards. Allow your children to work in the business, part time, from an early age.

Your children may be more flexible, responsible and independent, and more organized and cooperative because of your choice to own your own business. These life skills will be invaluable in obtaining work in the future, with either their *smart* moms or someone else.

Gladys Sarens set up her business to run in conjunction with a business her two sons owned and operated. "There is a pride and joy to see them use good business ethics and make choices based on the morals I taught them," she says. "Working this way gives me a balance of time with them while getting on with my work."

Smart Woman Valerie Hussey of Kids Can Press said, "My family is happier because I am happier." She tries to set family as a priority, and schedule in consistency: everyone must be home for dinner every night; every Friday is family night out; and weekends are spent at the cottage. The constant deadlines of the publishing world are not allowed to take precedence over commitment to family.

She is expressing a theme that permeates this area of experience. We heard many versions in which *Smart Women* spoke of the knowledge/wisdom they have acquired from running their businesses and have applied in teaching lifelong lessons to their children.

Linda Maul: "My children have learned to follow their dreams."

Laurie Peck: "My children have learned not to work at something they don't like."

Rhoda Herring: "My children have learned that failure is not bad, it is just a learning experience."

Let your kids be your cheerleaders. If they are going to yell anyway, it might as well be a cheer for you.

- **How do I get my husband to like this?** Generally, the women interviewed said that their partners are the ones that most often get the short end of the stick. You need to recognize that this is not always a negative. In choosing to own a business and move away from the role of prime caregiver to your children, you are creating opportunities for your spouse to grow and enhance his own life.

"My husband gained from being around our children and became younger at heart."
Gladys Sarens
Sunshade Products Ltd.

Mary Dixon: "My husband was forced to learn new skills, to pick up the slack at home. As a result, he has become more rounded [balanced]."

Many others spoke of how hard it is to juggle schedules and find time for each other. The favorite solution is to schedule a weekly unbreakable "date" with your partner, taking turns choosing the activity of the evening.

Loretta Mahling: "My husband reminds me that family is important too. I decided to take Saturdays off. Amazingly, the business didn't stop running because I wasn't there."

A great many women feel operating their own business has actually enhanced their relationship with their spouse.

Karen Farkas says working with her husband all the time allows her to appreciate his strengths and his weaknesses more. They both realize that their livelihood depends on their ability to work well together.

Loretta Mahling: "My husband is happier because he likes a lot of quiet time. Before I focused my attention on my business I was always dragging him somewhere he didn't want to go."

• **How can my friends help?** Over 50% of our *Smart Women* position their women friends as a top priority. So much for the myth about women hating other women. Their peers provide them with the encouragement, contacts, ideas and the sounding boards necessary for survival. Good friends are crucial—friends who are there at 2 a.m. and with whom you can be totally honest. Over 60% of the women talked about having longtime friends in their lives. Some dated back as far as elementary school.

> **"I see very thin lines between my personal and professional life and in many instances they intersect."**
> *Peggyann Boudreau*
> *JDP Computer Systems Inc.*

Shelley Stewart: "I can't hide from them so they keep me honest. It's so comfortable to be with them. I still have three friends with whom I attended high school. They know my history, know exactly who I am and what I have done."

Donna Bell: "My spirituality is built on friends who are empathetic, and who validate me and aren't afraid to 'kick me in the ass' when I need it. My friends remind me of how much I have accomplished and this is an important part of finding balance."

Most of the women have support groups of 10 to 15 women, with acquaintances added for various occasions. Because interests change, because they all are growing and because people move away or move on, they constantly have their antennae up, searching for new friends. When they look at the amount of time they have for friends and the amount of time and energy they put into keeping their business growing, they realize they must make tough choices about the friends they keep. They no longer believe that "Girls have to be nice to everybody." If a person constantly drains their energy or takes without giving anything back, they choose to let go of the relationship and replace it with one that gives them affirmation, stimulation and joy.

Zandra Bell: "When I reached a certain level of success, some of my old friends stopped calling. They didn't feel comfortable with me any longer. I had to find new friends with whom I had more in common, and who understood the demands of my business."

Jacqui MacNeill: "When I tried to discuss business problems with some of my longtime friends, they interpreted my success to mean I shouldn't have any problems. They would try to make me feel responsible for every problem. They weren't able to understand. I had to find new friends who were in business. Ones who realize that just because there is a problem you need to talk about, it doesn't mean you caused it.

6. Can I run away from home if it gets to be too much?

When all the responsibilities get to be too much, you should run away from home. Realize that free time—days when your briefcase doesn't call to you from the trunk of the car, are essential for restoring creativity. Running away from home is about giving your conscious mind a complete rest, thus enabling your subconscious mind to begin dealing with your challenges more effectively. Running away from home is not about running to other work, it's about leaving your cares behind.

You may want to leave a note!

Many women use the word "hide" to describe how they feel about ducking their workload for a while. Some don't run far.

Gaetanne Riopel: "I take a day off and hide at home with only the cell phone for emergencies."

Barb Housser: "I go to a nearby health ranch. It is better than a week in Hawaii, and quite affordable, especially in the off-season. I get new, good habits started while I'm there."

The majority run away to a retreat once a year to be totally by themselves, but choose to run away with family the rest of the time.

Lori Donovan: "We choose not to work on weekends and arrange to do special family activities like skiing and boating. These activities keep us close."

Susan Vertefeuille: "It's a reward to me for working hard. The whole family escapes frequently for a special treat like a night at a hotel with a water slide. We take turns picking."

Deb Hagman: "Our home is our business. Owning an adventure tourism business that is run from our home makes it hard to keep customers and kids separate. Most of the time we like it, but sometimes we just have to run away. We do it for a week at a time. And in the summer we take a full month."

The financial rewards that come with running a profitable business can pay off personally when they provide you with money for permanent retreats and adventure holidays.

Maureen Wilson bought a home on an island. She takes time away from her business in chunks. She goes to the island for several days, winds down, replenishes her spirit and then goes back to the mainland to work. "When I am in the city, my time is concentrated around my business. I work full speed ahead, because I know the island is there waiting."

Judy Harcourt: "I go to the cabin and the rule is no work goes with me. I plan my work so we can get away every second weekend and for blocks of time when the kids are on holidays."

If, in the early days of your business when cash flow is limited and you can't afford a place to run away to, try Carol Ann Fried's creative solution.

"I found a cabin to rent on an annual basis and asked three friends to rent it with me. We each book it exclusively for our own holidays and share it on other weekends; often we invite other friends to join us, which helps cover the cost of the food and ferries. It has worked so well that even though I can afford my own cabin now, I prefer sharing."

Many of the women are choosing to invest in time shares and trade their weeks with friends, or combine weeks and friends.

When you are a busy woman, even running away from home takes planning. Most say the important trick is to know your business's down times and schedule holidays six months to a year in advance. Paradoxically, by "locking yourself in," you ensure you will get to run away.

> Gladys Sarens: "We plan a trip every winter to balance the hectic pace of seasonal work. If you have it scheduled you stick to it. Otherwise you just let the days fill up with work."

Many *smart* businesswomen combine conferences and business at the front end of family "getaways" in order to take advantage of the business expense portion as a tax write-off.

> Gladys Sinclair: "I do 15 to 20 large craft shows each year in Ontario, so I try to make it a working holiday as much as possible with husband and/or children. Life is too short to spend it in cheap hotel rooms so we treat ourselves to a little luxury and some fun.

Nurturing your inner being creates the rock-solid foundation on which to build a profitable business. When you combine spirituality with the care of your body and the development of your mind, you attain an inner serenity that helps you deal with the daily crises. Your compassion and caring attitude will attract and keep good people in your life. Your belief in the abundance of the universe will help you invest in your business and enjoy the blessings of a high return.

The WHOLE PERSON
Action Plan for Nurturing Your Spirit

1. a)   What is balance to you right now? How good do you feel about the division of your time and attention? Where are you resenting spending time?

   _____

   _____

   b)   What are you going to change?

   _____

   _____

2. How can you become more in touch with your soul?

   _____

   _____

3. a)   Take time now to do a 10-minute meditation. Set down this book (did I say that?), close your eyes, relax, breathe deeply, move into your inner self and close off outside distractions.

   _____

   _____

   b)   Write a mantra that is meaningful to you. Repeat it over and over to help you quiet your darting mind (e.g., *"I am enough, I am all I need to be"*—Val Petrich).

   _____

   _____

4. Write out a description of a personal two-day retreat[4] you will take this year. Where will you go? What will you do there? What will it cost? Schedule it in your day timer.

   _____

   _____

[4] Many convents and monasteries offer retreat space at very low rates. They provide simple, quiet space for you to be alone. Check your Yellow Pages.

Conclusion

What trends are developing in women-owned businesses?

1. Leadership

Increasingly women in politics, arts and business are being used as role models by women who wish to learn leadership skills. This will result in a shortened learning curve for younger woman business owners. Two major trends appearing in women's leadership styles are putting their personal values foremost in making business decisions and claiming the label of *bitch* as a refusal to be intimidated.

a) Value-Based Business

Huge numbers of women-owned businesses, represented by 75% of the women interviewed, consider their spiritual philosophy an integral piece of the foundation on which their business is built. As more spirituality is breathed into the heart of these businesses, we will see it manifested in more genuine concern for others. Entrepreneurs will place increasing emphasis on their need to seek staff and customers with similar values; and to create the opportunities to more openly discuss their values in order to encourage others to adopt them. This trend will escalate with the steadily increasing number of women-owned businesses. The impact of their values on the business community is already being felt, as employees strive to meet these new guidelines, clients are screened for their values, and competition becomes more spiritually aware—in order to keep abreast of the trend. Growing spiritual awareness in the marketplace will parallel the new emphasis North Americans are placing on purchasing value-based experiences rather than material goods.

b) Bitches Are Beautiful

Women are going to assert themselves more. As a result, many people will feel the pendulum has swung too far. While learning to stand up for themselves, some women will make the mistake of being aggressive and emotional. This will lead to increased tension between the sexes and escalating public friction. Only when women feel comfortable about asserting themselves will societal tension dissipate. Unfortunately, it's going to take a few years of transition.

2. Management

Women are wrapping their minds around bigger systems. They are becoming less and less intimidated by traditional male territory.

a) Techno-geekess

Not "goddess" but "geekess" is here to stay. Women are rapidly catching up and in fact surpassing their male counterparts in their use of technology. Some experts say the computer is the great equalizer between the sexes. All of us can become "chipheads." As computers become more user friendly, women are eagerly looking at how they can use them to make their lives easier.

b) Money Matters

We are in the midst of a developing trend, as financial institutions are waking up to the impact of their refusal to deal fairly with women. They are changing their attitudes and approaches to win back the huge number of women entrepreneurs they have driven away. The new policy is just beginning to trickle down to the people on the front line. It will take years to overcome the damage. But, as financial institutions hurry to catch up, we will see the following trends develop:

• **Money Lingo:** Financial institutions will have to communicate in plain words, because women clients will insist on it. A new "money spiel" will result. Women will reject the "fiscal terms" that tended to exclude them. There will be a new emphasis on fair lending terms and access.

• **Micro Loyalty:** Women feel no loyalty towards financial institutions. Their loyalty is given to person X within it, who is willing to help them make their vision happen. If person X leaves, the woman client will follow, whenever possible. If she is forced to find another bank manager, she will search for person Y, not a particular financial group. This micro loyalty will predominate in the next decade. In order to keep these clients, financial institutions will place greater emphasis on character traits (empathy, people skills) in their loans staff and less on "bean counting."

c) New Stats

Another impact we will see over the next decade will be larger businesses owned by women. This will be the result of easier access to financial sources to fund growth and increased knowledge about how to grow.

We will also see an increase in the amount of land owned by women, as they access money to build their factories, hospitals and schools more easily.

Women will increasingly borrow from new kinds of venture capital groups, co-ops and other allies. Low interest rates will bring a new surge of private investors to small business. Many new investors will want a small piece of the action in case their own job disappears. Women are moving quickly to create and borrow from these new financial sources.

Women-owned businesses will become more profitable as women work smarter to secure their future. They will place a greater emphasis on making and saving money for their own retirement years.

3. Self-Development

As women's confidence continues to grow, the resulting self-esteem will cause a whole-person effect. Women will take better care of themselves, be willing to put their needs higher on the list and expand their sense of connection to the universe.

a) From T & A to Pecs and Glutes

Women are being educated on the necessity of maintaining strong, healthy bodies to meet their goals of longevity and quality of life. Education about the ability of muscle activity to burn fat is putting new emphasis on developing and maintaining a more muscular body. Over the next decade, the image of "tits and ass" will disappear. The new feminine ideal will be a streamlined body with well-defined muscle. Women will be working to develop pecs and glutes.

b) From Global to "Universal" Connections

Women are spending increasing amounts of time on voyages into their psyches. They are exploring who they are and why they are. They are trying to answer the universal question, "Why do I exist?" One of the newest tools they are developing for this search is synchronicity—the awareness of universal energy, sometimes identified as coincidence. Women will use synchronicity, along with other tools, to tap into what they want.

c) Segmenting

A huge number of women are rejecting society's definition of balance, choosing not to do it all. They are moving towards segmenting their lives and focusing on one major role at a time. These segments will be separated by significant periods in which the women will re-educate and rejuvenate themselves.

List of Smart Women

Margo Almond
Clearway Computer Consultancy and Training Limited
technology / computer applications and training

Hermante Ayotte
Clinique De Médecine Industrielle & Preventive Du Quebec Inc.
medicine / occupational health consultant

Denise Bagley
The Learning Edge Inc.
business training and consulting

Barbara Balfour
The Gallery
potter / contemporary clay retail and classes

Nicole Beaudoin
Quebec Business Women's Network Inc.

Donna Bell
Blue Dawn Originals
contract / customized industrial sewing

Zandra Bell
at wit's end
ultimate customized comedy

Brenda Blunderfield-Boernsen
B's Fine Coffee & Teas
retail specialty coffee and tea blends

Bonnie Bond
Seagull Pewter Ltd.
pewter and silver manufacturing / wholesale and retail

Peggyann Boudreau
JDP Computer Systems Inc.
computer consultants

Wendy Brownlie
Clinical Physiotherapy Services
physiotherapy

Angela Bucaro
Angela Bucaro Designs Inc.
garment design

Leslie Campbell
Campbell Communications Inc.
Focus on Women magazine

Lise Cantin
Fishbowl Restaurant
restaurant / food service

Terry Chang
Body Works Training and Rehab Centre
bodyworks fitness centre

Eveline Charles
Bianco Nero
beauty salons / spa

Carmel Cochrane
Town Textiles (Inc.) Timmins
dry goods store / retail

Jane Cotter
Heavenly Bodies (HB)
garment industry

Diana Courtnier
. Starting Point
internet café

Debi DeBelser
Northwest Pipe Ltd.
pipeline supplies / oil industry

Meredith DeGroat
Totally Tropical Interiors Ltd.
silk plants and accessories

Mary Dixon
Peguis Publishers Ltd.
educational publishing

Elaine Donald
Delaine Holsteins
dairy industry

Lori Donovan
First Step International Ltd.
shoe manufacturer

Helen Douglas
Classic Flowers
flowers / retail

Jocelyna Dubuc
Centre de Santé d'Eastman
spa / hospitality

Bev Durvin
Benkris & Co.
retail kitchen supplies / cooking classes

Karen Farkas
Heart Smart Foods
health foods / wholesale

Carol Ann Fried
Friedom Training Services
training and empowerment services

Renate Geier
La Raffinage Spiritual Day Spa
spiritual spa service

Signa Gilchrist
Gilchrist & Co.
certified management accountant

Norene Gilletz
Gourmania Inc.
food consultant / cookbook author

Monica Gross
Sarah's Corner Ltd.
retail gift and home accessories

Deb Hagman
Hog Wild Specialties
wild boar sausage and hunting

Joy Hanley
Fine Food Investments Ltd.
wholesale / retail food manufacturing

Judy Harcourt
Harcourt & Associates
personnel agency

Bea Harks
Visions of Beauty
cosmetics

Rhoda Herring
Rhoda's... Elegance Again
consignment clothing for women

Meg Herweier
Dovetail Enterprises Home Improvements
contractor / builder

Barbara Hodges
Spadina Industries Inc.
manufacturer futons/mattresses

Barb Housser
Sam's Deli
delicatessen food service

Phillipa Hudson
Mineral World & Scratch Patch
retail and wholesale geo products

Valerie Hussey
Kids Can Press
publishing / children's literature

Karinna James
Catalyst Insights Ltd.
service and training

Sue Jiang
Shangri-La
well-being products / services

Beverley Keating MacIntyre
BKM Research & Development Inc.
technology training company

Anne Kramer
Current Technology Corporation
hair-growing technology

Elaine Kupser
Impact Magazine
health and fitness magazine

Donna LaChapelle
Coldwell Banker Accord Realty
real estate company

Lara Lauzon
Lauzon Consulting Inc.
consulting/wellness field

Joan Macdonald
J.V.I. Commercial Driving
driver training for truckers

Jacqui MacNeill
Escents Aromatherapy
aromatherapy wholesale and retail

Loretta S. Mahling
Enchanted Forest Retail Group Inc.
retail kitchen, Christmas gift
products

Cindy Maloney
Groomingdale's Pet Salon Ltd.
dog grooming

Valerie March
V. March Associates
financial planner

Devon Mark
Dr. Devon Joy Mark
psychologist

Linda Maul
Corporate Source Inc.
service—recruitment and development

Alandra McLaren (Captain)
Sea Sisters Charters
charter services / transformation training /
sailing retreats / Usana Distributor

Bev McMaster
WeCare Health Services Inc.
health services / home support / nursing

Danielle Medina
Medina Foods Inc.
food-quality-control measurement
system

Beatrice Meili
Saskatoon Book Store Inc.
book store / learning centre

Pauline R. Melnyk
Les Portes Auto Magique Inc.
automatic doors

Anne Miner
The Dunvegan Group Ltd.
research and marketing consultants

Dorothy Murray
CrossXtrainers
health and wellness service

Linda Naiman
Linda Naiman & Associates Inc.
design marketing communications

Lillian Neaman
Paper Gallery Ltd.
retail gift shop / custom invitations

Susan Nicol
Lilyfield Communications
advertising / journalism / corporate
communications service

Elizabeth Noonan
Elizabeth Noonan & Associates
marketing / advertising / communication

Tannis Ortynsky
CompuTemp's
supply staff for any industry

Marlene Pearce
Marlene Pearce and Associates
interior decorating / service

Irene Pearson
RobRene Ltd.
retail hardware outlet

Laurie E. Peck
Listen International Speakers Network
Inc.
speakers bureau

Val Petrich
The Yoga Studio
yoga training

Manon Pilon
Europe Cosmétiques Inc.
cosmetic distributor / hair salons /
esthetics school

Simonne Power
Sunny's Family Restaurant
family food restaurant

Dulcie E. Price
Optimum Agra Services Ltd.
grain broker

Valerie Pusey
Northern Passage Gallery
graphic production and display art gallery
and retail art sales

Helen Read
The Clothing Refitters
alterations and fashion design

Vivian Reid
Viva Optical Contact Lens Centre
fashion eye wear / contact lenses

Judy Richards
Davidson's Jewellers Limited
jewellery / retail

Gaetanne Riopel
Party & Masquerade
retail costume rental / party decorating /
character deliveries

Gladys Sarens
Sunshade Products Ltd.
aluminum sunrooms / patios

Shirley Schwab
Earl Beebe Trucking Ltd.
trucking company

Charlotte Semple
Victoria Women in Need Society
secondhand retail / training and education
drop-in centre for battered women

Faralee Shipley
CrossXtrainers
fitness trainers

Gladys Sinclair
Naturals Handwoven Clothing
handwoven and custom-made clothing

Ashley Smith
Charles Ben Studio
hair salon

Gail Spencer Lamm
CrossXtrainers
fitness trainer

Shelly Stewart
A La Mode Fashions Inc.
retail women's clothing

Mary Sutherland
Sutherland Books
retail book store

Lynne Sutton
Totally Pets
pet supplies and services
dog grooming

Doris Tan
International Beauty Services
wholesale cosmetics Aveda

Joan Teskey
Wajo Studios Ltd.
school photography

Kate Thrasher
KTG Enterprises Inc.
pr and marketing
strategic planning and teaching

Donna Tremblay
The Art Mart
craft supplies / classes / retail

Hélène Tremblay
Destination Montreal
relocation service

Gaye Trombley
The Avalon Group Ltd.
human resources consulting

Julie A. Tubman
Tubman Funeral Homes
funeral services and supplies

Mary Ann S. Turnbull
Turnbull Learning Centre Ltd.
education services

Susan Vertefeuille
Dr. S. Vertefeuille
optometrist

Arlaina Waisman
Nutrawise Enterprises Ltd.
manufacturing health jams

Alison (Babe) Warren
Babe's Honey Farm
honey and beeswax production and
pollination

Maureen Wilson
Sweat Co. Studios Ltd.
aerobics fitness training / personal training
studio

Renate Wowchuk
Renate's Hair Designers
hair salon

Liz Wyman
Office Compliments Ltd.
office overload service

Resource Directory for Women Entrepreneurs

Provided by Partners in Enterprise, a leader in small business sources and advice[1]

Business Development Bank of Canada (BDC)

The Business Development Bank of Canada (BDC) attempts to help potential and existing entrepreneurs develop and build successful businesses. Programs and services are designed to meet the needs of high-technology and knowledge-based companies, women entrepreneurs, aboriginal businesses, exporters and other emerging sectors of the economy.

Local BDC branches may be contacted at over 80 locations across Canada or by calling 1-888-463-6232. Web site is *http://www.bdc.ca*.

Small Business Central

Small Business Central is a small-business resource directory with as many as 84 links involving finance, management support and Web resources associated with topics such as startup, marketing, new products, expanding businesses, acquiring businesses (including franchising) and tools.

[1] Partners in Enterprise, Phone (403) 444-3339.

CANADA BUSINESS SERVICE CENTRES

The Canada Business Service Centres (CBSC) reduce the complexity of dealing with various levels of government by providing a single point of contact to a wide range of information on government services, programs and regulations. The CBSC's initiative is a result of cooperative arrangements with 28 federal business departments, provincial governments and in some cases, the private sector, associations and academic and research communities. Each CBSC offers a variety of products, services and expert referrals to help businesspeople obtain quick, accurate and comprehensive business information.

As a gateway for Canadian business the CBSC offers the following services:

- *Service on the Web* – The CBSC Internet site at *http://cbsc.org* contains collections of the latest information on federal, provincial government services, programs and regulations that can be searched.

- *Service by telephone* – The CBSCs provide toll-free telecentres to help business reach business information officers that are ready to help find answers to business questions and problems.

- *Service in person* – CBSCs offer an extensive collection of reference material as well as access to external databases that business clients can research on their own or get help from trained business information officers.

- *Service by fax* – The CBSCs respond to business needs by providing a toll-free, fax-on-demand service that allows businesses to order documents to be faxed to them using a touch-tone telephone, 24 hours a day, any day of the year.

- *Pathfinders and Info Guides* – These overviews describe services and programs organized by topic (e.g., exporting). *Pathfinders* are available from the CBSCs, on the Web or through the fax-on-demand service.

- *Toolbox* – The CBSCs have recently collaborated in the development of several innovative products. The Interactive Business Planner is a revolutionary, new business planning tool designed specifically for the Internet. It is available at *http://www.sb.gov.bc.ca*. A major new on-line service also has been created for Canadian businesses seeking export information. ExportSource is available on the Internet at *http://exportsource.gc.ca*.

The locations of the Canada Business Service Centres are the following:

Alberta
The Business Link
Ste. 100, 10237-104 Street
Edmonton, Alberta
Phone: (403) 422-7722
Toll-Free: 1-800-272-9675

British Columbia
Canada/British Columbia Business
Service Centre
601 West Cordova Street
Vancouver, British Columbia
Phone: (604) 775-5525
Toll-Free: 1-800-667-2272

Manitoba
Canada Business Service Centre
330 Portage Avenue, 8th Floor
P.O. Box 2609
Winnipeg, Manitoba
Phone: (204) 984-2272
Toll-Free: 1-800-665-2019

New Brunswick
Canada/New Brunswick Business
Service Centre
570 Queen Street
Fredericton, New Brunswick
Phone: (506) 444-6140
Toll-Free: 1-800-668-1010

Newfoundland
Canada Business Service Centre
90 O'Leary Avenue
P.O. Box 8687
St. John's, Newfoundland
Phone: (709) 772-6022
Toll-Free: 1-800-668-1010

Northwest Territories
Canada/NWT Business Service Centre
P.O. Box 1320
8th Floor Scotia Centre
Yellowknife, NT
Phone: (403) 873-7958
Toll-Free: 1-800-661-0599

Nova Scotia
Canada/Nova Scotia Business Service
Centre
1575 Brunswick Street
Halifax, Nova Scotia
Phone: (902) 426-8604
Toll-Free: 1-800-668-1010

Ontario
Canada—Ontario Business Call Centre
Toronto, Ontario
Phone: (416) 954-4636
Toll-Free: 1-800-567-2345

Prince Edward Island
Canada/Prince Edward Island Business
Service Centre
75 Fitzroy Street
P.O. Box 40
Charlottetown, Prince Edward Island
Phone: (902) 368-0771
Toll-Free: 1-800-668-1010

Quebec
Info entrepreneurs
5 Place Ville Marie
Plaza Level, Suite 12500
Montreal, Quebec
Phone: (514) 496-4636
Toll-Free: 1-800-322-4636

Saskatchewan
Canada/Saskatchewan Business Service
Centre
122-3rd Avenue North
Saskatoon, Saskatchewan
Phone: (306) 956-2323
Toll-Free: 1-800-667-4374

Yukon
Canada/Yukon Business Service
Centre
201-208 Main Street
Whitehorse, Yukon
Phone: (403) 633-6257
Toll-Free: 1-800-661-0543

CANADIAN BUSINESS WOMEN'S NETWORK

This network supports and promotes women entrepreneurs through networking and information dissemination including a directory that lists women's businesses and a directory of business resources.

The Web site address is *http://www.cdnbizwomen.com.*

CANADIAN YOUTH BUSINESS FOUNDATION

The Canadian Youth Business Foundation (CYBF) is a nonprofit, private-sector initiative designed to provide mentoring, business support and lending to young Canadian entrepreneurs who are creating new businesses.

The Web site address for CYBF is *http://www.cybf.ca*

SMALLBIZ CANADA

SmallBiz Canada is a Web site supporting small businesses in Canada. It has informational articles, success stories, books in brief and links to other sites such as management consultant firms on tax issues and very interesting U.S. small business sites.

The Web site address is *http://www.microsoft.com/canada/smallbiz/*

STRATEGIS

Strategis is Industry Canada's business information site on the Web. Strategis is used by over 140,000 people on a regular basis.

Strategis can be accessed at *http://strategis.ic.gc.ca* .

WOMEN BUSINESS OWNERS OF CANADA INC. (WBOC)

WBOC's raison d'être is to increase business opportunities for women-owned businesses in Canada. This will be done by providing linkages to information, services and support through a strong network of peers.

Phone: (416) 366-9669
Fax: (416) 366-9663

WOMEN ENTREPRENEURS OF CANADA

Women Entrepreneurs of Canada focuses on the needs of established women business owners.

Phone: (416) 361-7036
Fax: (416) 862-0315

WOMEN INVENTORS PROJECT

The Women Inventors Project is a nonprofit organization working to increase the number of successful women inventors and entrepreneurs in Canada. The Women Inventors Project provides education, advice and encouragement to innovators of all ages.

Phone: (416) 243-0668
Internet: *http://www.ics.bc.ca/wip*

ASSOCIATION OF ATLANTIC WOMEN BUSINESS OWNERS (AAWBO)

The AAWBO is a nonprofit organization. It is a resource group of women business owners committed to sharing information and supporting and encouraging each other.

Phone: (902) 422-2828
Internet: aawbo@dbis.ns.ca

WESTERN ECONOMIC DIVERSIFICATION

Western Economic Diversification (WD) provides a number of programs and services across western Canada to help small and medium-sized businesses grow and create jobs. WD's Web site has information regarding business planning, tax information, small business regulations, labor market data, business financing, exporting and selling to the government.

The Web site address is *http://www.wd.gc.ca*

WOMEN'S ENTERPRISE INITIATIVE

Four nonprofit associations have been established to assist women to start or expand their businesses in western Canada. They are funded by Western Economic Diversification. These associations, although different from one another, all participate in lending and training activities to support women entrepreneurs. For example, the Alberta Women's Enterprise Initiative Association's Web page has over 80 links to women entrepreneur Web sites.

Locations and contact details are given as follows:

Alberta
Alberta Women's Enterprise Initiative
100, 10237-104 Street
Edmonton, Alberta
Phone: (403) 422-7784;
and
260, 800-6 Avenue SW
Calgary, Alberta
Phone: (403) 777-4250
Toll-Free: 1-800-713-3558
Internet: *aweia@compusmart.ab.ca*

British Columbia
Women Enterprise Society of
British Columbia
Ste. 7, 2070 Harvey Avenue
Kelowna, B.C.
Phone: (250) 868-3454
Toll-Free: 1-800-643-7014
Internet: *WESBC@silknet*

Manitoba
Women's Enterprise Centre
Main Floor; 130-240 Graham Ave.
Winnipeg, Manitoba
Phone: (204) 988-1860
Toll-Free: 1-800-203-2343

Saskatchewan
Women Entrepreneurs of Saskatchewan
112, 2100 - 8 Street
Saskatoon, Saskatchewan
Phone: (306) 477-7173;
and
2124B Robinson Street
Regina, Saskatchewan
Phone: (306) 359-9732
Toll-Free: 1-800-879-6331